The Ethiopia Book of Travels

Author

Of His Imperial Majesty's Aides-de-Camp
Imperial Commissaire to Bulgaria
Lieutenant General Azmzâde Sadık el-Müeyyed

Edited and Translated by
Gıyas Müeyyed Gökkent and Family

Published by G M Gökkent
2021

Copyright ©2021 by Gıyas Müeyyed Gökkent
All rights reserved. No part of this publication may be reproduced, distributed, or transmitted in any form or by any means, including photocopying, recording, or other electronic or mechanical methods, without the prior permission in writing of the copyright holder, except in the case of brief quotations embodied in reviews and certain other noncommercial uses permitted by copyright law

Published by Gıyas Müeyyed Gökkent
Edited and translated by Gıyas Müeyyed Gökkent
This hard cover edition first published in 2021
Visit website at www.menah.org

ISBN 978-1-7371298-9-9
Printed in the United States of America

Jacket Cover Image: 'Taraf eşref Hazret Padişahiden memuriyet mahsusa ile olaca Habeşistan'a izam buyrulmuş olan yaveran-ı hazret-i padişahi'den al yom Bulgaristan Komiseri Ferik Sadık Paşa Hazretleri ve refakatlerinde bulunan Refetlû Talip Bey ve Çavuş Yasin Efendi' [His Excellency Lieutenant General Sadık Pasha, the Bulgaria Commissaire today, and Refetlû Talip Bey and Sergeant Yasin Efendi in his company who have been ordered to go to Abyssinia on special assignment by His Imperial Majesty, the noble Padishah] in *Servet-i Fünûn*, 28 Teşrin-i awwal R1320 [10 October 1904], No: 707, page 68, Alem Matbaası Ahmed Ihsan ve Şürekası in 1956 SB 501 Volume 28, Number: 707, 0039, National Library of the Republic of Turkey
Other Front and Back Jacket Cover Images: Sadık Pasha's seal and signature courtesy of SALT Araştırma (Research), Osmanlı Bankası Arşivi (Ottoman Bank Archives). Sadık Pasha's photo is from the family collection

Ali Cengiz Gökkent

(1932-2016)

Mutlak bir gerçek varsa	If there is an absolute truth
bu evrende	in this universe,
nedir ?	what is it ?
Değişimden, değişmeden	Other than
başka?	transformation, transmutation?
Zamanın belirlediği	You learn the past
tek yönlü	in this unidirectional
bu yaşam sürecinde	continuum of life set by time
geçmişi öğreniyorsun	And sometimes you remember
Bazen de hatırlıyorsun	you live the present,
Şimdiyi yaşıyorsun,	You assume it will never end
Hiç bitmez sanıyorsun	And sometimes you say, please
Bazen de aman ne olur	Let it never end, or
Hiç bitmesin ya da	let it end as soon as possible
bir an önce bitsin diyorsun	You anticipate the future
Geleceği umuyorsun	with unbelievable longing
İnanılmaz bir hasretle	You wait
Bekliyorsun	It is not clear whether it will come, or not
Gelir mi, gelmez mi	
belli değil	Yet, time has already been set
Lakin, kurulmuş bu saat bir kere	It is flowing relentlessly,
Amansızca, tüm coşkusuyla,	with its full fervor,
tüm hışmıyla akıyor,	full fury
sonu bulunamıyor!	Its end cannot be found!
Değişimin kilometre taşları	The milestones of change

CONTENTS

Foreword	viii
Azmzâde Sadık el-Müeyyed Pasha	xi
Selected Dates in Ottoman-Ethiopian Relations	xix
Preface	xxii
Departure from Istanbul	1
The Red Sea	12
Arrival to Djibouti	17
Djibouti	22
Departure from Djibouti	31
Dire Dawa	42
Somalia	44
Departure from Dire Dawa	48
Arrival to Harar	56
Harar	59
Departure from Harar	66
Haramaya Base Durgu	70
Qersa Base	75
Yekka Base	78
Chalanko Base	82
Derru Base	84
Tullo Base	86
Debbesu	89
Quni Base	91
Bedesa Base	93
Gelemso Base	99

Laga Hardim	101
Katyinwaha Base	104
Fantalle	107
Tadecha Malka	111
Choba	114
Menabella	116
Balchi	118
Tchefe Donsa	122
Akaki	124
Chula	127
Addis Ababa I	131
A Summary of the History of Ethiopia	134
Brief Description of the Geography of Ethiopia	139
Types of People and the Administrative Division	141
Addis Ababa II	144
Addis Ababa III	152
Types of Penalty and Trials of Afa Negus	154
Courts	156
The Ethiopian Law Called Fata Negus	157
"La Basha", or the Detective Exposing the Thief	157
Ishi - Beru Hatyu, Aftun Hatyu – Three Brides and a Groom	158
Battles Between the Ethiopians and Disciples of the Mutemahdi	160
The Death of Negus Yohannes in the Battle of Qallabat	164
Addis Ababa IV	166
History of the Calendar	169
The Religious Order	170
Types of Wedding	172
Diseases and Treatments	173
Music	174
Addis Ababa V	176
The Cordial Relations Between Ethiopians and Muslims During the Rise of Islam	177
Addis Ababa VI	182

Buda - Affliction of the Evil Eye -	184
Tfu Tfu Means the Evil Eye is Warded off	184
Monsieur Ilg	185
Addis Ababa VII	188
The Language of the Ethiopians	190
Addis Ababa VIII	193
Military Service in Ethiopia	195
Addis Ababa IX	203
His Imperial Majesty Emperor Menelik	207
The One Who Wards Off Misfortunes and Hardships	209
Her Majesty the Empress Taytu	210
Addis Ababa X	215
Addis Ababa XI	218
The Princes of Shewa Province	221
Akaki	223
Dubbi Base	226
Menabella Base	228
Tadecha Malka	229
Fantalle	231
Laga Arba	233
Laga Masu	235
Lost in the Forest	236
In the Middle of the Desert	239
Gota Base	240
Tuma Base	243
Arrival to Dire Dawa	246
Medal Warrant, Letters	249
Departure to Djibouti	253
Departure to Suez	257
Occupation of Massawa	258
Battle of Dogali	259
Calamity of Monsieur Salimbeni and His Companions	260

Occupation of Eritrea	262
Mareb Convention	265
The Reason for the Announcement of Martial Law in Hamasen	267
Announcement of the Annulment of the Treaty of Ucciale	268
Battle of Halaya with Batha Agos	268
Battle of Koatit	270
The Senafe Incident	272
Occupation of Tigray	274
Defeat of Amba Alagi	276
Mekelle Siege	278
The Agame Revolution	283
The Lina Incident	284
The Alekeye Incident	285
Battle of Adowa	288
Famous Ethiopians	294

ILLUSTRATIONS

Ali Cengiz Gökkent	iii
Azmzâde Sadık el-Müeyyed Pasha	x
Haqqi Al Azm and Rafiq Al Azm	xviii
Captain Émile Guépratte	11
Faces of Somalis	47
Somali Women	55
Our Servants and Soldiers	74
Monsieur Ilg	187
Ethiopian Army Battle Formation	201
A Warrior from the Imperial Guard	202
His Imperial Majesty Menelik	213
Her Imperial Majesty Taytu	214
Map	303
Order of Solomon Medal Warrant	304

*Indicates editor's notes in the text

Foreword

Survived a lightning strike, slept with deadly scorpions and snakes, invited to an audience with Lady Desta and her thirty slaves, spoke to the English agent Ármin Vámbéry, called on by Baron Maurice de Rothschild, met with sultans and emperors. These were all in a day's work for my great grandfather Azmzâde Sadık el-Müeyyed, an Ottoman officer and statesman.

Sadık Pasha traveled widely from Kosova to Chechnya, from Libya to Ethiopia. He supervised the construction of the Hejaz telegraph line for which a monument still stands in Marjeh Square in Damascus, Syria and the Hejaz Railway, submitted for inclusion in the UNESCO World Heritage list by Saudi Arabia in 2015 and for which a monument stands in Haifa today.[i] Sadık Pasha was appointed as the commissaire to Bulgaria in 1904 and served as the governor of Jeddah[ii] in 1910. Sadık Pasha was a renaissance man, publishing on subjects ranging from chemistry to photography, from history to children's books.

The Ethiopia Book of Travels takes you to June 1904 to accompany Sadık Pasha on a mission for Sultan Abdulhamid II to go before Emperor Menelik II, the ruler of Ethiopia. One of three missions to Africa by Sadık Pasha to counter the scramble for Africa by West European powers, this volume should be considered a companion to *Journey in the Grand Sahara of Africa*, republished with contributions from his descendants in *Journey in the Grand Sahara of Africa and Through Time*. I hope you enjoy the journey.

I am grateful to Sonia Muayad Al Azm, Esma Günay Gökkent (Azm), and İklil Azmzâde for participating in the editorial board. Missing sections in the Ottoman text were completed using Haqqi and Rafiq Al Azm's

---

[i]   https://whc.unesco.org/en/tentativelists/6026/
[ii] In modern day Saudi Arabia

Arabic translation through the efforts of Amina Sanaa Al Muayad Al Azm, Hassana Almuayad Al-Azem, Ghaith Almuayad Al-Azem, Sonia Muayad Al Azm, Omar Khoja, Samia Azem Aidi, Ghassan Aidi, Maria Saseh, Sufian M. Azm, and Nouwar Azem. In particular, it would have been impossible to complete this task without the encouragement of Amina Sanaa Al Muayad Al Azm and Hassana Almuayad Al-Azem.

Rawia Alsasa, Nora and Randa Barazi, Zehra, Lilah, and Adnan Khoja, Lara Aidi, Nedim Koray, Cem Şendil, Mehmet Rasin Sirel, Esin Otağ and Mayssa Mohamed Ali Al Azem helped with other aspects of the book. I am grateful to Asım Jeyan Ülkü and Arda Falahat, life long friends, who sent me some of the source documents and to Tolga Falahat for his comments on cover design. Nilgün and Sena Gökkent were patient and supportive.

İklil Azmzâde provided a number of key documents such as civil registry records, photos, the medal warrant bestowed by Emperor Menelik II upon Sadık Pasha and drew my attention to Haqqi and Rafiq Al Azm's Arabic translation. Sinem Gülmez from SALT Research Ottoman Bank Archives kindly provided the image for the seal of Sadık Pasha. Saeed Ibrahim at the Egyptian National Library provided a copy of Haqqi and Rafiq Al Azm's *Rihlat Al Habasha* that included the map of Sadık Pasha's journey. It was Nora Barazi who made it possible to obtain a copy of this map. Finally, my thanks also go to Elisabeth Biasio, Peter Gerber, Felix and Vreni Ilg, Daniela Zurbrügg who showed an interest in this work.

The translation uses current place names and dates, but, in spite of long sentences and occasional difficulties in translating verbatim, deliberately follows the original text closely to reflect Sadık Pasha's spirit and his era.

This book is dedicated to my father, Cengiz Gökkent, because he inspired me to translate Sadık Pasha's work.

Dr. Gıyas Müeyyed Gökkent
Bodrum, April 2021

Azmzâde Sadık el-Müeyyed Pasha
(1860-1910)

Source: Family collection

Azmzâde Sadık el-Müeyyed Pasha

Azmzâde Sadık el-Müeyyed was an Ottoman officer and statesman born in Damascus in 1860.[i] He was one of eight children of Azmzâde Salih Izdeshir Bey.[ii] His mother's name was Safiye. He lived in Al Jisr Al Abyad, Damascus during childhood. After spending his early years there, he is likely to have studied at Collège Saint Joseph in Antoura[iii] near Beirut and then in Al Madrasa Al Wataniya[iv] in Beirut. He enrolled at the Military College in Istanbul in 1880 and graduated in 1883.

After a brief period in the regular army, Sadık Pasha began his career as an aide-de-camp of Sultan Abdulhamid II. In 1887, seeking to prevent further loss of Ottoman territory in North Africa in the face of a West European scramble for colonies, the sultan sent him to Jaghbub as an envoy to Sayed Mohamed Al Mahdi Al Senusi, the leader of the Senusi movement, known as the Ikhwan or Brotherhood.[v]

In 1888, Sadık Pasha attended the coronation of Kaiser Wilhelm II as part of the Ottoman delegation. In the same year, he traveled with the Russian Czar's brother Grand Duke Sergei Alexandrovich to Jerusalem. In May 1891, he went to Germany for further military training.

Sadık Pasha went as an envoy to Sheikh Senusi for a second time in 1895, this time to Kufra in the Grand Sahara. His prominence at this time is reflected in his appearance on the cover of *Le Petit Journal* published in France.[vi] His diary on his travels in the Sahara was published as a book in 1897 and serialized in the *Servet-i Fünûn* weekly in 1898. In the same year, he was in Thessaloniki on an assignment in the aftermath of the Greco-Turkish war in 1897.

In 1900, Sadık Pasha supervised the construction of the Hejaz telegraph line. In 1902, he became deputy to Marshall Kazım Pasha, the Minister of Hejaz Railroad Construction and Works. Both of these projects were crucial for facilitating the Haj pilgrimage and for more rapid, secure links with the holy lands.

In 1904, Sadık Pasha headed a delegation to the court of the Ethiopian Emperor Menelik II to thwart Italian colonial ambitions. After this mission, he was appointed as imperial commissaire to Bulgaria towards the end of the same year. He served in this capacity until 1908, a year which saw the restoration of constitutional monarchy and culminated in the deposition of Sultan Abdulhamid II early in 1909.

Sadık Pasha was appointed as the civil and military governor of Jeddah at the start of 1910, but passed away in mid-October at his home in Istanbul where he had come for treatment for a bacterial infection on his back referred to as şirpençe, literally translated lion's claw.

During his career, Sadık Pasha received a gold Imtiyaz medal awarded for extraordinary loyalty and gallantry, a silver Imtiyaz medal, four Osmani, four Mejidi medals, Russian order of Saint Anna of the first rank, the Ethiopian order of the seal of Solomon of the first rank, German Red Eagle order second class, and the German imperial order of the crown third class.[vii] Sadık Pasha traveled to far-flung parts of the Ottoman Empire and had a wide range of interests. Besides his own legacy, Ottoman and other official records, as well as a growing volume of academic research, a close glimpse into his early career and the man himself through English eyes can be found in *The Letters from Constantinople*, published in 1897.[viii] Sadık Pasha spoke Arabic, Turkish, French, and German. He published seven books, ranging from his books on the Sahara and Ethiopia to compilation and translation of books on chemistry, photography, history and even children's books.

Sadık Pasha was married to Azmzâde Esma who was extraordinary in her own right as a recipient of the imperial order of charity of the second rank and, later, of the first rank. In the early 1900s, they lived in Teşvikiye, Istanbul with their three children, Masune, Celaleddin, and Gıyasiddin, my grandfather.[ix]

Selected Dates in the Life of Sadık Pasha

- Born in Damascus - 1860[x]
- Enrolled in the Military College in Harbiye, Istanbul - 15-09-1880[xi]
- Graduated with the rank of Mülazım-ı thani -Second Lieutenant-1883
- Joined imperial aides-de-camp - Mülazım-ı evvel - First Lieutenant - 1884[xii]
- Promoted to Yüzbaşı - Captain - 15-01-1885
- Promoted to Kolağası - Major - 1886
- Visited Jaghbub as envoy to Sayed Mohamed Al Mahdi Al-Senusi- 03-12-1887[xiii]
- Visited the German Empire as a part of a delegation representing the Ottoman Empire on the coronation of Kaiser Wilhelm II - 15 June 1888
- Accompanied Grand Duke Sergei Alexandrovich, the Russian czar's brother, to Damascus and Jerusalem - June 1888[xiv]
- Awarded German imperial order of the crown third class-04-08-1888
- Promoted to Binbaşı – Lieutenant Colonel - 26-08-1888[xv]
- Awarded a silver Imtiyaz[1] medal -1888
- Military training in Berlin, Germany - 28-05-1891[xvi]
- Promoted to Kaymakam - Colonel - 29-07-1894[xvii]
- Traveled to Kufra as envoy to Sayed Mohamed Al Mahdi Al Senusi – October 1895
- Awarded medal - 22-12-1895[xviii]
- Miralay – Brigadier, Report on Benghazi - 14-01-1896[xix]
- On duty in Birecik - July 1896[xx]
- On duty in Deir-ez zor - 10-12-1896[xxi]
- Awarded Mejid medal of the second rank - 07-05-1898[xxii]
- Awarded German Red Eagle order second class - 21-08-1898

---

1   Literally translated 'distinction'

- Presented his book titled *Bir Osmanlı Zabitinin Sahrayı Kebirde Seyahati* [An Ottoman Officer's Journey in the Grand Sahara] to the padishah - 27-02-1899[xxiii]
- Promoted to Mirliva – Major General - 15-03-1899[xxiv]
- Traveled to Skopje, capital of the Kosovo Province[xxv] - 11-03-1900[xxvi]
- Assigned to construction of the Hejaz telegraph line -15-03-1900[xxvii]
- Awarded gold Imtiyaz medal – highest military award for extraordinary loyalty and gallantry - 23-04-1900[xxviii]
- Visited Jerusalem - 28-06-1900
- Hejaz telegraph line extension from Ma'an to Mecca -14-10-1900[xxix]
- Awarded Mejid medal of the first rank - 09-01-1901[xxx]
- Transferred from Mecca to work as deputy to the Minister of Hejaz Railroad Construction and Works Marshall Kazım Pasha - 01-01-1902[xxxi]
- Promoted to Ferik – Lieutenant General - 25-07-1902[xxxii]
- Awarded the Order of Saint Anna of the first order by the Russian Czar 06-11-1902[xxxiii]
- Awarded Ottoman medal of the first rank - 7-11-1902[xxxiv]
- Visited Pecha[xxxv] - 04- 05-1903[xxxvi]
- In Thessaloniki 14-9-1903[xxxvii]
- Headed delegation to Emperor Menelik II - 28-04-1904[xxxviii]
- Awarded Order of the Seal of Solomon of the first rank
- Traveled to Chechnya 05-09-1904[xxxix]
- Posted to Sofia as Imperial Commissaire in Bulgaria - 01-11-1904[xl]
- Visited Berlin with a delegation - 28-05-1905[xli]
- Published *Habeş Seyahatnamesi* [The Abyssinia Book of Travels], 1906
- Visited Kosova - 21-10-1906[xlii]
- Promoted to Birinci Ferik - General - 01-02-1907[xliii]
- Posted to Jeddah -Vali Kaymakam – Governor - 31-01-1910[xliv]
- Passed away at his house in Teşvikiye, Nişantaşı - October 1910[xlv]

Publications

- *Fernando* - Translation, Esad Efendi 20. Matbaası, H1300 (1883), EHT 1961 A279, National Library, Republic of Turkey
- *Al-Kimya fi Tahlil Al-Hawa wa'l Ma* [Chemistry in the Analysis of Air and Water] – Translation, H1301 (1884), NEKTY07003, Istanbul University Rare Works Library, Turkey
- *Tarih Al Futuh Al Sham* [The History of the Conquest of Sham], Translation of a work by Al Imam Mohammad Al Waqidi, Tercüman-ı Hakikat Matbaası, H1302 (1885), EHT 1960 A443, National Library, Republic of Turkey
- *Fenn-i Fotoğraf* [The Science of Photography], NEKTY04364, Istanbul University Rare Works Library, Turkey
- *Küçük Hanri* [Little Henry], Translation of a work by Christoph von Schmid, Kasbar Matbaası, H1307 (1891), EFKDP065911, Edebiyat Fakültesi Kütüphanesi, Istanbul University Library, Turkey
- *Afrika Sahra-yı Kebirinde Seyahat: Bir Osmanlı Zabitinin Sahra-yı Kebirde Seyahati* [Journey in the Grand Sahara of Africa: An Ottoman Officer's Journey in the Grand Sahara], Alem Matbaası - Ahmed İhsan ve Şürekası, H1314 (1897)[2], NEKTY04526, Istanbul University Rare Works Library, Turkey
- *Habeş Seyahatnamesi* [The Abyssinia Book of Travels], İkdam Matbaası, H1322 (1906)[3], EHT 1971 A89, National Library, Republic of Turkey

---

2   Translated to Arabic in *Rihlah fi al-Sahra al-kubra bi-Afriqiya*, Silsilat al-Dirasat al-Mutarjamah, 1998. Translated to modern Turkish script by Idris Bostan, *Afrika Sahrâ-yı Kebîri'nde Seyahat*, Sâdık el-Müeyyed, Çamlıca, 2008

3   First partly translated to Arabic by Jamil al-Azm and later in full by former Syrian Prime Minister Haqqi al-Azm and author/politician Rafiq al-Azm. More recent edition in Arabic published as *Rihlat al-Habashah, min al-Asitanah ila Adis Ababa* by Azm, Sadiq Basha al-Mu'ayyad, Beirut: al-Mu'assasah al-Arabiyah lil-Dirasat wa-al-Nashr, 2001. Part of the original text is available in modern Turkish script as *Habeş Seyahatnamesi*, translated by Mustafa Baydemir, Kaknüs, 1999

Endnotes

i   Based on civil registry records in Syria. However, an alternative reference cites 1858 as his year of birth. See Bostan, Idris translation of *Afrika Sahrâ-yı Kebîri'nde Seyahat* by Azmzâde Sadık el-Müeyyed, Istanbul, 2008

ii   Salih Bey remarried after the death of his first wife and altogether had eight children. His name may be written in modern Turkish script as Azmzâde Salih İzdeşir el-Müeyyed

iii   In family records, the schools he attended are listed as Madrasat Antoura and Madrasat Al Boustani. See http://www.alazmfamily.com/notables.htm . However, the first is likely a reference to Collège Saint Joseph located about 20km from Beirut, https://www.csja.edu.lb. Officials at the school could not find a record of his attendance, but indicated that the records may not be complete. The second is likely a reference to the famous Madrasat Al Wataniya at the time whose founder was Mr. Al Boustani. This school was also located in proximity to Sadık Pasha's grandfather's summer house which is where the American University of Beirut Medical School stands today

iv   In Zokak Al Blatt in Beirut. The building is currently a ruin

v   Located in modern day Libya

vi   *Le Petit Journal*, Supplement du Dimanche, No:262, 24, November 1895

vii   There is also a reference to a medal for the Greco-Turkish War of 1897 citing state annals. See Bostan, Idris translation of *Afrika Sahrâ-yı Kebîri'nde Seyahat* by Azmzâde Sadık el-Müeyyed, Istanbul, 2008

viii   For a more personal account of Sadık Pasha refer to Müller, Georgina Adelaide (Mrs. Max Müller), *Letters from Constantinople*, Longmans, Green, & co, 1897

ix   Syrian civil registry records list their address as number 62 in Teşvikiye, Istanbul, but a fire burnt their house either in late 1902 or early 1903. It is not clear whether number 62 was their residence before or after the fire. They are likely to have continued residing in the same neighborhood after the fire, although they also had a summerhouse in Bostancı, Istanbul. Sultan Abdulhamid II bestowed an imperial grant of 100 Lira to Sadık Pasha after the fire. See Republic of Turkey Presidency Directorate of State (Ottoman) Archives Ref: ML.EEM 1372-69, R-6-11-1308. The archive date is incorrect and should be 1318 since Sadık Pasha mentions that the fire occurred a year before his visit to Addis Ababa in his *Habeş Seyahatnamesi*. Refer also below for other earlier residences near the Yıldız Palace where the aides-de-camp offices were located

x   Courtesy of İklil Azmzâde from civil registry records, Damascus, Syrian Arab Republic

xi   'Yaveran-ı hazret-i şehriyarileri kulları : Binbaşı Sadık Bey kulları bin Salih', NEKYA90964/4, Rare Collections Library, Istanbul University

xii   Republic of Turkey Presidency Dir of State Archives Ref: MB.İ. 131-22, H-13-08-1301

xiii   Republic of Turkey Presidency Dir of State Archives Ref:Y..MTV.29-15,H-17-03-1305

xiv   Republic of Turkey Presidency Dir of State Archives Ref:DH.MKT1561-18,H01-03-1306

xv   Republic of Turkey Presidency Dir of State Archives Ref:İ.DH1094-85804,H-18-12-1305

xvi   Republic of Turkey Presidency Dir of State Arch Ref: Y.PRK.MYD 10-48, H-19-01-1308

xvii Republic of Turkey Presidency Dir of State Archives Ref: İ.TAL.57-65, H-25-01-1312
xviii Republic of Turkey Presidency Dir of State Archives Ref:Y.PRK.UM34-27,H-05-07-1313
xix Republic of Turkey Presidency Dir of State Archives Ref: Y.E. 9-13, H-28-07-1313
xx   Republic of Turkey Presidency Dir of State Archives Ref: İ.Mİ. 18-45, H-11-02-1314
xxi Republic of Turkey Presidency Dir of State Archives Ref: İ.HUS. 50-132, H-05-07-1314
xxii Republic of Turkey Presidency Dir of State Archives Ref: İ.TAL. 137-20, H-15-12-1315
xxiii Republic of Turkey Presidency Dir of State Arch Ref:Y.PRK.MYD21-106,H-16-10-1316
xxiv Republic of Turkey Presidency Dir of State Archives Ref: İ.TAL 168-7 H-03-11-1316
xxv Capital of present day Macedonia
xxvi Republic of Turkey Presidency Dir of State Archives Ref:Y.PRK.MYD23-7H-09-11-1317
xxvii Republic of Turkey Presidency Dir of State Archives Ref: Y.MTV. 201-29 H-07-12-1317
xxviii Republic of Turkey Presidency Dir. of State Archives Ref: İ.TAL 207-54, H-22-12-1317
xxix Republic of Turkey Presidency Dir of State Arch Ref:DH.MKT2414.73,H-19-06-1318
xxx Republic of Turkey Presidency Dir of State Archives Ref: İ.TAL 237-23, H-18-09-1318
xxxi Republic of Turkey Presidency Dir of State Archives Ref: İ.ML 48-14, H-21-09-1319
xxxii Republic of Turkey Presidency Dir of State Archives Ref: İ.TAL 281-9, H-18-04-1320
xxxiii Republic of Turkey Presidency Dir of State Archives Ref: İ.TAL 289-5, H-25-04-1320
xxxiv Republic of Turkey Presidency Dir of State Archives Ref: İ.TAL 289-1, H-05-08-1320
xxxv In modern day Kosovo
xxxvi Republic of Turkey Presidency Dir of State Archives Ref: HH.İ. 157-51, H-06-02-1321
xxxvii Republic of Turkey Presidency Dir of State Arch Ref:Y.PRK.ASK204-10,H21-06-1321
xxxviii Azmzâde Sadık el-Müeyyed, *Habeş seyahatnamesi*, Ikdam Matbaası, H1322 and Republic of Turkey Presidency Dir of State Archives Ref: HR.TH. 302-27M-27-04-1904
xxxix Republic of Turkey Presidency Dir of State Arch Ref:DH.MKT886-30, H-24-06-1322
xl Republic of Turkey Presidency Dir of State Arch Ref: A.MTZ(04)122-69,H-22-08-1322
xli   Republic of Turkey Presidency Dir of State Archives Ref: HR.SFR799-31, M-28-05-1905
xlii Republic of Turkey Presidency Dir of State Arch Ref: BEO 2930-219731, H-03-09-1324
xliii Republic of Turkey Presidency Dir of State Archives Ref: İ.TAL 413-59, H-17-12-1324
xliv Republic of Turkey Presidency Dir of State Archives Ref: İ.DH 1479 – 37, H-19-01-1328
xlv Republic of Turkey Presidency Dir of State Archives Ref: HR.UHM. 79 – 50, M-07-11-1910 and Ref: 14-6, H-27-09-1330

Haqqi Al Azm
(1864 - 1955)
First Prime Minister
of the Syrian Republic
1932-1934

Rafiq Al Azm
(1865-1925)
Author, Politician

Missing sections in the Ottoman version of this book were completed using the Arabic translation of Sadık Pasha's *Habeş Seyahatnamesi* published under the title of *Rihlat al Habasha,* Sarai Barudi Printing Press, Cairo, 1908 by his relatives Haqqi Al Azm and Rafiq Al Azm.

Selected Dates in Ottoman-Ethiopian Relations

- Ottoman forces under Özdemir Paşa capture Massawa - 1557[4]
- Monitoring of English and French ships travelling along Hejaz, Ethiopia and Yemen coasts and monitoring of missionaries - 1849[5]
- Elimination of export levies for Ethiopian products that will be transported from Massawa Port - 1850[6]
- Troops and ammunition being transferred for the conquest of Ethiopia from Egypt -1857[7]
- The loyalty of the clans and tribes on Massawa Island on the shore of Ethiopia and islands until Bab Al Mandab to the caliph - 1862[8]
- Massawa captured by Italy - 1885
- Thanks of the Ethiopian Emperor due to the permission for the construction of a church in Jerusalem for the worship of Ethiopian priests and nuns - 1886[9]
- Investigation of Italy's transport of troops to Ethiopia to determine if it could be for the conquest of Tripoli - 1887[10]
- Ban on exports of animals from Syria demanded by Italy for the army they transferred to Ethiopia - 1887[11]
- Step by step conquest of Ethiopia by Italians and prevention of the capture of Ethiopian mountains which feed the fertile waters of the Nile - 1890[12]

---

4   See Sarınay, Yusuf, *Ottoman Archives and Ethio-Ottoman Relations*, DSA, Ankara, 2001
5   Rep. of Turkey Dir. of State Archives Ref:A.MKT.MHM16-19,H-12-09-1265[1-8-1849]
6   Rep. of Turkey Dir of State Archives Ref: HR.MKT. 37-82, H-03-02-1267 [8-12-1850]
7   Rep. of Turkey Dir of State Archives Ref:A.MKT.UM269-20,H-01-06-1273[27-1-1857]
8   Rep of Turkey Dir of State Archives Ref: A.M.26-40, H-29-06-1278 [1-1-1862]
9   Rep. of Turkey Dir of State Archives Ref: Y.A.HUS194-19,H-07-11-1303[7-8-1886]
10 Rep. of Turkey Dir of State Archives Ref:Y.PRK.MŞK12-50,H-24-02-1305[11-11-1887]
11 Rep. of Turkey Dir of State Archives Ref: MV. 26-65, H-22-03-1305 [8-12-1887]
12 Rep. of Turkey Dir of State Archives Ref:Y.PRK.TKM19-24,H-02-03-1308[16-10-1890]

- Defeat of Italians in battle with Emperor Menelik - March 1896[13]
- The desire of England to subjugate the region from the Cape of Good Hope to Central Africa and the necessity to act against England with Ethiopia - January 1897[14]
- The reception of Prince Ato Joseph sent by the Ethiopian Emperor Menelik - August 1897[15]
- The satisfaction of the padishah with the gifts sent by the Ethiopian Emperor and the goodwill shown to Muslims and reciprocation with gifts - February 1898[16]
- Candelabra and valuable gifts presented to Ethiopian Emperor Menelik II - May 1898[17]
- Friendship letter of Emperor Menelik II - July 1899[18]
- Receipt of Amharic note sent by the Ethiopian Emperor, a tiger and a lion and query on where they should be delivered - August 1900[19]
- Note on the goals of Italy and England regarding Tripoli and Ethiopia[20]
- Lieutenant General Sadık Paşa, Binbaşı Talip Bey and certain personnel from the rifle brigade, as well as Ibrahim Bekir Bey traveling to Ethiopia - May 1904[21]
- Note on the establishment of an Ottoman consulate in Ethiopia - January 1910[22]. An Ottoman consulate was opened in Harar in 1912. Following the dissolution of the Ottoman Empire, Republic of Turkey opened representative offices in 1926

---

13 Rep. of Turkey, Dir.. of State Archives Ref: Y.EE.118-29, H-27-09-1313 [12-3-1896]
14 Rep. of Turkey Dir. of State Archives Ref: Y.PRK.HR23-1, H-01-08-1314 [5-1-1897]
15 Rep. of Turkey Dir. of State Archives Ref:Y.PRK.PT16-6,H-21-03-1315 [20-8-1897]
16 Rep. of Turkey Dir of State Archives Ref: Y.PRK.NMH.7-66, H-11-09-1315 [3-2-1898]
17 Rep. of Turkey Dir. of State Archives Ref: HH.İ.114-69, H-25-12-1315 [17-5-1898]
18 Rep. of Turkey Dir. of State Archives Ref: Y.EE.62-41, H-25-02-1317 [5-7-1899]
19 Rep. of Turkey Dir of State Archives Ref:Y.PRK.MYD.23-38,H-18-04-1318[15-8-1900]
20 Rep. of Turkey Dir. of State Archives Ref:Y.MTV.239-13 H-21-10-1320 [21-1-1903]
21 Rep. of Turkey Dir. of State Archives Ref: HR.TH.302-27, R-25-02-1320 [8-5-1904]
22 Rep. of Turkey Dir of State Archives Ref:HR.HMŞ.İŞO53-11,R-07-11-1325[20-01-1910]

The Ethiopia Book of Travels

Author

Of His Imperial Majesty's Aides-de-Camp
Imperial Commissaire to Bulgaria
Lieutenant General Azmzâde Sadık el-Müeyyed

Published in series in the İkdam newspaper after
approval from the High Domestic Printing Authority

Dersaadet - İkdam Printing Press
1322 [1906]

Preface

His Imperial Majesty the supreme benefactor whose rule is the source of success and the salvation of the country and state ensured the beginning of my success with the knowledge that I have gained that has come by registering at the military school where I completed studies and graduated with a diploma thanks to imperial support and again through imperial grace I have traveled to various locations, the last of which was my humble assignment to Ethiopia, so that given both this work and the owner of this work have resulted from the imperial grace of our benefactor, our master the mighty Padishah, I declare my gratitude and thanks.

Of His Imperial Majesty's Aides-de-Camp Lieutenant General
Azmzâde Sadık el-Müeyyed

Thursday, April 28   Departure from Istanbul

Departure from Istanbul • Piraeus translators • Two nice hours in Napoli • Arrival to Marseilles • Automated waiter and water bearer • Arrival to Port Said • The skills of Red Sea sailors • Continuing on the way

On the twenty-eighth day of last April at ten o'clock, we departed from Istanbul, with Major Talip Bey of the Imperial Second Division officers and honorary imperial aides-de-camp and Yasin Efendi of the sergeants of the Imperial Supreme Guards Rifle Division accompanying me, by embarking on the "Orenoque" ship of the Messageries Maritimes Company so as to get on the first ship going from Marseilles to Djibouti since I was assigned by the supreme order of the noble guardian of the caliphate to deliver an imperial letter to His Majesty the Ethiopian Emperor Menelik II from the most noble, His Imperial Majesty, the supreme sovereign. Our ship was big and quite clean. It was traveling thirteen miles per hour. One strolled amply in the lounges, deck since there were hardly twenty-five, thirty male, female passengers in first class.

We arrived to Çanakkale at night. After stopping just enough to pick up and deliver mail, the ship continued on its way. The weather was quite nice and calm. Arriving to Izmir at half past seven o'clock alaturca time[23]

---

23   *Alla Turca in Italian, à la Turca in French, or alaturka in Turkish was used to refer to time keeping in the Ottoman Empire. Under this system, time was set at 12:00 at sunset. Sunset

the next day, Friday, the ship anchored off the pier and quite a lot of cotton, eggs, figs and grapes began to be loaded to take to Marseilles. That Friday, I went out to the city and obtained some missing items required for the journey. Although I had taken voyages before to Africa, one time to Jaghbub, once to Kufra, from Damascus to Hejaz due to the assignment for the Hejaz telegraph line and on duty to imperial Anatolia and had sufficient tools required for travel, the necessary equipment for the journey had to be procured again since our house, with all the things inside, burned down last year.

After our ship completed loading at half past seven o'clock following an interval of twenty-four hours' rest in front of Izmir, we departed towards Piraeus. While we were having dinner, the weather had worsened and the ship started to sway excessively and everyone lost his cheer. Leaving their meal halfway, the passengers began to retire to their cabins one by one. I was also forced to retire to my cabin and sleep at one o'clock since I still had not become used to stormy weathers despite having traveled at sea numerous times and encountered ferocious storms.

Our ship arrived to the port of Piraeus on Sunday morning. After obtaining clearance as usual, the inside of the ship filled with hotel translators and brokers, other travel translators, boatmen. They surrounded the cabin passengers. Of these translators who spoke various languages, some spoke English, French, some Greek at the same time. Of the ones falling to my humble share, I was assuming that the one speaking in French spoke Turkish, the Turkish speaking one spoke French. They are using all articulation and eloquence to take the passenger outside to tour Athens. After a translator who had guided a person from among my friends who had passed from here on duty before me showed his business card and the reference written behind it, I went outside the ship in his company together with the other passengers. Getting on a landau[24] so as to look around freely and stop where desired, we set out towards Athens. As we stopped in front of antiquities and other places worth seeing, the translator started putting

---

in Izmir was at 18:56 on April 29th, 1904. The Ottomans referred to the European time keeping system as alafranga

24 *A convertible four wheeled carriage

on strange demeanors, pointing right and left with his hands, imitating the historical characters in the events that he was telling and providing descriptions, more than necessary explanations.

Anyhow, after touring Athens by carriage a few hours, we returned to Piraeus by getting on a train. We found the third class passenger deck quite crowded when we boarded the ship. We departed from here at six o'clock alaturca time. A rumor began to go around in the ship: "A storm will apparently break out in the evening!" Evening came. However, this storm that had been announced before did not break out, fortunately. On the contrary, the weather was nice in the evening. This night passed comfortably. I learned something new at dinner. Let me mention it here: I had read that horse meat was eaten in Europe and had even seen large mules which had been skinned in butcher shops in Paris with the label "fat mule" written on them. However, I did not know that donkey meat was also eaten. In effect, there should not be a difference between horse, mule, donkey meats logically and scientifically. It is possible that their meats are similar to one another since they are fed with the same nourishment. For this reason, he who eats horse meat, possibly also eats donkey meat, too. However, I had not heard that they were numerous enough for consumption since donkeys are only kept in zoos in most European capitals. At dinner that day, a quite thick, but thinly sliced sausage with a nice appearance came before the soup. Without touching it, I made do with olive, butter, and sardines since I did not know its kind. A rather fat, affable priest who was next to me and whose familiarity with delicious dishes was apparent from his face and healthy appearance recommended it, telling me: "Definitely eat from this sausage, it is made from mule and donkey meat. It is very delicious!" and those at the table affirmed. Thanking them, I apologized.

We passed through the Messina Strait between Italy and Sicily at midnight. We saw the island and town of Stromboli on our left side the following morning, on Tuesday. We passed the time for a while by watching the smoke from the volcano on it. We sailed between Capri Island and the shore of Napoli at five o'clock alafranga time. There is a natural tunnel one can pass from one side to the other on a big rock near Capri island: it is visible from the ship. It is being recounted among the passengers that the famous Krupp, the owner of the big artillery plant in Germany, had died in his mansion on Capri Island and His Imperial Majesty Wilhelm II had come here for the purpose of touring twenty days ago.

We entered the natural harbor of Napoli, created by the hand of God in the most beautiful way, at six o'clock alafranga time. The harbor is in the shape of a very big egg and the sea protrudes into the land from the open side. Mountains surround it and the famous Vesuvius Volcano is seen on its right side. Besides this natural harbor, the region has a nice pier.

Musician girls and boys welcomed the ship with boats upon approach, playing instruments, singing beautiful songs. The enthusiasm and deray of the musicians was increasing as coins were thrown by passengers to the inside of the umbrella that the most beautiful of the musician girls had opened towards the ship to collect money, presenting a beautiful scene with the view of the country and the setting of the sun. Especially the basket after basket of flowers in some of the other boats… Above all, a type of quite beautiful, layered white carnation that I saw for the first time in my life… Fruits in other boats…Especially the numerous quantities of cherry baskets…The boats drew up alongside the ship. The music and cheer increased. The musician girls finally began to dance in the boats. Leaning to the side of the ship, all the passengers were immersed watching this.

I was among those settling for watching the country from outside since the ship was only going to be staying for two, three hours. Health checks were conducted with great care and at length. Most of the deck passengers departed from the ship to transfer to another ship.

Although the flower, fruit, dance, music boats retreated one by one with the evening, the lights of the city, the beauty of the scene was giving the soul an alternate pleasure. The ship continued on its way after taking and dropping off some cargo.

The weather was cloudy, the sea choppy on Wednesday. I was among those who could not eat lunch. At six o'clock in the afternoon, we left the Monte Cristo Island, which had earned fame because Alexandre Dumas had selected it as the stage for his famous novel, on our right. Most of the passengers retired to their cabins early since the ship continued to sway.

Sighting the coast the next day, Thursday, we started approaching Marseilles. We entered the famous Joliette port of Marseilles at half past four o'clock in the afternoon. Leaving all our belongings other than our handbag at customs since we were going to be transferred to another ship, we became guests at the Hotel Genève located on Canebière Street that the Marseillais consider a source of pride even against Parisians. While much can be written on the scenery of Marseilles, its location, my observations there, I made do with recording only the things that attracted my attention most since this travel book is on Ethiopia.

Leaving my bags in my room at the hotel, I started looking for a ship that would go to Djibouti or Aden. I went to the English company named Peninsular. They stated that they had a ship going to Aden the next day, could not say whether ships operated between Aden and Djibouti or not, and this point could be learned from agencies in Port Said. I decided to depart with the aforementioned ship with the intent to wait to embark on the first ship to Djibouti in Port Said if it could not be learned in Port Said whether there were ships between Aden and Djibouti.

On Friday morning, while we were sitting outside the café on Canebière Street immediately adjacent to the shore that had been mentioned and looking around, the waiter lowered the awning almost near the ground by loosening the ropes of the canvas above us and we could no longer see the surroundings. I asked for the reason. He pointed towards the clock on the wall. I looked at the clock that showed half past seven. I understood the reason somewhat later. It turns out that the awning is lowered every day at this hour as protection from the sun. However, the weather was quite cloudy today. Nonetheless, the 'automatic' waiter had not thought of this and had supposedly done his duty. A story similar to this came to my mind as I was drinking my coffee:

We were strolling with a number of my officer friends on a Sunday fourteen years ago while I was in Berlin. The weather suddenly worsened. It was obviously going to rain hard. It became necessary to get in somewhere. We went to a friend whose house was the nearest to the place where we were. It really began to rain quite hard, the waters began to flow in the form of a stream on two sides of the road. Everybody was scurrying around. As for us, we were looking from the window to the big street in front of us. After coming until the water tap on the road with his two-wheeled barrel pulled by an animal and filling the barrel with a hose, a municipal official, charged with pouring water on the road, went to wherever the road had been watered till and started pouring water on the road from there onwards. He poured water under that violent rain until he completed the section that was his share. He did not care even though he was soaking wet. At that moment, the host came to our side. We asked what this man was doing. He regarded this situation as normal, saying "He is doing his duty!"

Transferring our heavy baggage at customs to a big ship of the Peninsular Company, we departed from Marseilles at noon alafranga time. I had seen the Messageries ship as big and orderly upon departure from Istanbul. It really is like that. However, I thought I entered a house bigger than one with ten rooms, a Hotel Continental or Pera Palace when getting inside this ship. Before departing from the ship, the agency official introduced me to the inspector of the company and the ship's security chief, who were traveling on the ship, because these two persons knew a little French. The ship's crew, which was about two hundred, could not speak a language other than English. Such a disinterest of the English to French was really very strange even though the French and English were neighbors such that a person could have breakfast in Paris in the morning, eat lunch in London, throw the cigarette that he had lit while departing from the French coast on the English coast after an hour and a half. There were a lot of French people on the ship. Those of them who did not know English like me were quite bored because not even one of the waiters knew a language other than English, as I mentioned. This situation cannot be a coincidence because it is customary to keep waiters who speak various languages at ships, hotels since there could be people from all countries. The opposite of this principal was abided by here.

As for the order, cleanliness, size, speed of the ship, there is nothing to say. With deadweight of twenty thousand five hundred and twenty seven tons, sixteen thousand five hundred horse power, it has four hundred beds for first class cabin passengers, one hundred and eighty beds for second class. Each class passenger eats at a different lounge. Although there are fixed chairs for four hundred passengers in the first class lounge, the distances between the tables, chairs have been abundantly calculated and arranged in a manner that there would be ten people at each table. The stairs of the ship are symmetric, sloped, decorated with carpets and quite ornate like hotel stairs. The ceilings are high. If a person did not look at the sea, one could believe one's self to be in a hotel. The upholstery and decoration in the dining, reading, cigarette and coffee lounges are excellent. The lounges are bright with electricity. Quite cool breezes can be created even in the hottest weather when the ventilator fans are working.

The tables are set four times a day. Meals are eaten at each. The passenger finds a printed list with the names of the dishes in front of him each time. Whatever dishes he desires from the list, those are brought. The baths of the ship are equipped with quite excellent and neat showers. The decks are quite large. A net is stretched around one of the decks towards evening. English passengers pass time with a ball game that they call tennis.

With quite a lot of Indians among the ship's attendants, those adhering to the Buddhist religion have worn hats, while some of the Muslims have worn a white trouser, put on a blue and long tunic, wrapped around a long and red turban and the other portion have worn a wide tunic, a wide trouser one of which is white and wrapped a big, red turban. A quite nice scene emerges on the ship when the crew is all lined up on roll call day. The company's inspector was on my right side at the dining table, two German merchants going to the Far East were on my left. We chatted a little bit with them during meal times and the inspector ordered my meal from the waiters if required.

Our ship was new and had set out on travel for the second time. It was moving at sixteen miles per hour speed, with the capability to go faster if necessary. A special map for the passengers to find out where they are in the sea exists such that the direction that the ship is following is drawn in red ink on this map and the present location is shown with the longitude and latitude indicated on the map each day at noon time and the date is being inserted there. In this way, the passengers see the distance that they have covered and understand the time of arrival to the port they are going to by comparison and calculation without asking the captain.

A person enters somebody else's cabin because of the abundance of cabins and the resemblance of the corridors if he does not look at his cabin number. Although all doors have locks, the cabins do not have keys, bolts. This precaution must have been taken with the consideration that everyone can rush out to the deck immediately to save his life without panicking to open the door in a moment of sudden emergency. Although I asked for a key from the waiter a few times, he did not understand or did not want to understand.

The day after our departure, in other words on Saturday, the weather was quite cloudy and the wind was rough. The sun did not appear at all. On Sunday, the sky cleared and pleasant weather followed. Monday was also nice since we were always heading towards the south. The following day, or Tuesday tenth of May, we entered Port Said two hours after midday, in line with calculations and estimates.

Leaving my belongings on the ship, I toured the agencies one by one. They informed me that a small ship sailed back and forth between Aden and Djibouti, but it had been under repair for some time and for this reason there was no other way than seeking a sailing ship to cross from Aden to Djibouti. No longer seeing a need to go to Aden, we checked into "Hotel de Post" after handing over our belongings to the warehouse of the Cook Company located seaside. I selected this hotel since they informed me that this hotel's owner had worked in hospitality in Djibouti for a few years and the hotel was clean and the scenery around it was nice.

If the question of why one would not go from Aden to Djibouti with a sail ship comes to mind, let me state that the sail ships on the Red Sea coasts and outside it, in other words those that sail back and forth in the Gulf of Aden, are not such big and proper ships and most almost consist of a barge with sails. I had boarded such a ship once from Rabigh until Jeddah when I was on the Hejaz telegraph line assignment. I only understood what it was at daytime and after having left the shore since I had embarked on the boat at night. The hull had been built so unevenly and non-uniformly that two individuals were forced to constantly empty water with buckets to the sea. The sail was ripped and torn from end to end during the journey. The sailors did not even have the needle, packing needle thread to sew this. Fortunately, we had these. The gendarmes who were with me stitched it so that we could complete our journey thus.

However, the skills of the Arabs in sailing are really worth mentioning: We were passing between corals since we were going parallel and close to the coast. A person sees nothing if he looks at the sea surface. However, it can be seen that one is traveling over a forest of coral if attention is paid to the depth of the sea. The captain would read from memory to the helmsman without pause, "Right! Now left! Avoid the branch at such place, the snag in another! We arrived at such place! We passed such place!" and the helmsman would maneuver according to that. Our boat was cruising at twelve miles speed with the strength of the wind and leaving a snake-like trail on the water in its wake.

Most ships that approach the coast in the Red Sea take such a specialist local Arab under the name of a guide (pilot). Most of those that did not take one have run their ships to the ground on the corals. The masts of these can still be seen here and there. One should see the rowboats that the Arabs on the coast use, too. Made from very long, solid wood, a person can hardly fit in the widest part. Getting in like this during the day, the coastal Arab fishes in the sea during the day, takes it to his hut in the evening, carrying it like a pole on his shoulder. He turns it upside down if there occurs a storm in the sea. In other words, he mounts it like mounting a horse and comes in that way. If the weather is good, he reverses it and gets into it. There is nothing inside that will be spilled, become wet. The boat has an oar the size of a showel, while the boatman has a cloth on his waist.

Thus, having seen these at the time, I did not long to travel with a small boat from Aden to Djibouti, in the Gulf of Aden and at the mouth of the Indian Ocean at all.

Since we would land on the shores of French Somalia and cross from there to go to Ethiopia, references had been written by the noble French ambassador His Excellency Monsieur Constans introducing my humble delegation, that had been ordered by his most noble, most honorable, supreme imperial highness, to the Governor of Somalia located in Djibouti and the French ambassador at the Ethiopian capital, and sent to the French consulate in Port Said to be handed over to me. I thanked both his excellency the ambassador and Monsieur Ledoux the translator of the embassy since these had been arranged and prepared by the honorable Monsieur Ledoux.

Since the consul was not in Port Said, his deputy Monsieur Joseph Khouri handed over the references to my humble self and treated me abundantly well and with deference. As a French cruiser prepared for dispatch to the Indo-China colonies of France was going to visit Djibouti by departing from Port Said after a few days, the necessary procedures to have us go with the mentioned cruiser and as guests were done and our departure from here on the fourteenth day of May was decided. We became acquainted and exchanged visits with Monsieur Guépratte of the naval captains through the aforementioned Monsieur Joseph before departure. Declaring that he had been the commander of the stationnaire of the Istanbul embassy a few years ago and later been honored with compliments and received imperial graces and rendered very happy with high medals from His Highness, the supreme Imperial Majesty, he mentioned His Imperial Majesty Hamid, the supreme sovereign with deep gratitude and praise and also indicating his special respect and affection for His Excellency Monsieur Constans, he said that he would be extremely pleased and happy for our humble delegation to be a guest on his ship and I relayed my thanks and satisfaction to the aforementioned for this courtesy and hospitality. I am seriously grateful for this service of the aforementioned at a time when we could not find a ship to go to Djibouti.

During the few days that we spent in Port Said, white clothes, sufficient provisions and food for the journey, vegetables, fruits in vacuumed boxes were obtained and placed in chests.

*Captain Monsieur Guépratte
Commander of the French Cruiser La Foudre*

Saturday, May 14   The Red Sea

Departure with the French cruiser named La Foudre • The hospitality of the captain and the officers • The attributes of the cruiser • A recollection from the Hejaz road • Flying fish • Heat of the Red Sea

Just as the captain of the ship sent a mouche[25] to pick up our belongings from the shore at eight alafranga time, he sent a commanding officer with another steamboat to pick us up at eleven o'clock. Monsieur Joseph also boarded to bid us farewell. Upon our arrival to the cruiser that had been mentioned named La Foudre, the hospitable captain met us with his entourage of officers in front of the ladder and, after the performance of the official welcome ceremony, presented his officers and hands were shaken with all of them. Just as he himself took me to the quarters assigned to me, another officer took Talip Bey to his cabin and the master sergeant was also shown a place. The place shown to me consisted of the biggest lounge of the cruiser, a dining lounge located outside it, a bed cabin, and a bathroom located opposite this such that quite a few guests could reside if required. Besides this, the captain showed the people who were assigned for service.

Going up to the deck after arranging my bags, I explored and toured the ship. The cruiser was maintained quite clean and orderly like other warships. The cannons, rifles on it were glittering brilliantly. With six thousand tons deadweight, eleven thousand five hundred horsepower, one hundred and eighteen meters length, and sixteen meters width, it had two large submarines, four regular torpedoes inside to be transported to Indo-China. Having a proper workshop to conduct repairs if required, its average speed is sixteen miles, but it can travel nineteen miles if required. Equipped with sixteen cannons, its crew is four hundred people. We departed at noon towards Suez at the speed designated for the canal, in other words five miles per hour. Large salts could be seen to our left and, on our right, the railroad stretching towards Suez and the fresh water canal that was being drained from the Nile. On coming across ships on the way, sometimes our ship stops and they pass and sometimes they stop and we

---

25   *An open excursion boat

pass. We met a Dutch warship towards evening that saluted us by having music played and passed.

The ships rent quite strong electric searchlights from the company and hang this in the front to see their way at night. These searchlights turn the surroundings to day since their light is quite strong.

We arrived to Suez the next day, Sunday morning at half past six o'clock. Stopping briefly, the ship picked up the firemen who had been hired before. European firemen cannot tolerate the heat since the temperature is too much in the Red Sea, the Indian Ocean. For this reason, ships always have fireman from locals present for these places.

Just as we were watching the shores of the Suez Canal yesterday, we are traveling while observing the shore of the Gulf of Suez, its mountain and hills today. Exiting from the Gulf in the evening, we entered the real Red Sea. I took off the wool undershirt since the temperature kept on rising and started wearing white clothes like the officers of the ship. Although I had not seen any cause for complaint from the Messageries and Peninsular ships, in truth time was passing nicer on the cruiser. Due to being a guest on the ship and the known hospitality of the French, starting from the captain to the private of the ship, each one was trying to do what they could to please us. Moreover, since weapon, cannon, fitness instruction drills and various military exercises were being undertaken in the cruiser in turns, watching and observing these was amusing us quite a bit. The temperature started to rise as we went south. The wind was not blowing from ahead, as usual in the Red Sea, but blowing from the north to the south. For this reason, it was not that much use in alleviating the heat, but, at least, it was increasing the speed of the ship.

A cool and nice wind was being produced in the lounges thanks to the wind fans operating with electricity. However, I was able to sleep in the bed cabin by having a hand fan on one hand and a handkerchief on the other to wipe the sweat. Mind you, the hospitable captain offered to install a fan in my cabin, but, thanking, I requested them not to get into this trouble and told him that my cabin was not hot to a degree so as to be a bother each time he asked.

I was following the direction of the ship on the map. Coming next to Hejaz ports adorned with clemency such as Al Wajh, Yanbu, Rabigh,

Jeddah, these and, parallel to these, the forts and places that were on the haj route were appearing in front of my eyes. I was absorbed for hours with memories of the time spent there. I stayed in a tent for six months at first in Beqaa, together with the construction platoon accompanying me, during the construction of the telegraph line between Syria and Hejaz. I had gotten used to the climate and weather conditions and made quite a lot of friendships with desert Arabs.

Summoning some Arab sheikhs to come before me through the might of his imperial majesty the supreme benefactor, we had eaten a meal together with them under a tent, at a sofra[26] and chatted. In brief, when I was in Mada'in Salih, I had brought together the sheikhs of the big clans named Al Ida, Al Faqir and Bali, who had been foes with each other for a long time, at my side at the same time. They had agreed [to a] 'ceasefire' among themselves for a year because they had to serve a grand purpose at the same time. The telegraph line was going to pass where Al Faqir and Al Ida clans roved and due to this, each of these tribes was going to carry both the provisions, the military equipment, as well as the telegraph poles, wires and other necessary things with camels within their boundaries. As for the Bali Arabs, they were going to carry the two thousand or so telegraph poles that were unloaded at the Al Wajh pier to the vicinity of Mada'in Salih that was at twelve days' distance, crossing these over quite steep, rugged terrain. Due to this situation, it was necessary for these people to make peace with each other and reconcile among themselves. Through imperial patronage, they came with one message from me and the tribes were reconciled. They performed the desired services. Each one was decorated and received high rewards in proportion to their service. In the official opening ceremonies of the centers, when they were informed that they would receive the honor of a reward and their garb of honor was bestowed, the shouts of imperial troops "Long live my padishah" and prayers of thousands of Arabs "May Allah help the sultan!" rose to the audience of God.

With imperial grace and blessing, many benefits and boons came about besides the main objective of communication in the establishment of the telegraph line. A traveler did not dare to separate from the haj

---

26 *A board, table or other setting on the floor on which dishes are set

caravan before the construction of the line. Those staying behind due to fatigue or another reason could not find the road trail later, turn here and there in the desert and thus many would perish from hunger, thirst. Now, each pole of the telegraph line has almost become a guide to salvation and safety, a security officer. Henceforth, there is nobody who confuses the way. Some poor come and go without waiting the caravan by walking along the poles from Syria to Hejaz, from Hejaz to Syria. I had seen this later at the time when I was on the duty of Hamidiah Hejaz Railway Line deputy supervisor.

I had written quite a lot of things during my assignment on the telegraph service, to a degree that could amount to a book of travels. However, these, along with their photos, burned, too and disappeared together with the house in the fire I mentioned before. Nothing remained other than memories. Consequently, I will insert, on occasion as the turn comes, what I remember here since the place where I am going is across from the Arabian Peninsula anyway.

As I write these lines, a light splash in the sea attracted my attention. First, I thought birds were flying on the surface of the water. I asked an officer who was looking in that direction when these disappeared. He said, "Look, they will come out now". A school of hundreds of fish really appeared from the water and after flying with a speed like an arrow, parallel to the water surface for forty, fifty meters, they suddenly disappeared together in the water. They came out again. Flew and submerged again. They continued in this way until disappearing from the eye. A different school of fish appeared from the other side. They call these flying fish, according to the statement of the officer. It is found a lot in the Indian Ocean. I was quite amazed since I saw a 'flying fish' for the first time in my life. Anyway, we had neared the Indian Ocean quite a bit today, in other words Wednesday eighteenth of May, because leaving Jabal Al Tair Island and lighthouse on our left at six o'clock in the afternoon, we came next to the lighthouse of Zubair Island at nine o'clock. With the weather very hot and humid tonight, a person sweated where he sat even though the fan was swaying on top of the deck. What are we going to do in Djibouti? I spent most of the night on the deck, on a linen chair.

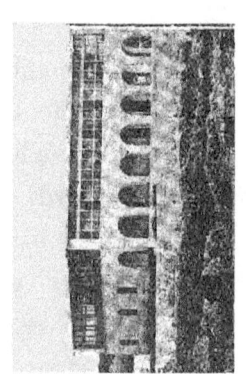

Djibouti. French Somali Coast

Thursday, May 19   Arrival to Djibouti

Arrival to Djibouti • Leaving the cruiser • Visit to the Djibouti Governor and the Ethiopian Consul • The joy of the Muslim community • Where to sleep best in open-air? • Memories of Medina • The hospitality of Arabs

When we woke up in the morning, I saw that gulls had surrounded the ship and flew alongside because we were approaching Bab Al Mandab. At nine o'clock, as the town of Sheikh Said and Parim Island appeared on our left and Gulf of Ras Siyyan on our right side, we were passing the narrowest point of Bab Al Mandab. The width of the strait here is exactly thirteen miles.

Arriving in front of the Djibouti pier at four o'clock in the afternoon alafranga time, our ship dropped anchor. Our belongings had been taken out from the hold before and were now about to be lowered to the steamboat. A steamboat was prepared by the officers' command for our humble delegation to board.

A lot of black Somali children came swimming to meet the ship. They get the coins that are thrown in the sea while the coins are going to the depths. They are very skillful in swimming and diving. They began to be afraid when I turned the camera towards them.

With the captain and other officers of the cruiser wearing their official uniforms and the crew lined up on the deck and the Ottoman flag decorating the ship's main mast, we bid farewell to the captain and officers and embarked on the steamboat. Upon the departure of the steamboat, the captain and the officers concluded the official ceremony with cannon shots.

The governor's office is at the head of the pier. Going there first, we met with the governor, Monsieur Bonhoure. The aforementioned was a quite polite and courteous person and honored and treated us highly and offered us ice coffee in huge glasses as was the custom there. I knew that the best drink to quench the heat in hot countries was cold and plain coffee from my experiences in both the African Grand Sahara and the Hejaz journey previously. I preferred this to all other beverages here, too.

After the governor, we visited the consul of His Imperial Majesty Ethiopian Emperor Menelik in Djibouti, Ato[27] Joseph. Since the aforementioned was the chief of the first delegation that was sent by his most noble highness, the guardian of his realm, His Majesty Menelik, we had become acquainted with him earlier when he had come to Istanbul. Just as the Governor of Djibouti reported our arrival to the consuls in Harar and their ambassador in Ethiopia's capital Addis Ababa, Ato Joseph immediately sent a telegram to His Imperial Majesty the Emperor.

There is a single hotel named Hotel Des Arcades in Djibouti managed by a Frenchman. We checked in there, too.

The local population that consisted of Muslims came in waves beside us the moment we set foot ashore and not settling with the words "Ahlan wa sahlan"[28], they stayed outside in large groups both while we were at the governor's office and with Ato Joseph and accompanied us going from one place to another. They did not miss an opportunity to express their satisfaction and happiness. If we said "a carriage is necessary", twenty of them would run altogether to bring a carriage; if we asked "how do we go to a place?", they would all want to guide us. However, there was no need for their guidance because following our arrival to Djibouti, the governor had offered his secretary to accompany us and to act as our guide. I had not accepted this offer and made do with the few police who accompanied us.

After retiring to the hotel, the front of the hotel filled up with the Muslim population. Muslims wanted to see the delegation sent by the most noble, his imperial majesty the guardian of the caliphate not just once, but observe as much as possible. This situation continued until darkness fell.

---

27 *In Amharic, equivalent to 'Mister'
28 *Welcome in Arabic

We were asking for ice continuously saying 'barrad' due to the harshness of the heat. Some of us were trying to quench the heat with coffee, some with soda. After having dinner, we lay on the beds that were in the balcony that surrounded the sides of the hotel all around, without a blanket, cover because it was not possible to lie in the rooms due to the severity of the heat.

They sleep outside in the summer in most places in Arabia. I had slept outside quite a bit in Birecik, Urfa, Diyarbakır, Hejaz. The most orderly and nicest method is in Medina. In most of the places mentioned, the people would see each other since the sides of the roofs were open. However, in Medina, let alone seeing one house from another, even the people who lie on the roof of the same house cannot see the others. This is because whatever the division of the house is in the middle and top floor, the same size and dividing walls are raised above the roof to a level to exceed human height, maintaining the same division. Extending from below upwards, the stairs come out to a landing. From there, everybody goes to the section above his room. Although the dividing walls are sealed by making them from brick or lime, depending on the construction type, the external wall is equipped with chess-like apertures like crenels which not only secure the view to the outside and provide cooling, but also preserve privacy like a cage.

The water-carrier goes up to the roof with full waterskins in the evening. He waters the surface of the roof abundantly. Mattresses are laid over quite plain, clean and nice divans (bedframes) made from date branches. Each family retires to their section at sleep time. Even the poor sleep on bedframes since bedframes are cheap. The better of these is bought for two mecidiye[29] quarters, the most expensive two person one for a silver mecidiye. In the summer simoom, water is drunk there frequently even at night. Consequently, numerous small and local water pitchers are kept at each section. As that hot simoom wind blows, the pitchers cool the water like ice. Meanwhile, the water in copper or tin pots heat the water like bathhouse water for ablution. When the simoom wind dies down and humid clouds spring up, the cold water in the pitchers begins to warm at

---

29 *Coin named after Sultan Abdulmejid who ruled between 1839-1861

that hour. If the cloud disperses and simoom blows again, the waters cool. In brief, the natural application of the subject of evaporation is witnessed there every day.

While I am talking about Medina with great satisfaction, let me also declare it here that the people of Medina, the rich and the poor, are people of the nature and know how to live well. Their clothes are quite nice relative to their climate and weather, their dishes are delicious and they both eat well and feed well. They are all generous, friendly and hospitable. They are welcoming. One does not tire from their gatherings, chats. They look for an opportunity to treat others. If someone invites two, three people to a meal, he will definitely have food cooked to feed thirty, forty persons. In this way, the needy also eat after the guests. If a guest comes to one of the community, he will immediately slaughter a sheep. If another guest comes after half an hour, he will have another sheep slaughtered even though the previous sheep has not been put on the fire yet. In short, each guest understands that another sheep has been slaughtered for him from the huge bowls of stuffed sheep that come to the table. Although they cook various kebaps, meatballs, cutlets at every invitation and banquet, a stuffed sheep or lamb comes in a huge bowl to the table before these.

If someone says, come on, who can afford this expense? Can food for a hundred people be cooked for ten people? Is one, two okka[30] meat not sufficient for two persons who come after feeding the other desert Arabs? Why is there a need for the other when one sheep has been slaughtered already? What if the owner of the house is a poor man? These are true. However, this is the custom of the country. They have to abide by it. He will borrow even though he does not have money. He hosts the guest.

I had been invited to a meal by the Sheikhs of the Belka and Adwan clans when I undertook the extension of the Hejaz telegraph line. A huge dish of approximately one and a half meters in diameter was first brought to the table by four, five people. There was a big sheep in it for my humble self. There were also five-six lambs for the number of other officers present at the table. The degree of hospitality of the Arabs is not known without living among the Arabs. I will include a story here as an example:

---

30 *1 okka = 1.3 kilograms

A poor Bedouin comes to town concerning a business with his quite nice and fast camel. An important person present there requests to buy his camel. He offers money to the Bedouin that is more than a few multiples of the value of the camel. The Bedouin does not accept to sell his camel no matter what since he loves it quite a lot. He takes care of his business in town and retires to his desert. The person in the town becomes more interested in the camel. He gives quite a bit of money to a few persons from the notables of the town to convince the Bedouin. He sends them to the desert where the Bedouin is located. These persons walk to the location where the clan is present. They ask for the tent of the Bedouin and go there directly. The Bedouin not knowing why these people have come runs to treat them, to their coffee. When it is evening, he brings in front of them a big dish (wooden, large deep dish), with abundant tirit[31]. He feeds them. The guests tell the Bedouin the purpose of their visit after drinking their coffee. The Bedouin says without hesitation, "Why did you not say this as soon as you came? The meat in the tirit you ate is that of the camel you wanted. I would not have slaughtered it if I knew!" They freeze like that and in astonishment.

Thus, a Bedouin who owns no other belongings, property in the world other than his camel slaughters his beloved camel without hesitation in abidance to hospitality and Bedouin custom because he has nothing else to slaughter for his guests that he knows nothing about even though he had not agreed to sell his camel for a lot of money with all this pleading and request of the most respectable, well-known person of the town and who, if necessary, could have done him a favor.

They say "One word leads to another".[32] While saying we lay on the balcony in Djibouti, we said how well one lies on the roof in Medina. Talking about Medina, we passed from the hospitality of its people and from there to the desert Arabs. Now, let us again cross to the other side of the Red Sea: Settling for the balcony in Djibouti per force, I fell into an uncertain rest.

---

31 *A dish with meat on a bed of bread

32 *The original text quotes 'Al kelam bjir al kelam' which is a saying in Arabic

Friday, May 20   Djibouti

The visit of the Somali delegations • The return visits of the governor, the consul • Djibouti railroad • Forty-one male children from four women, one father • The ships that stop by Djibouti • Import and export • Kinds of Dangalis • Banquet at the government building • Fans of five-ten meters

Checking the chests in the morning, I separated some extra clothes and items to leave in Djibouti and, in the evening, I prepared the items that would go to the railway station because there exists a three hundred and ten kilometer long, narrow track railroad from Djibouti towards the capital and after covering this distance by train, passengers complete their journey by riding mules. Information regarding this railroad will be provided later.

Coming next to me, the waiter said that some of the headmen of the community had come to visit and waited below. I said, "They are welcome". He went to call them. Let me describe the waiters here until they come. When I said Hotel Des Arcades is the largest, let not Pera Palace, Summer Palace, and when saying waiter, an attendant with a black fabric tailcoat, a European shirt and white necktie come to mind. The waiters here are from almost half naked, barefoot, bareheaded men and their clothes consist of an apron and a vest or a tunic. Some of them put on a cap on their head. They are not European. Most of them are fifteen, sixteen years old, intelligent and skilled in service.

The headmen came by the time I wrote these lines. The visitors, consisting of seven, eight people, are the leaders of clans called Iyessa and Dangali of the Somalis and some are walnut color, while others are darker, coffee colored. All of them are tall and quite well built. They are seriously majestic and dignified faced people, with some in a long tunic, a cap, while others are with an apron and bare headed. Their hair is frizzy, almost like a big turban on their heads. A long skewer-like wooden arrow is stuck between their hair on their heads like those that European women fasten their hats with. Since their nails arrive at their scalp through the bushy and curly hair layers with difficulty they scratch their heads with this arrow if required. A few of them had gone to and returned from Hejaz and speak Arabic. The Arabic of the remainder is slight.

Standing respectfully after greetings, these persons prayed for the continuation of the life and health of Our Mighty Protector and Master His Imperial Majesty and blessings for the increase in glory and might of his caliphate. Talking and chatting about the situation in Istanbul, the number of its residents, its mosques and sacred places, where I would go, and from here and there, they declared that a delegation of those from their tribes near Djibouti would come to perform a welcome ceremony in the evening.

At this moment, Governor Monsieur Bonhoure came to visit with some of his entourage and in his official uniform and later, the Ethiopian Consul Ato Joseph. We chatted with them for a while, too. While the governor had already informed us and given invitation yesterday for an official banquet that would be arranged in honor of the delegation this evening, he reminded us of our evening talk and then left. There were two cavalry gendarmes in front of the governor's carriage. Ato Joseph and the headmen also retired later. These headmen had dressed in a primitive way. Some were barefoot. Some wore pattens like those worn in Hejaz. Despite this, they left an imposing impression on a person. The governor shook their hands when he saw them. He inquired after the health of all of them. Although they are headmen, each looks like a statue from bronze of the symbol of warriorship.

Two more visitors came after the governor and Somalis retired. These persons had come to the hotel immediately after our arrival here and gained my acquaintance through Ato Joseph. These persons were Iskandar Ghaleb Efendi and Bashar Ghaleb Efendi who were originally from the Beit Shabab town of Lebanon. One is thirty, the other twenty-eight years old. After completing their education in schools in Beirut, they went into business and had come to Djibouti after engaging in commerce in many African countries and briefly in Dahomey. They had become one of the most respected merchants here in a few years and gained a good reputation on the coasts of Ethiopia and in the interior, even before the emperor. With integrity and reliability, they had gained the trust and confidence needed by merchants and made a fortune. In truth, their good fame and characters are pleasing. They presented themselves to provide any kind of guidance and service to our delegation. I obtained information regarding Somalis and Djibouti from them, taking advantage of their guidance and their knowledge of the surroundings. I toured the region and its surroundings with a carriage under the guidance of Iskandar Efendi. I wrote the information on Djibouti since there was still quite a bit of time until the evening banquet:

The French state had bought the location named Obock, outside the strait of Bab Al Mandab and north of the Gulf of Tadjoura, from the local chiefs in the Gregorian year one thousand eight hundred and sixty-three. The aforementioned location had become a center to provide coal and provisions to battleships in the war that had begun with the Chinese in the year one thousand eight hundred and eighty-three and a government had been formed there to bring security. Following the benefit seen during the war, this location had gained much importance and become a port for ships going to and coming from Indo-China. However, ships are forced to anchor quite far away since the sea is very shallow on the Obock coast. This situation has caused limited availability of provisions and food there. Moreover, there are high and difficult to pass mountains that make it difficult to come and go to the interior. All these drawbacks had made it necessary for a center more suitable than Obock to be looked for. Now, however, Monsieur Lagarde, ambassador before the Ethiopian Emperor, had discovered the Djibouti location that was across from Obock, with the guidance of some of the local sailors. The waters of Djibouti are deeper. It is both easier for ships to shelter here and to go to the province of Harar.

For this reason, it was decided to establish a center here and to move the capital here. With the support of government on one side, the efforts of the merchants on the other, the town slowly grows and takes the form of a quite important, large commerce center today. Trade caravans come and go from Djibouti to Harar, which is a city of Ethiopia, and from Harar all the way to the capital Addis Ababa. Thus, the importance of Djibouti is increasing even more.

A person named Monsieur Ilg, who is originally Swiss and has been in the service of the Ethiopian Emperor for a long time, has obtained the right to operate a railroad for a period of ninety-nine years from Ethiopia and ending in Djibouti and he executed a partnership agreement with a person named Monsieur Chefneux who has also been in Ethiopia in merchandise trade for a long time and is competent in the formation of companies. Going to France immediately, Monsieur Chefneux obtained the right from the Minister of Colonies for the extension of the line from the location named Ali Sabih, situated on the border of Ethiopia and French Somali, to Djibouti in the distance that comprises ninety kilometers.

After preliminary surveys that were done with a lot of difficulty, construction works began in the year one thousand eight hundred and ninety-six. The importance of Djibouti increased steadily from that moment on. Abandoning the local huts, the arriving merchants began to construct stone buildings. A French company was set up with the objective to construct buildings to rent to the population. Free lands were given to those who wanted land to construct buildings and shops. The Muslim merchants coming from Yemen, Hadhramaut for the purpose of commerce also have a lot of property here. Some of the Somalis from the local community have left their shrub and grass huts after constructing stone houses for themselves by copying others. The most respected and well-known person of the local community is a philanthropist named Haji Dide Adla who had come to visit me with other respected Muslim merchants. He is seventy years old, fit and strong. With the blessing of forty-one male children from only four wives, his relatives admire him.

The company that has been established to produce ice by bringing water to the town had opened wells on a flood bed located seven kilometers from the city, raised the water to elevated pools with steam pumps and distributed water to the city with pipes and this task had finished four years ago. Taking free lands, Arab gardeners who came from abroad had dug wells and established gardens on the aforementioned flood bed and in the location named Ambouli. They are growing crops such as tomato, cucumber, eggplant, purslane, zucchini, watermelon and melon and competing with tin gardens. The people refer to tin canisters as tin gardens.

The port of Djibouti is divided into four main quarters. The first of these is Hay Al Murabat (the French mispronounce it as Mrabou), or the Murabat quarter where a holy person named Sheikh Siraj resided for a while and was buried there after his death, a lodge was made for him and this quarter was remembered after him.

The agency building for the Messageries Maritimes Company, coal warehouses, vehicles, tools, workshops and the like are present in this quarter. I saw a lot of Russian owned ship coal there to be sent to the Far East for the Russian navy. The construction of a pier that extends five hundred meters towards the sea from the shore where the agency building is located has begun. Ships will dock at this pier when construction is finished.

The second quarter is the section named Mesitah Al-Hayye (the French call it Plateau du Serpent), in other words Snake Square, and the main large buildings such as the railway station and the other buildings belonging to it, the monasteries of Franciscan priests and nuns, and the municipal hospital are in this quarter.

The third quarter is the Djibouti quarter where the city's establishment had first begun and formed. Principal buildings such as the government office, customs, police offices, the shops and headquarters of the Arab and European merchants, and hotel are located here. A wide, orderly and tourable, one kilometer long street passes between the Djibouti quarter and the Plateau du Serpent quarter. Separate government offices like public works, post office, and the courthouse are located on half of this street.

The fourth quarter is the quarter of the Somalis and while the dwellings consist of huts from fences, bamboo, and reed, the streets are straight and orderly. At one time, permission was given for the construction of huts such as these. Now, when a hut collapses by itself, a good building is constructed in its place. Construction of huts is forbidden.

There are two quite large, stone mosques in Djibouti. One of these is that of Somali Haji Dide Adla mentioned before. The second is the work of the late philanthropist named Al Sayyid Hasan Al Baz from Massawa. The imams were making the children read the glorious supreme Qur'an when I visited these mosques.

The number of residents of Djibouti increased day to day during the construction of the railway and even reached a population of twenty thousand in the year one thousand nine hundred. However, when construction stopped at Dire Dawa, just as the engineers, workers and contractors naturally returned to their countries, the hoteliers, vendors, grocers and the like, who catered for them, also left. In the current situation, its residents are about seven, eight thousand people comprising Arabs, French, and Somalis.

While there exists a quite rich salt basin named Buhaira Asb or Assal behind Gulf of Tadjoura, it is approximately thirty kilometers from the Gulf of Tadjoura coast and cannot be benefited from that much in the current situation since its heat is quite harsh and its snakes are abundant. I will relate the information I gathered regarding the ships that stop in Djibouti and its commercial life here to encourage Ottoman merchants. Namely:

Three of the ships of the Messageries Maritimes Company that go from Port Said to the south and three that go from the south to the north stop once a month in Djibouti. Two of the ones going from the south to the north are affiliated with the Madagascar line, while one is affiliated with the Indo-China line. One of the ships of the National Company going to Indo-China only stops when going there. The ships of the French company named Havre Peninsular sailing to Madagascar and Rangoon stop by once a month, both coming and going. One of the company ships that operate from England to the Gulf of Basra stops by once a month, only while going south. A Russian ship stops by Djibouti once every two months, both while going and coming and this ship is recommended for merchants from Istanbul, Izmir and Syria. This is because after departing from Odessa and laying over in Istanbul, Izmir, Beirut, Haifa, and Port Said, the ship in question also stops by Djibouti and from here it goes to the Gulf of Basra and returns the same way.

All the mentioned are scheduled ships. Moreover, the Messageries Maritimes, Afrique Oriental and other unscheduled ships transporting coal to warehouses are not included in this number. There is also a small, three hundred gross ton French ship that comes and goes between Djibouti and Aden that carries Djibouti's post and a lot of commercial merchandise and passengers. This ship was in repair when we came to Djibouti.

All kinds of goods come to Djibouti from the outside for sale domestically. The goods that are sold most to Somali and Dangali tribes are Indian rice, white corn and tumbak from Arabia, dates that come from Baghdad and Basra, textiles that come from England like calico and linen. Linen, known with the name Abu Jadid around here and a cloth used a lot on the Somali coast and Ethiopia, is of American manufacture.

The goods that are sent most from the coast to Ethiopia are all types of cotton and silk cloth, drapery, iron tools and equipment, Persian rugs and carpets, European kilim which are imitations of these, all kinds of firearms, silver and copper items.

Embroidered carpets, decorative goods like curtains and rose oil are sent from imperial domains[33], especially from Istanbul.

Mixed silks with cotton, the silk cloth referred to as "Kutnu" and clothes manufactured from cotton only are being sent from Syria.

Sailing ships loaded with coffee, salt, grains and wicker come from Yemeni coasts. Selling these, they buy various goods. All the one hundred or so local sailing boats that come from both Yemen to Djibouti and come and go between Djibouti-Aden-Zeila-Berbera carry the Ottoman banner.

On the other hand, the products that come from Ethiopia through the Harar route are all natural products. These are the coffee of Harar and Kaffa, ivory, yellow gold, wax, cardamom, and domesticated animals like cattle, goat and sheep and some quantity of wild animal leather, and goods like the oil that is extracted from the misk cat (what the Europeans call civet).

The Gallas obtain the gold by the method of filtering river and stream sands. Two million francs worth of gold is coming to Djibouti annually. One kilogram of misk oil is sold for three hundred francs.

---

33 *A reference to the Ottoman Empire

There are Ottoman subjects numbering more than two hundred, consisting of Hejazi, Syrian, Yemeni and Armenian communities in Djibouti and some of these are merchants, while some are shop owners. There are those who come and go to Harar.

When it was late afternoon and the weather worsened a bit, I was both writing these lines and having ice brought by telling the waiter "barrad" and drinking the water glasses mixed with plain coffee because Djibouti's weather is quite hot, the sun scorching. In other words, if one of the whites were to stay without an umbrella in the sun for five-ten minutes, sunstroke would immediately kill him. Incidents like this are common occurrences.

A melodious sound came from afar at around ten o'clock alaturca time. They informed me that the Iyessas' delegation of Somalis had come. I went out to the balcony. I saw a community of four-five hundred people coming, half naked above the waist, equipped with a spear and cane, each huge like a bronze statue, proportionately tall, and each of whom could be a model for a sculptor. Tahlil[34] and takbir[35] and battle songs were heard in turns as they were coming. A large group from the community had surrounded them to watch. Giving greetings and after performing the welcome ceremony in their own language, they constituted a big circle and some were dancing with a song, while some were performing imitations of combat and battle inside the circle. The ferocity and toughness of their countenance, the lightness and speed of their presence and movements show that they really are a warrior race. After these persons displayed various performances and revelry for a while longer, the Dangalis came and they finished their turn, too. Then, the local Arabs came with drums and also left after darkness fell. They all left satisfied under imperial patronage.

With alafranga time approaching eight o'clock, I wore my official white uniform and went with my friend to the government office where we were invited. Two rows of gendarmes had lined up at the door. Being from the local Somalis, their clothes are white pants till their knee, white jacket, a red fez on their head decorated with a star in front and their legs are bare below the knee. The local people here can be gotten used to wearing

---

34 *La ilaha illallah – Literally translated means there is no deity, but God

35 *Allahu Akbar – Literally translated means God is Greater or Greatest

clothes. They cannot be gotten used to shoes. Going around barefoot has been their custom and ease. Accompanying us from the reception hall respectfully, his excellency the governor took us to the adjacent balcony because the guests were gathering there. Both the gate of the government office and the corridor and halls were adorned in quite a nice way with colorful flags, lanterns, natural and artificial flowers. Ottoman banners and flags of victory were flying at the big door of the hall and French flags could be seen opposite.

As the invited government officials came with their families, they were introduced. We moved to the table when mealtime came. The table was quite sumptuous and lavish. A meter wide, large fan they called paiqar, hanging on the ceiling across the length of the table, began to move to allay the heat. The ropes this was tied to had been taken outside the lounge by means of pulleys. It was being moved by servants who were specially there pulling and releasing the ropes. The top of the glass spheres over the candles of the chandeliers found above the table were covered by metal cages with a lid so that they would not be extinguished by the wind that was created. These were being made in India for this service apparently. It was not possible to eat if the big fan above our head had not been there. Anyway, most of Djibouti's houses, shops are equipped with these fans. Whites cannot live without these.

Our meal consisted of fish, the meats of sheep, cow, birds, vegetables and dessert and so on and was excellent. A more than abundant variety of fish are caught in Djibouti. However, theirs is not like the taste of the fish in Istanbul. Standing at the end of the meal, the governor wished better and more abundant health and welfare for His Imperial Majesty the Sovereign Padishah and those present repeated praise and compliments altogether. Upon customary ceremony, I undertook the required reciprocation.

After the meal, we smoked, drank coffee and beverages with ice and chatted for a while on the balcony of the building and then everyone dispersed to his place.

Saturday, May 21   Departure from Djibouti

Departure from Djibouti • The characteristics of the road • Chat with Somalis at the stations • Somali huts • The loyalty and affection of Somalis to His Majesty the Guardian of the Caliphate • Soot instead of soap • Miswak instead of cigarette • Arrival to the border of Ethiopia

We came to the station in the morning at half past five o'clock alafranga time. We said goodbye to the persons who came to bid us farewell. The train departed at six o'clock. Since the surroundings of Djibouti are barren, grassless, sandy, I was assuming that the terrain would continue like this. The opposite of what I expected happened. Enough grass for animal herds to be able to graze and even enough shrubs that could be burned instead of wood began to appear after leaving the city four, five kilometers. I saw the wells, pumps and water wells that I mentioned before when we reached the Ambouli station located at the seventh kilometer. I had mentioned that the city's water went from here. Our train continued on its way after taking its water.

Although part of the terrain after Ambouli is volcanic, it is not devoid of vegetation even if it has less grass and shrubs than before and is partially suitable for agriculture. The terrain and the surrounding hills began to appear lush green after traveling a little more. Beautiful pastures for animals appeared. The soil appears deep red like the soil of Hauran[36],

---

36   *A region in Southern Syria

and soft like henna. Nice and productive farms would form if the stones on the surface are collected and spread to the surroundings at intervals.

During a chat that I had had previously, the governor said that he had the idea of establishing villages and settlements in the land around Djibouti that were suitable for agriculture, at a time when the colony finances allowed, by taking out water through artesian wells and transporting it with canals. A lot of crops would be harvested from the soil if he can really implement his idea because the soil of the land has not been cultivated yet and has been fortified with the manure of domesticated animals which have been grazing God knows for how many centuries.

There is the grave of an engineer on the nineteenth kilometer. He is one of the foreigners who were killed by the local people during construction. We crossed a large valley here with an iron bridge. As we waited a little before crossing the bridge, desert dwelling Somalis present there who saw my fez ran and surrounded the wagon with happiness. After chatting a few minutes with those who spoke Arabic, they complained about the railroad. Upon my saying, "Come on, is this not better than your camel?", one of those who could speak most raised all kinds of strange objections like "No, it is not good, the camel does not harm a person on contact. If a camel gets excited, at most foam will come out of its mouth. (Pointing to the locomotive with his finger) Whereas this shreds whatever it comes across, whether human or animal. When it gets excited, its sound scares our camels, sheep and even goats. Our loaded camels get scared and topple their baggage. (Pointing to the smokestack of the locomotive) When it gets excited, it belches smoke, fire, sparks from its mouth. It leaves ashes from fire where it passes. A camel's meat can be eaten, milk drunk, it has offspring, multiplies. What to cut on this, what to eat of it?"

When I said that there were trains in imperial domains and that a railway was being constructed even on the blessed Hejaz road, he only allowed for ours by saying, "In that case, yours is not a European curse". Then, the train departed, the talk was interrupted. Saluting with their hands, they disappeared from the eye.

The conductor declared that the local community had created a lot of difficulty for engineers and workers during construction. Fights between them sometimes resulted in death and, for this reason, all of the foreigners could [only] continue work armed. [This was] because the travel of the caravans between Harar and Djibouti used to be done with the camels of the local community before the railroad and so the railroad seemed like a rival to them.

As the color of the shrubs started changing at seven o'clock, all the grass and shrubs of the surroundings and the region took on a color of silver. Stopping at the location named Alaile at half past seven o'clock, the train's engine, axle and so on were lubricated.

There are a few Somali huts with irregular walls made from rubble stone in Alaile, with their roofs consisting of grass, shrub and reed. I wanted to take a photograph of some children. Their father begged me saying that they would die. I gave up since I was unwilling for them to die!! After departing from here, we came across numerous camels that were white, completely clean, elegant, beautiful, cute like a gazelle, light like a dromedary similar to the camels that I saw in Benghazi's Barqa Desert at one time, as well as a herd of goats that were completely white, with tight bellies like a gazelle. I watched them grazing as much as could be seen from the train. At eight o'clock, we arrived at the location of Holhol that is found on the fifty-second kilometer. This station consists of three rather large huts that are separate from each other and a Somali village with forty-fifty huts is located around it.

Since Somalis are cattle owners like various desert Arabs, they live from their yield, in other words fees from transporting loads with their camels, the offspring of their sheep, goat, camels and their milk. They go to wherever it rains and wherever they find abundant pasture, stay there until the pasture is consumed. Each tribe roams and travels within its own borders. Consequently, they are nomads. However, they do not have tents made from hair like the desert Arabs of Damascus, Baghdad, Aleppo, Hejaz in the Arabian Peninsula, the Bedouin of Tripoli and Benghazi. They immediately make a dwelling wherever they are forced to camp. They make a muddy and often dry wall if there is stone, of approximately two meters' diameter, irregular, round, and with a height of one and a half meters and cover its top with tree branches and later soft, thin grass. A family can make itself a house in one day in this way.

In places where there is no stone, both the wall and the roof are completely from tree branches. A round, half sphere shaped ridge is constructed on its top with grass. In places where there are also no tree branches, each homeowner possesses at least four canes or poles, each with a height of two, two and a half arşın[37]. After the canes are tied to each other and set up, it is nothing to cover the shrubs and grass around it. When the tribe goes from one pasture to another, everyone carries his dwelling that consists of four, five poles and five, ten kıyye[38].

Since there are mostly pastures in the vicinity of this station and, moreover, they earn money by selling things like yogurt, ayran to those coming and going, the Somalis appear to have immediately abandoned a nomadic life as they have fortified their huts quite a bit and formed a village here without being forced.

Somali girls brought yogurt, ayran in small waterskins, baskets when the train stopped. They sold these to passengers who wanted. I bought a small container of ayran, too. Esteemed readers will say: "Come on, can ayran, yogurt be sold with baskets? Would a basket hold ayran?!" Those who read the Grand Sahara Book of Travels may recall that the people living in Awjila and Jalu oases weave the leaves of date trees, after turning them into a thin band, like a thin thread. Then, they knot the thread putting it one on top of another and again weave it with date leaves.

In this way, they manufacture lidded boxes of various sizes and shapes, in other words spherical, elliptical, round, to put sundries, round boards for eating meals on top like big trays and even pitchers to a degree that can hold yogurt, ayran and water. These containers are used to cool the water since the pores of the fibre tissues leak water a little. So, in this way, the Somalis here weave and use bowls, containers from a thin, soft, quite strong grass instead of date branches.

After weaving the container, they hold its inside against smoke for a while specifically for liquids desired not to leak. A layer of soot blocks the pores, after fumigating like this occasionally, the inside becomes almost like a glazed jar. Anyway, they do not wash containers like this. If something

---

37 *Cubit or 1 arşın = 68 centimeters

38 *1 kıyye = 1,283 gram

else is going to be placed in the yogurt container, they soot the container. Its tar goes away. In this way, as the container gets sooted over and over again, its inside becomes like a jar.

I found the yogurt I bought too sour and kind of bitter. I asked them how they made it. They fill the milk that they have obtained today in a large sooted container without boiling and adding yeast. The next day they add the milk that is left over from their food on top of this. In sum, they take old milk from a container supposedly as yogurt on the one hand. On the other hand, they put fresh milk. They do not know how to boil and ferment. For this reason, although their ayran, yogurt are not quite drinkable things for us, I kept on drinking ayran continually with the effect of the heat on the road.

Surrounding me here, too, the men chatted quite a bit with happiness and affection. The men wore waistcloth, the women were with quite low cut neckline clothes[39], and the children were completely naked. They all have proportionate figures and are graceful. Most speak Arabic.

We passed over a big iron bridge after leaving the station. Quite nice and cute white goat herds are visible on our right and left. It looked like thrown cotton balls from afar. As we got further from Djibouti, a little coolness was felt, or more correctly the heat was easing since we were rising above sea level. Otherwise, what chill yet?

Towards nine o'clock, the grass, shrubs started to be fewer in the land we passed. Volcanic nature had beaten the power of plants to grow here. Black stones had begun to be seen frequently.

Arriving at the station named Dasbiya located on the seventieth kilometer at exactly nine o'clock, the locomotive obtained its water here.

The vicinity of this station was quite populated and there were a few Somali huts around it. A Somali child had improved his craft and was selling coffee that he had prepared before the train came to the passengers in big cups.

Quite beautiful trees like ague attracted my attention after this station. I asked its name. Like other plants in this desert, these grow on their own

---

39 *The term décolleté is used in the original script. The Arabic translation of the text gives this as bare-chested

and are trees named farhi. Apparently, miswak is being made from its branches. It turns out that the pen-sized sticks that I saw here and there in most Somalis' mouth that they held like a pipe that they in turns sucked and rubbed on their teeth were from this tree. Old and young, the Somalis are so keen on this tree that a stick is almost in all their mouths, almost like a whistle. He takes it in his hand when he wants to speak. Then, he puts it in his mouth again and holds it tightly like cigarette between his two lips. Sometimes he sucks it, sometimes moves his lips right and left – as though washing his mouth. He keeps on rubbing the miswak against his teeth without holding it by hand. This behavior of theirs has now deviated from its original objective of cleaning teeth and turned to an addiction like a cigarette. The miswak sticks that they use are not dry like the miswak sticks we know. They are fresh, green and its bark is on it. It is obvious that the sap of this tree is giving them some joy.

We reached the Ali Sabih station located on the ninetieth kilometer at quarter to ten o'clock. This is the border between French Somalia and the Harar province that is under the rule of Ethiopia. Besides the station, there is a fort like building that overlooks the surroundings on top of a hill. A French official resides there together with his entourage. Since the land is quite barren and almost devoid of plants here, it is empty of people dwelling in huts.

We arrived at the Douanlé station that is located on the one hundred and sixth kilometer at quarter past ten o'clock. The Somali huts around this station have constituted a village. There is a guard post here that is fitted with the Ethiopian flag above it. The flag is made of a rainbow (in imitation of heavenly signs) and consisted of three different color fabrics that are stitched lengthwise. The one on top is green, the middle yellow, and the bottom is red. Standing outside, the soldier at the guard post saluted the delegation. The rifle in his hands is the Garra rifle that the French have sold to the Ethiopians. His clothes are an underwear, a tunic, and a cover similar to the ikhram that the North Africans of Tripoli wrap themselves in. However, theirs is from American cloth. There is nothing either on their head or on their feet on any of them.

The train stops here for a meal for forty-five minutes on the way from Djibouti. When the Somalis understood that I had been ordered to set out by the most noble guardian of the caliphate, they ran to my side with great enthusiasm and eagerness and prayed for His Imperial Majesty, our mighty Padishah, our master as had happened everywhere and respectfully declared their welcome to our delegation. The Somalis multiplied in number and became a great crowd until the train departed. The arrival of our humble delegation here was deemed a special holiday by them as it were. Thousands of Somalis at stations were showing their bond and affection for our master His Imperial Majesty the Caliph of the glorious Prophet.

The Djibouti Governor had mentioned when we were in Djibouti the extreme attachment and affection they always had for His Highness, His Supreme Imperial Majesty the Guardian of the Caliphate and the extraordinary happiness that would result when our humble delegation would be seen.

The train moved on at eleven o'clock. They requested me to inform the stations on my return. After crossing an iron bridge over a valley, we arrived to the Adeyle station located at the one hundred and thirty second kilometer at ten minutes to twelve. This station is small and there are a few Somali huts around it. We passed a plain full of Somali camels as far as the eye could see at twelve o'clock. Goats, donkeys were grazing between the camels. The huts of the owners can also be seen between the camels.

We came to the Aysha station located on the one hundred and forty first kilometer at ten minutes to one o'clock. This station consists of three huts and there is a small Somali village named Lasari in front of it consisting of twenty, thirty huts. With the land flat and grassy here, those nice Somali sheep are grazing as much as they want.

We arrived to the Adilgala station located on the two hundred and first kilometer at two o'clock. There is a small workshop of the company and some number of Somali huts here. At three o'clock, a lot of soil piles similar to Somali huts began to be seen while passing through an almost smooth plain.

I asked the conductor, he explained: These were the nests of a type of white ants. The entire plain is full of these nests. There is a distance of forty, fifty meters between one ant nest and the other, sometimes more and some of the nests are one and a half meters, some two meters high, with a diameter that is about the same as its height and quite strong and petrified so that a person can only demolish this with a spade.

Big tiny creatures! In our time, at what multiple is the height of the buildings that man constructs, what multiple of his own volume? If compared to the construction of the big structures that is a multiple of these creatures' heights, volumes, humans lag far behind.

This white ant must be of the same kind as the white ants found in the Hejaz desert in Hejaz, Medina, Mecca and known there as qarza on account of their whiteness. Although the ones in Hejaz do not construct a structure above and live underground, the work they do above ground do not lag behind those of their kind here. Being from quite destructive pests, they gnaw and destroy trees. If they shelter under a traveler's chest for one, two days, they eat the bottom of the chest and destroy the goods inside it. If attention is paid to the big poles in room ceilings in Medina, a line from mud can be seen on them. First plastering the mud layer, the ants begin to eat the tree without being seen. Since they had damaged the bottoms of some of the poles we had erected for the Hejaz telegraph line, the poles were later re-erected after the rotten places were cut. Although technical personnel had decided for the aforementioned line's poles to be from iron against the inevitable damage from this pest, wooden poles were later erected due to the distance and difficulty of transportation.

However, since the Hamidiye Hejaz Railway construction is progressing day-to-day through the public works of His Imperial Majesty our supreme benefactor, it is obvious that iron poles will, of course, be erected from now on instead of the wooden poles and as the line reaches the desired sacred target Supreme Allah willing, it is obvious that all the poles will be from iron.

Let us again return to our subject: Crossing an iron bridge of about twenty meters length at half past three o'clock, we entered a plain full of those beautiful, green miswak trees, surrounded by mountains on its left. Remembering the sands of the Libyan Desert and the Grand Sahara, I saw these places as an example of heaven compared to there.

We arrived to Milo station located on the two hundred and forty first kilometer at quarter to four o'clock. There are Somali huts here as well. We reached Harewa station at twenty five past four. The Somali huts here were more regular, larger and greater in quantity and had almost taken the form of a village. When we arrived there, Somali women were busy milking those nice, white as cotton, delicate goats with their arms bare and revealing. As for the men, some were rubbing the miswak stick between their lips against their teeth. Some were sucking on their mazga.

Let me describe mazga: They mix green tobacco or tumbak[40] with some ash. They make a paste from this that is rather larger than the chewing gum that children chew. It is squeezed between lower teeth and lower lips while the teeth are shut together and it is sucked thoroughly. It is taken out of the mouth when bored. Where to put it? There is no pocket. They attach it between the top of the ear and the head. If they get bored of chewing the miswak, they jam the miswak to their rough, dense and fluffy hair.

We came to the El Bah station located on the two hundred and eightieth kilometer at ten past five o'clock. There are no residents here even though there are grass, shrubs and even trees and it is also suitable for the residence of Somalis. The Somalis obviously do not like the shade because they are always used to standing under the sun. Someone who wants to rest at daytime, stretches and lies under the sun, leaving the shade of a tree or wall. The shade affects their body.

The terrain is a bit rough in the vicinity of the El Bah station. Growing steadily, the trees of the land that we passed after this station almost took the form of a beautiful forest. Other than the miswak trees that are green like emerald, this place is full of numerous wild trees the names of which I do not know. The surface is covered with grass and shrubs. When the railway was being constructed here, numerous trees were cut, their logs are still lying on the side of the road.

Plants such as wild vines, ivy, Honeysuckle, Bindweed are climbing the trees in this forest. A variety of wild ivies are present more than abundantly and the arbors, tunnels, deep green canopies that they constitute together with trees would leave even the most skilled gardener in awe. Their variety is also changing as the train moves. Let me briefly describe a few to the degree that my pen allows:

---

40 *Persian tobacco

Imagine a big tree: Its branches, shoots have spread around equally and in a round shape like an umbrella tree relative to the height of its body. After covering the body of this tree, a variety of ivies have dangled from the sides of the branches vertically down to the ground. After arriving on the surface, it has given root again on the ground. The buds that have sprouted from here have climbed over the previously dangling ones. In this way, a wall that is green like an emerald, rendering even the entry of sunlight difficult, has been woven around the tree and together with the tree a natural arbor has resulted. Or else, ivies have wrapped around a huge cut tree trunk and its branches; it has created irregular shades depending on the position of the tree, its enormity. Besides this, the grass on the surface of these arbors is not rough and big like the grass elsewhere. The grass here is soft almost like fresh turf, short and like a carpet that is emerald green because the heat of the sun is, obviously, not able to penetrate the surface here.

It is the first time I see such beautiful views since I landed on the African coast. I forgot that I am in Africa. For the first time, I am seeing wild pigeons, doves, birds resembling quails, and others, names of which I do not know, fly from tree to tree, hearing their songs.

As our train was advancing between trees since the El Bah station and I was watching and observing these beautiful nature scenes and on the other hand occupying myself with recording what I had seen, the train stopped. I saw a lot of Ethiopian officials and soldiers around. In this way, I noticed that we had arrived to Dire Dawa station that was the terminus located on the three hundred and tenth kilometer.

The time had come to six o'clock alafranga time. This means that the three hundred and ten kilometers from Djibouti to Dire Dawa was covered in twelve hours, including stop times.

Here is something that attracted my attention: The white ants are not like the Somalis, one likes the sun, the other shade because although I saw a lot of ant nests in the forest, I did not see a single Somali hut.

There were a lot of people at the station. About two hundred Ethiopian soldiers were lined up in salute. A young, handsome, courteous, polite youth came beside me when the door of the wagon opened and told me in French that he was Ato Biyana, the son of the governor here who was Ato Mersha, and that because his father was not in the region, he and the officials and soldiers had come to meet us as his representative and he presented the officials in his entourage. After the welcome ceremony was performed, we went to the hotel in front of the station, managed by a Greek. This was the only hotel that was present there. Before leaving my side, Ato Biyana placed guards outside the residence where we were, out of respect.

It is necessary to describe the hotel a bit to explain its exterior doors. The hotel consists of a stone single storey building, with two sections that are perpendicular to each other. The square has been completed by erecting a fence on the two other sides to the empty part of the building. This way a garden has been created inside. Each room has a door both to the cloister with a gazebo, to the corridor, and the street since the rooms, lounges, and so on are surrounded by the street.

This hotel was probably better than the hotel in Djibouti. Perhaps it was the nice view of the surroundings, the presence of trees and the relative coolness of the climate that reflected its superiority. The hotelier came and met us at the station because he had been informed about our arrival by the government. He said that he had prepared rooms and a separate dining lounge for us. This hotel was really clean and good relative to Dire Dawa.

After some rest and a meal, we fell into a nice sleep due naturally to the fatigue of travel and with the help of the relative coolness here.

Sunday, May 22   Dire Dawa

Dire Dawa • Preparation for the land journey • The display of the bond of the local Somalis to the Exalted Court • Somalia and Somalis • Oil, earth cosmetics • A grand apology

The easy part of the journey finished in Dire Dawa. We had to see to travel preparations since we were going to go on camel and mule henceforth and as the rainy season had started arriving immediately, it was necessary not to lose even an hour, let alone a day.

In the evening, we had only taken our bags and a few small things to the hotel from our baggage in the wagons. Our first task today was to bring the chests of imperial gifts accompanying us, together with other belongings from customs. The deposit chests had been made quite big in Istanbul, to a degree that they could not even be loaded on camels, let alone on mules. It was necessary to make the chests again. Although it was a Sunday and the day of Pentecost, each chest was turned into two by making four European master carpenters work with extra pay, standing over them until the evening. They became as small as possible. The items were divided accordingly. Their tops were coated with zinc so as not to let rain penetrate.

Since Dire Dawa is taking the form of a city that is growing, progressing day by day because it is the terminus of the railroad, the railway company even has a workshop and due to this, master builders, carpenters and blacksmiths are found. I was really quite delighted in the evening when I saw that all the chests were in a state that could be loaded on mules and that there was not any impediment for us to depart the next day because many people had advised me to be patient quite a bit both in Djibouti and when I arrived in Dire Dawa. They say that I am not in Europe and time has no value at all for the native population here. On my arrival to Dire Dawa, when I say "two days" to those who ask me "how long are you going to stay here?", they are laughing. "You are fortunate if you can depart in a week" would be the response.

Let me state that despite all this work today, I had to attend to arriving visitors occasionally and keep Talip Bey and Sergeant Yasin over the task.

While the Arabs came and left in fives, tens, I understood the Somalis numbered around five, six hundred when they were still half a kilometer away from the cries of tahlil and takbir and the battle songs that, in turns, rose to the sky. Continuing in this way, they gathered with the same tune and harmony in front of the hotel, first repeating prayers of welfare for the longevity and prosperity of His Imperial Majesty, the supreme Padishah and later performing the official welcome ceremony to the delegation, they began battle performances.

The front of the hotel became extremely crowded because a lot of people had gathered to watch these persons. The Europeans who were there stated that it was the first time they were seeing so many Somalis perform games together, that such a revelry and official reception had not occurred until now. I toured the city a little in the evening. I also obtained some information from the arriving visitors.

Dire Dawa is actually a village at ten minutes' distance from the place where the station is located. Prior to the arrival of the railroad here, the crops that were produced in the region were being collected in Harar and transported to Djibouti through Jaldessa on camelback. The mentioned items began to come here after the arrival of the railroad due to the proximity of Dire Dawa to Harar. This place gained importance since the goods that come from the sea are also transferred to the interior from here.

The Europeans and the railway company had given it the name of Addis Harar, with the belief that this place would replace Harar and even registered it with this name on some of their maps, but the emperor had not agreed to this name change and they had retained the Dire Dawa name.

Since the word addis in the Ethiopian language means "hadith" in Arabic, or "yeni"[41] in Turkish, Addis Harar means New Harar. In sum, its population rose day by day with the arrival of a lot of men here from abroad as the importance of Dire Dawa increased. Its current population is around two thousand. Most of these people are Muslim and members of the Somali tribes of Gurgura, Galla. There are also merchants who have come from Yemen, India. Although the principal officials of the railway are French, Muslims are present in their retinues. As for the tribes residing

---

41 *'Yeni' means 'new'

in the surroundings: The community between Djibouti and Dire Dawa are the Iyessa people of Somalis. Those who reside between Dire Dawa and Ortu, that is at twenty kilometers' distance and located in the west, are from the Gurgura who are from the mixture of Somalis and Gallas. I am putting below all the information I collected about Somalis since they have been mentioned a lot and their population is large:

Somalia

The Somali people occupy extensive lands starting from the north of the Gulf of Tadjoura that is outside the Strait of Bab Al Mandab, along the Gulf of Aden coast of Africa, until near the Zanzibar[42] border following the coast.

The smallest part of these coasts and the hinterlands are under the control of the French. Beyond here and the part extending near the end of the Gulf of Aden is under the control of the English. The small part at the end of the coast of Gulf of Aden and the large part that extends towards the Zanzibar border are under the control of the Italians. These places are shown in maps with the names of French Somalia, English Somalia, Italian Somalia after the names of these states.

It had been mentioned that a part of the Somali people are in the country of Ethiopia. The Somali people are divided to Iyessa, Dangali, Galla and numerous other branches. Some are enemies of each other. Attacking each other like other Bedouin people, they pillage cattle, animals. In this way, bloody battles take place between them. It is estimated that their population is around one and a half million.

Somalis are not originally African. In the eleventh century in the Gregorian calendar, one of the Indian Rajas, coming by sea to Bab Al Mandab with a large army, invaded the coast of the Arabian Peninsula, then the African coast on the other side, from Assab to Zanzibar and made these places his homeland. The Somalis are their descendants.

Although this conquest continued until the thirteenth century, the Emir of Muscat had crossed the Red Sea in the mentioned century to avoid paying tax and conquering the coast of Somalia in the name of Islam had brought it under his sovereignty and made the people accept

---

42 *Zinjibar in the text using the Arabic name

the Mohammedan religion of Islam. He destroyed some monuments and temples belonging to idolatry, turned the suitable ones to mosques. English officers who were trying to map Somalia have found some traces of Indian temples. Researchers who are working in linguistics find a complete resemblance between the Somali language and the Deccan language and show a lot of words and examples regarding this.

The Somalis are Muslims and most perform the prayer ritual, but some have become infamous for shedding blood and atrocities since they have not yet adequately received religious instruction. They have savage customs such as the husband beating his wife with a whip, sometimes making her bleed, ostensibly to render her obedient on the first nuptial night. The Somalis used to be engaged in the slave trade before, but they do not do this much any more.

Before travel with train, it was possible to go from both Djibouti and Zeila until the Ethiopian border with the protection and guidance of these Somalis in ten-sixteen days, over quite hot terrain. When travelers and merchants requested permission from government to go from the coast, the government used to license it under the condition of not being responsible for any harm or losses that may come to their lives and goods. In this way, the traveler had to give gifts, even if small, to the sheikhs of the lands they passed, besides the fee for the animal. Besides this, he was also dependent on the protection of a cameleer named Eban and the company of a few guards.

If a traveler came across a Somali desirous of marriage and, in particular, if that traveler was white, he would be exposed to a big danger. This was apparently because some Somalis could only ask for a girl to get married by first killing a man and sending a part of him to the parent or guardian of the girl.

There is always a pride in the behavior and demeanor of Somalis like other Bedouin people. They have a tough demeanor and are patient. They endure all kinds of hardship and tolerate it. For this reason, they retain their pride against the city dwellers that live in prosperity and benefit from the blessings of civilization. They even look at their prosperity and comfort in a condescending way.

Even the Somalis who provide menial services such as porterage, servitude, boating on the coast, stoking in ships do not regard the Europeans superior and maintain their behavior and pride despite seeing the progress of the Europeans, their big achievements. They never use alcohol. They are quite brave. They can bear hunger and thirst. Their weapons consist of a spear that is as long as their height, a shield, and a dagger at their waist. They are very skilled at using weapons. As they can hit their enemies where they want even with a spear from a far distance, they hunt gazelles, rabbits with spear. A Somali goes against wild animals like tigers and elephants alone, attacks and kills them.

Their spears are always in their hands. They walk leaning against it. Since they are used to this, they carry a cane at that height when they are not carrying a spear.

They do not engage in farming and agriculture. Since they live on animal husbandry, they almost do not have any work when they do not work as cameleers. They are very keen to get news and tidings from everywhere, from those who come and go.

Some carry a rosary with huge pieces on their necks. Their women and men rub a lot of butter and ghee on their heads instead of lavender.

After glistening their hair with butter, the men plaster it with thin soil. Whatever the color of the soil where they are, the plastered hair takes that color. It is sometimes red, sometimes completely white like lime. The head of those who rub the white soil resembles a statue head or those who used to wear wigs made from white hair in old Europe. Their hairs are curly from birth. However, it stretches down, preserving its curliness, when combed and exactly takes the form of a wig due to the effect of the paste or plaster made from butter and soil. Just like inviting each other to a meal is a treat, if a Somali invites another Somali to his house, in other words his hut, and plasters his head with butter, he would have given a treat proportionate with the quality, paucity-abundance of the butter he rubs. If one was to commit a crime infringing on the honor and dignity of another, he takes him to his hut and greases his head abundantly to atone for his fault. There cannot be a bigger apology than this.

The Somalis are not all of the same color. They are of various colors starting from the Ethiopian color close to tan to dark black. Their foreheads are high and wide; their eyes are big and beautiful.

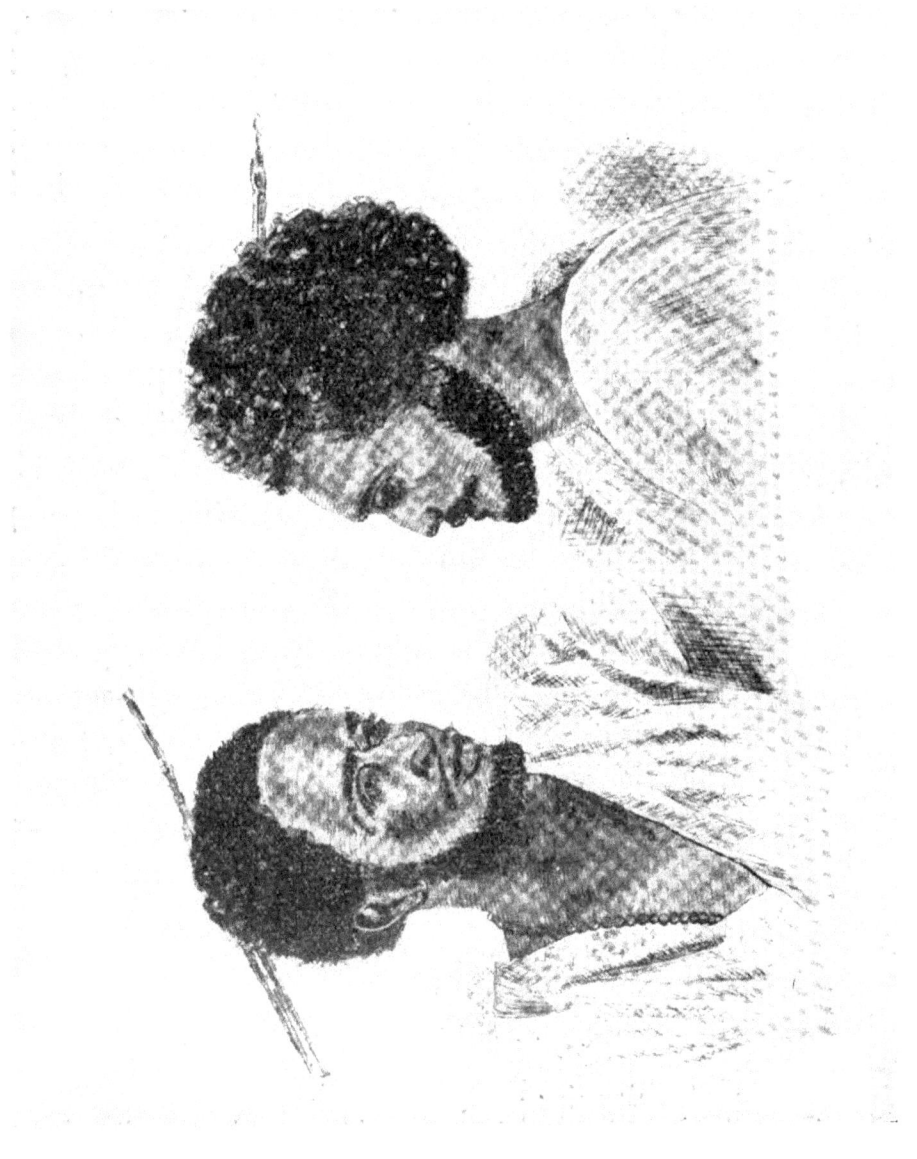

Faces of Somalis

Monday, May 23   Departure from Dire Dawa

Departure from Dire Dawa • Both saddle and hut • Big toe stirrup • Honor parade • The diligence of women • Rubber tree • Wood pickaxes • Lake Haramaya • Naive wild birds • Harsh cold • Those who came to greet

Since our departure today had been decided from yesterday, the mules reserved for us to ride, the camels required for the baggage had been hired from yesterday through Ato Biyana. Coming in front of the hotel early in the morning, these persons began to load the baggage. Our cameleers are Somali. As an example of their ability to produce and procure their essential needs as much as possible without depending on the outside and the craftsmen in the town, let me describe the camel saddles that I saw over and over while passing by train:

Somalis are not men who have ever given money to either saddle makers, or rope makers. The part of the saddle that makes up its soft section consists of rough wickers that they have woven from grass. They place three, four wickers one on top of the other so that the load does not hit the camel. The wooden part is composed of four units of rather long, sturdy canes. Each two of these canes are tied to one another to form an angle, in other words, a fork. The two ends of each of these two forks are also tied to the two ends of the other fork. After these are placed on a mat on the camel's back, the lower ends are tied tightly with a rope, like a girth, from below the camel's belly. In this manner, a quite light, sturdy and simple saddle is created. The baggage is loaded quite securely since the ropes of the right half of the baggage that are tied to the right fork are tied to the upper ends of the left fork; the left half's ropes are again tied to the upper end of the right fork. Since the baggage is resting on the forks, it does not harm the camel's back, belly.

As for the ropes used for travel, these consist of ropes that Somalis weave from a type of soft and sturdy grass. Saddles have another important use, too. The mentioned canes are placed against each other diagonally when the caravan stops in the evening. Its top is covered with straw mats. Perfect huts emerge for the cameleers. If there are extra straw mats left, they spread these in the huts under them. So, you see, they know the method of hitting two birds with one stone.

Had I seen this saddle method before, how it would have served me. Since the saddles of the camels of the desert Arabs between Syria and Medina are devoid of wood, consisting of two grass pillows adjacent to one another, it would not have been possible to load telegraph poles on these. This had resulted in the necessity of sending wood saddles all the way from Damascus with the effort and assistance of the province and this situation was causing both more expense and loss of time.

It was eight o'clock alafranga time by the time the camels were loaded and the horse saddles that we brought together from Istanbul were fitted to the mules and prepared. Since Governor Ato Mersha had returned to the city in the evening, he had come to visit and bid us farewell with his son Ato Biyana, some officials and some number of soldiers. Their mules were also ready. The saddles of their mules resemble old Ottoman saddles. However, with the stirrups so small and narrow so as to fit the feet of only five, six year old children, I was, in turns, casting an eye at their feet and the stirrups. We finally got on the mules. The Atos took off their shoes consisting of laceless footwear when they were about to mount. They gave them to their servants. Getting only their toe in the stirrup, they mounted from the right side. It turns out that it was customary for only their toes to be placed in the stirrup. The reason for them to mount from the right side is that generally the Ethiopians do not wear their swords on the left side like us, but tie it tightly to their waist with a strap on the right side.

It becomes almost like one with their body. Consequently, it is customary to mount from the right side since it is not possible to mount from the left side of the animal. Thus, our mules must have been surprised at our approach from the left side because we could only mount after a lot of effort and having their heads restrained by one or two people.

We set out on the road with forty, fifty people at eight o'clock. Since the track of the railroad by itself continued a few hours beyond Dire Dawa, we followed it.

Putting their hands behind the Atos' back and shoulders of mules, a servant was walking on both sides, embracing their Atos from the back and quite a few soldiers were going ahead of us, behind us, barefoot, bareheaded, weapon at shoulder, as they wanted.

The Muslims of the Ethiopians who came across us are passing after saluting. As for the Christians, standing on the side of the road, they are making a display of homage by placing their left foot in front of their right foot, bringing together their arms and bowing their heads until their knees.

As for the women, they were passing in groups, some with a huge load of grass, some a huge load of wood and their loads tied to their shoulders with straps and with some holding chicken, some milk, butter, honey, and so on even in their hands. These women were exempt from the display of homage. Who knows from what distant villages these wretches had woken up in the middle of the night and were coming to town barefoot, bareheaded to sell the things at hand. In truth, it was not possible not to pity them. I see from now that almost all the hard tasks here have been burdened on women.

There was an Albanian fellow traveler beside us named Bekir Ibrahim Efendi, one of the servants in the retinue of His Imperial Majesty the Emperor, who had been residing in the capital for a few years and occasionally came and went on these roads. I showed him this hardship of women. He said, "Yes, the wretch's husband, father or brother takes the money she will earn. He buys rifle rounds before everything else. He empties these in the air at a moment of happiness or when they cheer up. The labor of a few days of the woman is in this way wasted and gone".

We passed the town. We passed the stream that flows to the city. I offered the Atos to now return once or twice, but they accompanied us for an hour's distance. After leaving the Dire Dawa Police Chief Ato Yomru and five soldiers in our company, the Atos returned.

We were crossing a forest and moving steadily higher. The women with loads were continuing. After following the track for two hours, we left it to take a shortcut and started to follow the old road, in other words an uneven, narrow trail. During the journey, we are seeing numerous birds whose kinds I do not know, alongside those we know such as pigeons, doves, turtledoves, quails, sparrows perched on trees that resemble cypresses and a large variety of pines and others. One tree, in particular, attracted my attention a lot.

I had seen a kind of plant of the prickly pear tree variety, with twisted branches, leafless, flowerless in some garden pots in Istanbul. Although the trunk of the tree that I was seeing in front of me was solid and looked like those of poplar trees, all its branches, shoots were of the kind of the big, thick leaves of the prickly pear; but narrow, thin and had burst upwards. It neither has leaves, nor flower. It stands like an artificial tree as though made from wood pieces and painted green. I asked its name, kind from Ato. He said its name was "Kulkaval" in Ethiopian and that we would come across many ahead of us and that the Europeans made rubber from its sap. Truly, an abundant sap appears from whichever of its branches is broken that is white like milk and quite sticky.

We were one thousand one hundred and ninety three meters above sea level when we were in Dire Dawa. We set out with our white clothes, assuming that the temperature would continue to be mild. However, we started feeling cold since we had ascended another thousand meters by steadily climbing mountains within a few hours. After passing a few Ethiopian villages on the road, we came across a vendor's hut at ten o'clock. We got down to rest a little and wait for our camels.

The soldiers on foot who were beside us were continuing the road with quick steps since our mules were going fast. I told Ato a few times that we should go slow. Laughing, he said they were used to going like this from morning until evening and that they would not tire and he brought the mule to a gallop with the excuse of having it cleaned before arriving to the tent and made two of the soldiers run uphill for about half an hour. In this way, he demonstrated their strength.

Once at the tent, the owner put a few empty kerosene chests in front of us instead of chairs and tables. Since there was a tree next to the tent, we sat between the tent and the tree because from here, the slope of the mountain at a lofty point, the land, the forest, hill and streams that we passed are visible ahead of us, as far as the eye can see. I could think I was in Switzerland, or towards imperial Anatolia's Adapazarı or in the mountains, forests between Trabzon and Erzurum if there were not the Ethiopians around me.

The vendors present in the tent were a young man and a rather pretty, young and cute woman. They ground and brewed coffee for us. They gave us pomegranate juice and ayran. Meanwhile, taking out our breakfast from the saddlebags, we ate. I said that they ground the coffee. I had seen the stones with which they ground flour, sesame in Djibouti. And now, I am seeing the stones where coffee is ground. The local community grinds the flour on their own since there are no big mills around here. Their mills are not from stones of equal size and revolving one on top of the other like the hand mills we know and one stone is round or rectangular and smooth. The grains are placed on top of this. Another round, long stone like a rolling pin is held with two hands from the two ends that are pointed and ground over the flat stone. The grain becomes flour in this manner. The stones that are especially for grinding coffee also resemble this, but are smaller. God help those wretched women. Let the women in Istanbul and other imperial regions consider themselves fortunate. There was even grilled pigeon, which we had shot fresh, in our breakfast. After a repose and rest here of exactly two hours, we continued on our way.

The beauty of the forest, the size of the trees is increasing as we climb the mountain. The forest finished upon arrival to the summit of the mountain. Suddenly, what do we see? : A broad land full of thriving and inhabited villages and farms is stretching in front of us as far as the eye can see. It turns out that we were not ascending a mountain, but climbing the skirts of this high plateau. The beauty of the scene gained an altogether different color. I thought I was in one of the most thriving, inhabited and prosperous parts of Rumelia or imperial Anatolia. The villages are close to each other, the huts orderly. Man, woman, young, old are working in farms. Running around with the young ones of animals, the children are playing innocently. The corn saplings that have grown to a height of half an arşın are being tilled with pickaxe made from wood. Yes, these hardworking people are doing all their work with a wood pickaxe. The farms are being tilled with wooden ploughs.

Cattle, cows, sheep, and herds of goats are rolling and playing on green emerald like pastures. The men are doing their work naked above the waist, while the women, girls have low cut neckline cloth. Wild pigeon flocks are flying from one farm to another.

These hard working people are all Muslim and members of the Galla. They appear to be a beneficiary of the natural wealth God has bestowed and happy. We also benefited by shooting a few pigeons here.

At half past two o'clock alafranga time, we arrived to the junction of the road that goes to Harar and the road that goes to Addis Ababa. We had only hired the animals until Harar. With the replenishment of expedition needs and also the loading of baggage on mules here, we followed the Harar road since it had been determined before to go to Addis Ababa from the Chercher road. There are three different roads that go to the Ethiopian capital according to the investigation we conducted and the most suitable one of these in this season is the Chercher road. However, camels cannot go from here because it is quite steep and with ascents and descents. Nonetheless, it is not hot, malaria-infested and with limited water like other places apparently. More information will be provided about the roads later, God willing.

The iron telegraph poles that continued since the coast began to be replaced by wood poles starting from the road junction. After going ahead a bit more and descending from a light slope, a quite nice, mirror like lake appeared in front of our eyes. Its name is Lake Haramaya. The surroundings and vicinity also appeared as we approached. Oh, what a beautiful and nice view! The sides of the lake are surrounded with emerald like green hills. The water of the lake has originated from the rainwater that numerous waterways have gathered and brought. Its water is sweet. It is approximately two and a half kilometers long and one kilometer wide. Thousands of wild geese and ducks are swimming on it. The nests and the young of most are visible on the shore between the reeds.

Although the young Albanian named Şevket Efendi, from the company of Bekir Ibrahim Efendi, fired a few rounds and shot two, three geese and ducks with each try, some of these were retrieved and others stayed in the lake. A Galla child showed that he was ready to serve us to bring the birds that were shot by taking off his tunic. I also shot a few. It came to about ten. The wretched birds are so inexperienced and naive that shots are being fired, but they do not flee. They do not know what is happening. They make do with Quack! Quack! Quack! They do not shoot birds here because cartridges are so precious for the people and meat is found so abundantly. It only happens once a year if a foreign traveler is passing. For this reason and since it was not necessary to have more anyway, we were contented with this much today. With Lake Haramaya at two thousand two hundred and fifty meters above the sea level, the chill increased due to the approach of the evening.

Big pits dug at intervals between the farms of the Galla collect rainwater. They both obtain their water from here and water their cattle. At this moment, a few horsemen who were subjects of the Ottoman state of Aydın, Kayseri, Kurd and Albanian [origin] residing in Harar came to welcome us. They had been informed of our arrival. After covering some more way together with them, we selected the slope of a high hill overlooking a running stream to stop in the evening. The wind is blowing cool and violently. We were quite cold until our camels and tents caught up. Lighting a big fire at the base, the meals were cooked. Our bodies warmed. We slept early. The surroundings became cooler since it rained at night. We wore our winter undershirt and clothes when we woke up in the morning. Those who came to welcome us said that the local government in Harar was preparing a big reception ceremony and that all the community, composed almost entirely of Muslims, was quite pleased and happy and that they would all come to greet us.

Somali Women

Tuesday, May 24   Arrival to Harar

Arrival to Harar • Preparation for the road • The features of Harar • Where does the name for coffee come from? • Beads, rainbow umbrella • Abdullah • The palace of Ras Makonen • Coat of arms • Friday prayer

Striking the tents early in the morning, we set out on the road. I gritted my teeth even though my body was worn out and feeble, suffering from rheumatism due to the cold I felt in the evening and the dampness from the rain at night. I was both watching the surroundings and obtaining information about the town from the greeters who came from Harar, both yesterday evening and today while traveling. These will be written after arriving in Harar.

When we came close to one and a half hours' distance to Harar, notables and respected individuals from Mecca, Medina; quite a lot of Anatolian, Arabian and Indian people were coming in waves mostly on the back of animals, those without animals as pedestrian, firing with their weapons, and their youths reveling. The plain had become congested with people as though nobody was left in Harar other than the old and women. Since they are dismounting from their animals and approaching me respectfully as they come closer, I, too, am being forced to dismount from the animal frequently.

The foremost among them were praying for our mighty Padishah, our master His Imperial Majesty, while those hearing this were saying amen. In short, the reception was quite brilliant and sincere because we have not yet arrived to the reception that the government has organized. The people had come out of their own accord and come this far. In particular, the greeting ceremony of the Indians was quite nice. They are trying to treat us in every way by spreading all kinds of lavenders on our delegation, pressing amber, musk perfumed silk handkerchiefs in our hands for us to wipe our sweat, and presenting flower bundles. So, you see, our contingent was approaching Harar in this way. The regent, mufti, imams of Harar were also among the community.

Upon coming to an hour's distance from the city, a company of Ethiopian soldiers under the command of an officer is joining us every quarter of an hour after saluting our delegation. When we approached the city, we found about two thousand Ethiopian soldiers lined up in a row outside the city, saluting. Dismounting from the animals upon approach to them, we headed towards the official delegation at their head. They walked towards us, too and we met at the large square. The most senior of these persons was the deputy of Ras Makonen, Qenazmach[43] Genemi, his second deputy Balambaras Sheti and the foremost of the officials. After Qenazmach Genemi conveyed that Ras Makonen had assigned him to meet us on his behalf before his departure to Addis Ababa, communicated the greetings, words of the aforementioned and introduced those in his retinue, we set off towards the city.

While entering through the city wall, cannons began to be fired from a tower that was at a high place. The city was like judgment day due to the sounds of cannons, happy clamor of the community and the throngs of people. The roofs were full of women and children. They were both watching the Ottoman delegation and saying "lu lu lu" altogether as high as their voices allowed as part of the display of welcome and their voices were reaching the sky. Amid this grandiose and flamboyant reception ceremony, we reached Ras Makonen's palace that was located at a high place in the city and had been arranged for our residence from before.

---

43 *Commander of the right flank

After the foremost among those who met us, qenazmach and government officials repeated words along the lines of "welcome, you have brought joy" and greetings for a few minutes here, too and showed the guides and servants who had been assigned to our service, they left. I expressed the desire to visit the government regent at the government mansion. Qenazmach responded by saying, "You are tired, let it stay for another day". The English, French, Italian consuls came one by one and visited. I obtained information by meeting them quite a while, too.

The guide informed us that a big cow, sheep, lambs, grape baskets, banana and so on had come from Ras Makonen's residence for our kitchen. I had the cow given to the soldiers and servants who were accompanying from Dire Dawa. They slaughtered it immediately. They skinned it. While the meat was still hot, they ate it raw with a full appetite. I retreated from the window so that they would not say, "Is there more?"

Our guide and translator was a young, pleasant, quite polite, well-mannered, respected person from here named Sayyid Mohammed Al Naqib who sought to cater for our every need and comfort. Starting the replenishment of some provisions and necessities for the road with his guidance and also turning over the task of hiring mules to take us to Addis Ababa to him, our departure was deferred to Saturday.

When a person wants to travel around here, he must find a head muleteer referred to as nejadi. This man procures the required mules, muleteers. If they have returned from afar, they do not set out again before resting the animals and grazing them abundantly because it is not customary to give forage to the animals. The animals live on the grass that they find on the road. Some travelers have only been able to prepare their caravans in ten, fifteen days in centers such as Dire Dawa, Harar. Other than the mules and muleteers, a cook and an apprentice for the kitchen, a sufficient number of servants who are used to go with travelers are hired to bring water from the location of a stream, to gather wood for the base, to pitch and strike the tent, in short these types of travel services. When we set out with the men that we will hire for these services, their names will be declared.

These preparations used to be done entirely on the coast before the railroad was constructed. Now, these are seen to in Dire Dawa or, even better, in Harar because Harar is a big center of commerce and a point that caravans target, as will be explained. When a traveler or an official like us comes here, those wishing to register as cook, servant submit references that they have obtained from persons they accompanied in previous journeys. These persons are not referred to as attendant or servant, but "eskeri". This word must be a corruption of the word "askari"[44] because from the day that they are included in the service of the person hiring them, they obey his every order, submit almost like a soldier. They will rush to death and every danger with one order. They stand guard in the evening. It is customary to have them armed.

Most African travelers can go to wild and dangerous places with the help of these eskeris. A person can take as many into his service as he wants, even hundreds of eskeri if desired. The government does not prevent it. While travel procurements like this are being seen to, let me now relay some of my observations during my period of residence in Harar.

Harar

Harar does not immediately appear into view when approaching from the north, in other words from the road we came, because of the high hills that surround the city from far and screen it since they are relatively higher. The town is among these hills on top of an elliptical, rather long and elevated hill. For this reason, the residence and its other buildings face and dominate each other. The defense of the city is easy because it is surrounded by an ancient wall.

Since our residence was at the highest point in the region, it overlooks everywhere. A person thinks himself in Arabia when looking from the top floor. Their houses are built from stone, mud bricks; their roofs are flat like Arabian roofs. One comes across veiled women on roofs a lot since there is no shortage of services such as spreading grains, drying, hanging laundry. Most of their headscarves are red.

The roads of the region are narrow, undulating and serpentine. Not a single plan was followed when this town was being established, everyone had set up his building at will and passages had resulted in between streets.

---

44 *Refers to the word soldier in Arabic

Its roads are not very clean. The region looks like Damascus or a mansion in the middle of a big garden since it is surrounded by gardens and green hills all around.

Fruits such as sugar cane, banana, coffee, grape, lemon and orange; and vegetables such as zucchini, cucumber, eggplant, tomato, peas and the like are grown in the gardens.

The top of the houses is open like Arabian houses. They have a relatively big courtyard. The trees in the courtyard, which surpass the roofs, are giving the region a further charm. The streets cannot be seen from where we are because they are narrow. As a result, a person could think this place empty if there were not the women doing chores on the roof, and the occasional camel sound, or dog bark was not heard.

There is a population of forty thousand residing in the town. Thirty-five thousand of these are Muslims. The five thousand who are Christian are from non-Muslim nations such as Ethiopian, French, Greek and Armenian.

Although one assumes that Harar's climate is quite hot because it is near the tenth latitude to the north of the equator, the weather is quite nice and mild due to being one thousand eight hundred and fifty-six meters above sea level, surrounded by orchards and gardens. According to the consuls' statement, the temperature almost never exceeds twenty-six degrees centigrade in the summer. The climate becomes mild with the effect of rainfall in the summer and the sun in the winter because it does not rain around here and in the regions of Ethiopia and Sudan in the winter. The rainy season starts from May and continues until the end of September. June, July August, September are the months with most rain. Coffee is grown in the vicinity of Harar and in the region of Ethiopia owing to this moderation. This natural crop is growing as forests towards the southwest of Ethiopia, especially in the Kaffa region. The conferment of the name Kaffa, which means coffee, is arising from the spontaneous growth of the plant here. Coffee is present in large quantities in the exquisite Harar gardens and around it.

A river with abundant water named Erer passes from Harar and covers a distance of a thousand kilometers, crossing Somali and Ogaden territory and disappearing in the sands before reaching the sea.

Lots of women come to Harar early every morning from the surrounding villages, hamlets. Some bring wood, some grass, some chicken, honey, butter and so on; sit at the square that becomes the marketplace and sell there. Those who have gotten permission from their guardian to spend a part of the money they earned cannot go before buying something here that will make them prettier, enhance their beauty.

These women first go to their jewelers, in other words to their bead sellers. Consulting, discussing with each other, and shying from those around, they put on one necklace, take-off another. They try an earring, a bracelet. They decide after turning it over and over at length, looking at themselves with hand mirrors, smiling by showing their extremely white teeth, grinning and they buy whatever they are going to buy. If the person who is buying a bead does not have a mirror, she will also buy a small mirror because she will show her ornament both to others and occasionally she will watch herself. It is rumored, by those who compile merchandise trade statistics, that one hundred thousand bead boxes, each containing six thousand beads, and three hundred thousand mirrors made in Germany and Trieste are sold annually in this way. The beads are made from the imitation of precious stones. Second most in demand after beads are the clothes made in Europe. Since the women at the center of Harar demand red, blue colors most and wear dresses made from the blend of these clothes, these are sold in high volume.

While there are French, Greek, Italian, Armenian merchants and vendors and so on, the bulk of the trade is in the hands of the agencies here of two big merchants located in Bombay named Indian Mohamed Ali and Taib Ali Akbar. The Europeans confess that they cannot compete with these because these people live here frugally and modestly and sell their goods with a small gain. We bought the required provisions and so on for our caravan from these persons, too.

The trade of the Indians in this vicinity is not new, but very old. European industrial products began to come to these coasts a lot after the opening of the Suez Canal. However, Indian goods have been coming to Africa from Bombay through Zeila from of old, prior to Djibouti. Is it not strange? While Egypt is so near, we could not find Egyptian rice here or even in Djibouti and settled for Indian rice.

The square that is the biggest marketplace of the region can be seen from the top floor of the residence we were in. A crowd is never absent here. There is shopping both in the square and in the room like shops around the square. Camel, mule, donkey, cow, sheep, goat, chicken, corn, onion, in brief whatever is found in the region and comes from the villages are sold in the square, all at one place. One cannot get enough from watching the crowds seen here.

Their dresses are of all kinds. While the shemma clothes that the Ethiopians cover themselves in are white, the shemma that the notables wear consist of three parts with two sides white and the middle red, so that those who wear it look as though they have wrapped themselves in a flag. Especially the very strange umbrellas that I see over the heads of some of the nobles are such that these are only hung above umbrella shops in Istanbul as a signboard and for advertisement purposes. The color of the fabric between each iron stick is different. In other words, one is red, another yellow, yet another green, the next brown so that the fabric of the umbrella presents a scenery of color groups. Such umbrellas are being made expressly for here. It is quite desirable. They are carrying these not to be protected from the sun, but as an ornament because most Ethiopians walk around with their head bare. The nobles, notables (Christians) have recently gotten used to wearing a hat.

The first high mountain that can be seen from here is named Gondor and is at an altitude of three thousand two hundred meters above sea level. Since the crops of the coffee trees that are seen around it had gone to Mocha at one time and from there to Europe, it is still sold in Europe under the name of Moka. Everybody assumes that coffee originates from Mocha (Moka). In fact, it is the produce of Harar and its vicinity. However, it was previously being sent to that port for it to be delivered to Europe. While Aden has now replaced Mocha, the name Mocha has still endured.

Rauf Pasha, one of the Egyptian commanders, had occupied Harar and its dependencies with the soldiers that were under his command in the year one thousand eight hundred and seventy-five, after being commissioned with the administration of the African Red Sea coast of the Egyptian Khedivate. During the sedition of the Mutemahdi in the year one thousand eight hundred and eighty-four, the Egyptians vacated Harar of their soldiers and left the city to a man named Abdullah who was the ruler of the city before the Egyptians occupied it. This conceited man started with hundreds of rifles under his command and lowered the Ottoman flag and raised in its place his own private flag and this ignorance reached [the point] that he dared and attributed the title of commander of the believers to himself and ordered sermons to be read in his name and, unsatisfied, he sent Menelik a prayer rug and jug and washbowl for ablution inviting him to embrace Islam and threatened to march on him if he did not respond. Menelik sent him an appeasing letter with soft words, but Abdullah did not listen to his words. So, war erupted between them in the year one thousand eight hundred and eighty-seven. This backfired on Abdullah [and] he fell captive in the hands of Menelik. Thus, Harar entered the grip of the Ethiopian Emperor and it still remains so until now. Emperor Menelik arranged for Abdullah a salary from government and ordered him to stay in Harar where he is now in seclusion, unable to meet people because he is ashamed and embarrassed from what arose from the lapses that caused the loss of his country. His brother came to visit me when I was in Harar. However, I heard the story of Abdullah from the Albanians and Kurds who came to greet us and who were present in all the incidents that occurred and learned these matters from the beginning to the end. Those who came to Harar with the Egyptians, when the soldiers of Rauf Pasha occupied it, got married here and reside here to this day.

In the Gregorian year one thousand nine hundred, a quite deadly cholera pestilence had spread in the vicinity of Harar and one third of the population had perished.

In ancient times, Harar was subject to Ethiopia. The Muslims came and opened the area in the Gregorian year one thousand five hundred and twenty-one, but Harar stayed autonomous under their partly independent administration until the arrival of the Egyptians and their occupation. However, due to the harmful actions of the aforementioned Abdullah and his insatiable greed, it again came under Ethiopian sovereignty.

The palace of Ras Makonen where we are residing is the highest, most splendid and the sturdiest among the buildings present in Harar. The building is from stone and consists of divans, halls, numerous rooms, stairs, terraces, balconies in the style of houses in Europe and Istanbul over three floors. While the rooms, halls are spacious and wide, the floors are not wood or parquet, but consist of a solid surface coat based on the Arabian method that they refer to as zarika in Syria, tabtab in Hejaz. The windows are small relative to the rooms so as to prevent too much light. There are fixed wooden pergolas above each window for the purpose of preventing the entry of light, like the sunscreens of taut fabric in Istanbul. Dark colors dominate the paint and embroidery inside the residence. There are carpets and rugs spread on the floors. The reception hall is furnished with big seats and chairs and decorated with Emperor Menelik's painting and the Ethiopian flag.

The big plot around the building is surrounded by a wall and a part of it is arranged as a garden, and another part, or the section in front of the palace entrance, as a courtyard. One first goes through the courtyard door, in other words the main gate, before entering the palace. An elephant tail is hung above the door, or to the middle of the arch, and lion statues from plaster have been erected on either side. The tail is the tail of an elephant that the chief killed during a hunt.

The biggest pastime of commanders and foremost government officials in Ethiopia is hunting. The tails of the wild animals that everyone has shot is hung to their house doors like a set of charms. This task of hanging is done with a flamboyant ceremony. The person who has killed a lion and so on wears its mane on his head as a sign of victory during official days. A person who has not killed such an animal cannot wear this distinguishing feature. If he does wear it, he would have committed fraud.

I paid return visits to the deputy of the ras, Qenazmach Genemi and then to the consuls on Thursday, May twenty-seventh. Qenazmach's residence consists of two floors. The residences of the consuls also consist of two floors and although resemble people's houses from the outside, a person forgets he is in Harar by the arrangement, cleanliness and order when entering their rooms. Excellencies the British Consul Monsieur John, French Consul Monsieur Gabriel Guigniony, the Italian Consul Captain Stroni honored and treated our delegation a lot. Although they wanted to arrange receptions, I gave an excuse and dissuaded them since we had very little time. They repeatedly declared that they were ready to provide all kinds of assistance to facilitate our journey.

Since we had completed our tools and equipment, our head muleteer, mules and muleteers, cooks, and our askaris were hired with imperial patronage, I reciprocated by thanking for this humane offer of the aforementioned officials.

Besides this, Monsieur Qarra, the deputy of Monsieur Chefneux who is famous in all of Ethiopia and among those that have earned an important position before the emperor in Addis Ababa, and Monsieur Adolphe Michel, the Harar Telegraph Director and the representative of Monsieur Ilg, came bringing greetings from their principals while we were in Dire Dawa and declared that they were ready for any kind of assistance. We also thanked them. Doctor Jan Quzma also visited a few times in Harar due to my illness. In short, we are honored with respect and esteem everywhere during this assignment due to imperial patronage.

With several mosques existing in Harar, we performed the Friday prayer at the Grand Mosque. Everyone's eye in the mosque was turned to our humble delegation. When the sermon was read to the name of the guardian of the caliphate for his longevity and health and increase in glory and might and quite eloquent prayers were given for the victorious guardian of the caliphate and I heard the Muslim community of about two thousand say amen sincerely to these prayers, tears welled up in my eyes from joy. There is such a natural situation in almost all parts of Islamic countries. However, after passing all these seas and deserts, it is not possible for a loyal subject not to be happy on seeing that sacred name's sublimeness is always mentioned with respect and honor. May God extend the life of His Supreme Highness in full health to a great age and ordain his glory and might to be lasting and forever. Amen. These prayers are one thousandth of the prayers I heard from the mouth of the people while leaving the mosque. Wherever those who believe in the oneness of God are present, I see once again with complete pride that their hearts are also always faithful to that divine office. What faithfulness, what a supreme religion! There cannot be a tie as strong as religious ties, that's that...

Saturday, May 28   Departure from Harar

Trial • Saddle from merchandise • Ethiopian mules • Departure from Harar • Members of the caravan, travel services • Our tents • Our durgu cook Haji Yusuf • What an easy bread • Confidential meal

Before this departure day, the muleteers were coming to our residence every day, reviewing our belongings one by one, weighing the chests by hand and making remarks like: "This chest is heavy; we cannot load it on the mule. This chest is big, the mule cannot carry this". As for us, we were implementing what they said as much as we could. If they can get away with it, they do not want anything loaded on their mules. Finally, the muleteers came alone early today. Lowering the chests and gear from above, they piled everything in the square inside the wall. Everyone wanted to take the lightest load since the mules were not the property of one person and some owned two, some three mules. A brawl, pandemonium broke among them. Unfortunately, I cannot understand what they are saying. An hour, hour and a half passed and they were all still calling and shouting. At last, I sent word to Qenazmach Genemi. He sent an official named Ato Jemanah from his side.

The clamor stopped as soon as the aforementioned came through the door. Voices were lowered. After communicating the greetings of qenazmach to me, sitting on the topmost baggage, crossing his legs, the aforementioned frowned at the men. Pressing his hat forward, he glowered at them. The men froze like idols. It turns out that he had now taken on his formal role and the others were now almost in front of a court. However, he had weighed all the baggage with his hand one by one before taking on this position.

Since each of the muleteers want to take the light load, nobody wants to take the big chests. They put forward the excuse that some of our chests could not be loaded to mules. However, they had come each day while the guide was present and seen the chests one by one and negotiated with him on that basis. We paid all the fees in advance based on this.

In this situation, the case became between the guide and the muleteers. The head muleteer and the guide sat in front of the Ato like defendant-plaintiff. The muleteer said that he would give one jar of honey for court damages. Since the guide knew that he would be proved right, he raised the court damages all the way up to the value of a mule. The muleteer could not raise the ante because whoever lost the case would pay damages. We are watching this pandemonium. I am occasionally asking where the business is from someone who knows Amharic. The head muleteer claimed that it was not possible to load a few chests and that he had not seen those in the negotiation. The guide showed the servants in the residence as witnesses and rejected the claim of the head muleteer. However, this court was proceeding much more strangely than usual.

While the defendant is talking, he alternately points with his hand and goes back and forth as though on a theatre stage, raising and lowering his hand up and down to give strength to his statement, shouting, screaming, raising havoc, showing all his fluency and eloquence. The plaintiff stays silent like an idol until the defendant's statement is finished, and then starts raising havoc. The witnesses were heard. Ato passed his judgment. The head muleteer who had flown into a fury with rage bowed his head when ruled against. Not a word came from his mouth. He became timid[45]. After Ato ruled that all of these chests would be loaded on mules, the chests and loads were replaced with chair and tables. The muleteers drew lots.

---

45 *The expression 'Sütü döken kediye benzedi', literally 'looked like the cat that spilled the milk', could loosely be translated as 'becoming timid as a mouse'

Everybody took their share, went to bring their mules. Ato stayed next to us until we set out.

Let me write the information that I obtained about case damages until the muleteers come: A person who is going to sue another makes threats saying "the court damages are this much" because if the defendant is ruled against, it is likely that he will be forced to pay a multiple of the amount that was the subject of the case. Whatever damages the plaintiff puts forward, the defendant is forced to accept. If the defendant knows that he will be proven right, he would further raise the amount and not only accept the set damages. If they escalate, the amount of the damages sometimes reaches a large total. Whoever loses the case pays the pledged amount or goods.

The mules finally came. The muleteers started to load the baggages. Their loading of the baggage is bizarre, too. Not seen anywhere else. All their animals are without halters, mule shoes. They first placed a panel instead of the saddle on the animal, with its front in the shape of [the Arabic] number ٨ tied to a single fork and made from leather. On top of this, two calico rolls each tied to the other and protected with a round canvas took the shape of a pad. The calico rolls were not ours. The muleteers had bought two rolls each for their mules. They are going to make an additional profit since they are going to sell these fabrics in Addis Ababa at a higher price.

As for the baggage, they loaded two of each small halves, the size of a fuel container, in the manner we know by placing them to the right, left of the animal. They placed the larger, even one arşın[46] high, one-meter long chests on the back of the animal as though placing it on the floor. After passing the quite long thongs, instead of rope, below the animal's belly and wrapping the chest a few times, the muleteers, with one on the right side of the animal and another on the left, tightened the riems as much as their strength allowed by putting one leg each on the floor and the other leg leaning against the belly of the animal, so that the wretched mule's belly shrunk as to almost touch its back. The riems on its belly became invisible. Big swellings between the two straps and deep, deep holes had formed

---

46 *1 arşın = 68 centimeters

where the riems were touching. Since the bellies of the mules have callused like this, the mules were inevitably bearing this situation. The loaded mules are left to their own. The mules with baggage alternately lay and stood until loading finished. Since the baggage became one with their body, not even one moved from its place. We departed one hour after noon. We were bidden farewell by qenazmach and officials. They added four Ethiopian soldiers in the company of a junior officer to our side.

Since the first stop is always going to be brief, we camped after having gone two hours' distance today at the slope of a hill named Qersa. There were more than forty mules in our caravan since besides the mules loaded by muleteers, our passenger mules, there were also relief mules.

I registered and recorded the present population after stopping. I am recording them here, as samples of Ethiopian names:

Members of the Caravan

Myself, Major Talip Bey, Sergeant Yasin Efendi, Ibrahim Bekir Efendi and his partner Şevket Efendi.

Accompanying Soldiers

Sergeant Abu Bakr, Privates Omar, Osman, Hasan and Atemi.

Muleteers: 15	**Eskeris or servants: 14**
Ayalla	Haji Yusuf the cook
Nejadi or head muleteer	
Lemma muleteer	Juma'a
Bukulla	Ahmad
Shefau	Mohammad
Belay	Abdul Rahman
Adis	Alamu
Hilu	Mohammad
Butghas	Gharadu
Agha	Noru
Buat	Doghuba
Ayalla	Wak Ghira
Kabir Mariam	Beshra
Ghoshu	Alamu
Zakar Tarada	Abdul Rahman cook's apprentice
Kazmu	

It is customary for some poor people who want to go from one region to another to frequently join caravans such as this to be able to go for free. A few people joined us, too with the reference of the servants. In this way, our caravan size reached forty persons and forty mules.

As soon as the caravan camped, some of the servants occupied themselves with setting up tents, some in placing chests and goods inside tents, some carrying water for the kitchen, and some bringing wood.

Wood and water services are quite an important service. Caravans do not always camp near water so as to be far from the path of wild animals. They camp seven-eight hundred meters away because tigers, wolves, and other animals come to water at night. Big fires are lit with wood on four sides of the base. The soldiers and servants on guard pay attention so that these do not die until morning and add wood to the fire. This is so that wild animals do not approach the base and attack the mules that are grazing in the surroundings. These wild animals are very afraid of fire and run away from where there is fire.

Haramaya Base Durgu

Let me describe our dwellings in the desert since this book of travels could give quite a bit of guidance to people who will go there if required or those who want to go:

Our dwellings consist of a tent each and a number of items that are required for us to shelter. I had obtained my tent large, long and with two poles in order to be able to receive visitors who come. It is separated into a bedroom and living room with a small partition. The four skirts of the tent are not stitched to one another, but buttoned, so that depending on the direction of the sun, rain, wind the desired side is closed. One skirt opens and is elevated with two little poles to serve as a canopy. The inside is furnished with a common Anatolian kilim. Since it is always necessary to camp on tall grass here, kilim is necessary to protect from the damp and small pests. A collapsible table, and again a collapsible board, five-six chairs made from iron, three linen armchairs, a leather storage bag and two leather chests with linen on top can be seen in the middle.

The traveler is in need of impermeable chests and a cover to wrap the bed no matter what because of the abundant and violent rainfall around here. The locals protect their loads from rain by covering them with big animal hides.

There is a light, sturdy folding X model bed, a small table, bags for writing tools and toiletries in the bedchamber. Temporary hooks had been attached to the pole of the tent to hang weapons, clothes and the neck bag. The top of our food and provision chests is covered with zinc. My tent is at the center. The other tents are set according to that.

I saw a few Ethiopian men, women with full hands come to our base one after another as I was writing these lines. Abu Bakr met them, brought them beside me. The person in front kneeled down to greet. Abu Bakr was translating for us. The first was the shum, in other words steward or the chief, of nearby villages and had brought 'durgu'. I asked, "What is durgu? To whom is he bringing it?" In response, Abu Bakr said, "Master, wherever the emperor's soldiers and guests pass in Ethiopia, the people have an obligation to feed them. Since you are the guest of the emperor, the news have been spread everywhere. The people will perform their duties". Since, thank God, under imperial patronage, there was more than enough food and equipment for us to come and return, I apologized and refrained from accepting the durgu saying there was no need for these. Convincing me by saying, "Although the people are bringing these, it is the property of the emperor because 'durgu' is on the list of imperial levies. Naturally, the emperor's treat is not refused", Abu Bakr's eyes were not parting from the fat chickens in the women's hands and from the provision baskets on their heads. Upon my saying, " Fine, I accept", the shum gave thanks such as "Azguhar astali dahnasayi astali dagnu" and submitted the durgu to Abu Bakr. A portion went to our kitchen. The biggest portion was left to the soldiers, servants. It should be remembered that it is not necessary to distribute tips to those who bring durgu and depends on the generosity of the guest. The durgu that was brought consisted of chickens, pita bread, eggs, honey and butter. It was covered with red fabric. It was presented with a ceremony. Their bread is not from wheat, but made from a quite thin kind of grain with the name teff. I could not eat it since it was unsalted. I preferred melba toast.

The servants and soldiers surrounded the fire and finished the durgu in one hour. Plucking the chicken, removal of the thin feathers, putting it on fire is a task of a few minutes. Our cook Haji Yusuf's stomach is stronger than all. He is eating raw the tallow of a sheep we slaughtered, like eating Turkish delights. While Haji Yusuf has gone numerous times with a number of travelers to Africa and he has seen works of advancement and civilization to be able to pronounce numerous culinary terms such as soft-boiled egg, rare chops, pasta with cutlets, macaroni and know their meaning, he could never give up raw meat, raw tallow since his stomach did not tend towards civilization.

Activity is still continuing after the base has been set up. Some of the muleteers are polishing the leather panels on the back of the mules with soft stones, then softening it by rubbing oil. Some were cooking bread, digging a ditch around the tent so that rainwater does not flood the tent at night. Their baking of bread is quite simple and easy. Prior arrangements like kneading dough, fermenting, spreading the dough do not exist. There is a big flask of water, a wooden container, teff flour inside a leather pouch next to the person who bakes bread. The bread saj is standing over three stones so that the pit is facing up and a wood fire is burning below. The breadmaker empties some quantity of flour from the leather pouch on the container made from wood or some other material. While pouring some water on it from the flask with one hand, he mixes it with the other hand. While watery in a filo dough consistency, he pours it inside the saj and rolls it continuously with his hand. He creates a pita with uniform thickness, of almost crumpet thickness and pores like it. When the part that is adjacent to the saj solidifies (in other words when it hardens), the breadmaker raises the pita by inserting a thin stick between the saj and the pita and, raising the pita, turns its other face to the saj. In this way, he prepares a large quantity of bread in a short time by both preparing the dough and baking the pita.

Now, I see the muleteers eating their meal. They have put their bread and the mixture consisting mostly of red pepper that they eat with in the middle. All of them are in a squat position. Then, throwing one of the shemma clothes over them to cover themselves completely, they ate their meal under it with great silence and calm. I would not know that they were busy eating had I not seen them before they covered themselves. How can it be known! Quite a few people have snuggled, squatted side by side, the sheet that is covering them completely is moving. Something is being done below. One cannot tell whether it is some kind of trick, so I asked the reason for this: Apparently, Ethiopians hide when they eat, drink because they are afraid of being touched by the evil eye. In fact, when I ask water, coffee, and so on, the servant brings it secretly, hiding it under his cloth as though it was a smuggled good. When I drink it, he prevents others from seeing by spreading his shemma cloth in front of me. I maintained my custom of eating and drinking in the open since I tired from the repetition of this by explaining that I carried my bead set, brought my blue glasses in place of the blue bead, received blessings before to prevent the evil eye and consequently would not choke when I eat and drink. The wilderness is quite beautiful. The scenery of the surroundings refreshes the soul. While it is a pleasure to eat outside the tent since the weather is mild, the cook, servants, guide, eskeris are recommending we eat secretly by covering the door of the tent.

Activity gradually slowed in the base after the meal. Although the fires are still continuing, everybody went to rest except for the guards. I was checking whether the guards were awake as I woke up during the night.

Our Soldiers and Servants

Sunday, May 29   Qersa Base

Piu piu piyu! Piu piu piu! • Heavy rain on the road
• Ethiopian oilskin • Nocturnal visit of wild animals

In the morning, while the tents were being taken down, the chests were being packed and loaded, we came near the kitchen fire and drank our coffee, meat broth. As the cook was gathering the pots and was about to empty the plenty of soup remaining from the evening, one of the servants filled the soup in a large gourd that they were using as a pitcher. His friends surrounded him. While laughing and cavorting on the one hand, they passed the pitcher from one person's mouth to the mouth of another and emptied it. Although the youngest of our servants is nineteen years old, they do not miss any opportunity to laugh, play, and jostle since they are all plain-tongued like children, without a worry, and merry.

After all the mules were completely loaded, our passenger mules were brought in front of us. We set out at quarter to eight o'clock alafranga time as each servant carried the items belonging to him. Just as it is not customary for muleteers and servants to ride here, they also carry an item of their masters' belongings.

Since it is not customary for well-known people like us to carry their weapons themselves, the servants are walking in front of us with one of them holding a sword in his hand, another a double barrel, yet another a flask, another a mess kit, the other a lunch basket. When we see game, he thrusts the weapon in our hand. Upon shooting the game, he runs, brings it. If the game that has been shot escapes, he keeps at it until he catches it. The young ones among the muleteers at least carry the pole of their own tents. They also hang a big water canteen on the pole. In this way, they both get accustomed to the load and lighten the load of the mules. The land we are passing is fertile, productive and anyway, it is full of villages, farms like the other lands of Harar.

Dismounting under a big tree with a nice shade, we ate and rested at quarter to twelve o'clock. It is quite cool and refreshing under the tree. The tree looks a lot like a big walnut tree. Its shell is like a walnut shell, its leaves have the smell of walnut tree leaves. We judged it to be a wild walnut for this reason. Besides birds with beautiful voices like canaries, blackbirds, nightingales singing both on this tree and the small trees around it, the strange sound of a bird that we had never heard of in our lives, that could not be seen because of the denseness of the tree leaves, was also being heard. Sounding exactly like a piano, it is making quite beautiful sounds like "piyu piyu piyu! piyu piyu piyu! piyu piyu piyu!" Naturally, we named it piyu piyu.

After resting until one o'clock alafranga time, we set out on the road again. Let it be known that we were not moving with the pack mules since their movement was relatively slow and we set out with the soldiers and servants and passed the baggage. These came while we were resting and passed. Henceforth, we will continue in this way.

With the sky becoming cloudy, thunder rumbling, rain started during travel. It became steadily more violent. We did not get wet thanks to our tarpaulin, boots. The soldiers and servants got soaking wet. "Will you not become sick?", I asked one of them. He laughed and gave the following response: "We get wet five times a day and dry five times. We are used to it. Rainfall makes us wet, then sun comes out, warms, and dries us".

In truth, the rain here comes suddenly and pours violently. After it continues for half an hour, the clouds disperse. The harsh sun that comes out afterwards dries the surroundings. Nonetheless, some of the mule riders we came across, in other words some of the Ethiopian travelers, had worn black broadcloth, some black and rough felt oilskin, and slipped on the hood on their head. Some of the pedestrians had covered their head, back with tiger[47] hide, protecting themselves from getting wet in this way.

The felt that they wear is not like the oilskin we know and is like a large one-piece cone. It has a slit. The head slips through there when there is no rain. The small section on one side of the slit reverses and stays like a hood. The hood is slipped on the head when it rains. The slit comes towards the face of the person. He can only be seen from here. The broadcloth cloaks or oilskins are neater and are the garments of the nobles. Qenazmach Genemi and some nobles had worn such as these in Harar. We rejoined our caravan after going for an hour under heavy rain. Coming across a quite beautiful pasture with abundant and soft grass, the greedy muleteers have camped here using the excuse of heavy rain. I snapped at them and scolded them for camping early. However, it was too late. Anyway, since it was not customary to give fodder to the animals on the road and these would feed as they went along, it was necessary to graze them.

The place where they camped is quite beautiful, surrounded by hills, elevated in the front, but very damp and humid. Transferring our tents, chests to the slope of a hill that was eight hundred meters distant, we set up our base here. We left the animals at their pasture. The muleteers carried our belongings on their back in order not to disturb the animals. When it was night, wolves, jackals, hyenas wandered around the base, but they could not get near. However, they disturbed us the whole night with their squeals. We gave this place the name of "Qersa Base" since where we camped is near the Qersa Village.

---

47 *The author likely referred to big cats in general since tigers are known to range in Asia

Monday, May 30   Yekka Base

The sunrise procession • Variety of trees and birds • Goats that hoe • Wireless telephone • Wild flowers • Exquisite scenery • The benefits of anti-dysentery powder • Yesterday night's visitors

Waking up early, we drank our coffee, broth. While we were watching and observing the paradise like surroundings and the sunrise from the hill that we were on, numerous young Galla girls were passing, singing with a high voice all at once. The mixture of their voices with their echo was creating a nice harmony. Apparently, they were going from the village to the fields. Rising from behind the hill at this moment, the sun combined its rays with the zephyr and dampness of the morning.

The song that the girls were singing happily in this way, the charm of the surrounding emerald like hills were forming such a beautiful scenery that only a skilled painter, a skilled poet would be capable of describing this. It can be seen that the health of these girls wearing a tunic each, walking bare feet over the meadows is much better than those of prosperous girls with the pampering and abundance of civilization.

With the baggage loaded by one o'clock, we set out on our way. Loading the baggages is hardly an easy task. It takes one and a half, two hours. Like their other fellows, our muleteers do not know the meaning of hurry. Hours, time have no value according to them. They are laughing when we say, "Hurry up, be quick". They do not deviate from their own ways. If the baggage is not loaded in front of our eyes and they are to left to their own pleasure, the odds are that they still would not be moving from their place even at mid-afternoon since they like pastures with abundant grass.

The two sides of our path are like a thriving farm today. After passing through planted fields for a while, we started climbing Qulubi hills and mountains. I started seeing myself in Swiss or Anatolian mountains, forests again. Some of the fir trees are more than twenty-five meters. The thuja trees are reaching ten, fifteen meters. Big wild olive and wild walnut trees almost the size of a sycamore are seen abundantly, with green grass underneath like emerald. There are numerous kinds of trees that we do not know the name of. As varied as the trees are, the types of birds that are flying on these, leaping from one branch to the next, singing are varied to that degree. It is as though this forest has been formed to display trees and birds as a sample by the Almighty. There is no need to open the umbrella as the rays of the sun can only be seen between branches. We are traveling in the shade throughout.

After continuing on the road for about three and a half hours, we spread our rug under the firs and ate our light breakfast in this pleasant garden of the Almighty and took a break and rested a little. Later, we passed through cornfields. There are a good many goats grazing inside these. However, what is strange is that these animals never touch the corn saplings and only eat the wild grass in between. In this way, they both fill their bellies and serve in the fields. They are trained in this way apparently. While eating, we are watching the goats in the fields, the cows, donkeys and sheep in the pastures, the birds on the trees and Galla children swimming in a water deposit at a pit.

Two caravans passed, both from Addis Ababa towards the coast and from Harar towards Addis Ababa. The caravan going to Addis Ababa was loaded with galvanized metal sheets with grooves for covering roofs and iron rods. They have begun to construct buildings in the new style there. They are covering the roofs with these sheets instead of dry grass. Being quite light relative to tiles, it has been preferred compared to others. Meanwhile, the caravan coming from Addis Ababa contains local products such as ivory, the hides of animals, beeswax. Ahead of us, two persons who are on two hills with a distance of nearly an hour between each other were speaking by shouting to the degree that their voices allowed. This custom also exists in Mount Lebanon. There are those who speak from even further distances. Those who have been there would have seen this situation repeatedly.

After eating, resting, and in this way watching and observing the surroundings during an hour and a half, we continued on our way. We started climbing a slope again. The trees began to grow, become denser. The sun became virtually invisible. We passed alongside and left of the highest hill of Qulubi during the journey.

Ras Makonen has a residence at the top of the hill. Ras Makonen has pavilion like residences in nice places between the capital and his own government center of Harar and spends the night at these places when he goes to the capital. There are only a few guards at residences like this. Ras also has farms among those that are suitable.

The places we are passing are at an altitude of about two thousand five hundred meters above sea level. When the trees thin, we can see the Dangali and Asisa deserts, which are adjacent to the slope of the mountain where we are, on our right as far as the eye can see. We appreciate how high the place where we are located is as we see the depressions of the plains. The right and left side of the road is full of wild flowers. A quite nice and sharp scented wild jasmine vine is giving a perfume to the surroundings. It must be that those living here clearly do not know the worth and value of the wealth they possess since they have destroyed many trees here and there with fire. It is not possible not to pity this.

The game that we come across most are the wild chicken herds, with each one the size of a turkey, referred to as pej. We shot a few of these. We camped at a valley named Yekka, with verdant and soft grass that was surrounded by fir covered hills. Besides the grass there are also cultivated farms in this valley. The scenery of the surroundings is quite nice. The steps of fir hills are rising as though piled one on top of another in a form resembling stairs the further away one is from us. Hidden among trees on one of these, some residences of Qulubi Village are visible. The animals are grazing on the meadows, pastures.

The durgu came one hour after our base was set up. This time Abu Bakr reviewed the food that was brought with a lot of attention before coming to my side. He complemented the shum in a courteous manner. Obviously having eaten a lot of raw meat or tallow, one of our muleteers began to roll on the ground with a quite bad stomachache. I gave a quite big cup of medicine from my pharmaceuticals. His pain subsided, he felt relieved, but I was only able to stop the diarrhea he had contracted with anti-dysentery pills. I had taken a box of these pills for the road before leaving Istanbul. Its extraordinarily definite benefit was seen repeatedly in diarrhea and dysenteries. I recommend it. The people here consult whites for their illnesses and all troubles. Whites are doctors, surgeons and capable of everything in their eyes. They do not respect white color, however.

The hyenas behaved quite impudently this evening. They started roaming around the base before nightfall while we were still eating dinner. They approached as close as twenty meters, snarling and growling despite the fires that were lit around the base. The guards confined themselves to drive them away like shooing away a dog and finally, after I came out of my tent and emptied one or two rounds, they cleared off, retreating afar. However, their sounds continued until the morning. They are waiting for us to clear out so that they eat the bones, food leftovers at the base. Above all, if they can catch a mule this evening, it is a big trophy for them.

Tuesday, May 31   Chalanko Base

Monkeys • Children are carried in sacks

A person with a velvet sword scabbard, on muleback and two servants behind him came beside us this morning as the baggage was being loaded. After bowing and saluting a few times, he declared that he was Ato Muhibbi and we would be his guests this evening. Thanking him, we set out at one o'clock alaturca time. We started climbing the Illanekki Mountain. The trees of the forest are so big, so dense, so nice that however much it is described, it cannot be portrayed like the reality. Jumping from one tree branch to another tree branch, the monkeys are chattering and watching us.

Frankly, we have been traveling as though touring inside a big farm since our departure from Harar. There could not be any aspect to complain about were it not for the extraordinary ruggedness, narrowness, excessive ups and downs of the roads. However, houses, domesticated and wild animals, pastures, people working on farms had begun to become sparse here.

The Illanekki forest has terror together with its charm. It is quite dangerous to turn right, left on the road, to enter the forest. One comes across wild animals like tigers. Since the tigers know their hides are desirable, they do not appear much, like the other small animals. They hide on one side of the road, between shrubs and lie in ambush. If a lone, weaponless and reckless traveler passes in the open, it tears him to pieces by jumping on him suddenly. They also go to streams to drink water in the evenings. For this reason, caravans always camp far from water.

We came across quite a few coffee loaded mule caravans going towards Harar while traveling in the forest. After traveling continuously for two hours, we laid our rug at a location facing a plain that had a quite beautiful and broad emerald-like pasture, under the shade of big trees, on emerald like green meadows and ate our meal while both listening to the singing of the birds and watching the scenery in front of us.

Some women passed beside us. Those of them with babies had tied their child to their back with a cloth sack like a soldier's bag. The women never separate their baby from their back when they are working on the fields, shepherding animals on the meadows, doing tasks in their huts. Only the head of the child can be seen. The heat of the sun does not affect even this little head. However, whites cannot stay under the sun even for five minutes without an umbrella. Since the sun here is quite harsh, it will cause a heatstroke, result in cerebral edema. It sends the person to the other world.

If the child cries while the woman is walking, she will drive the sack to her right or left side. She breastfeeds the child from the side that it is on. She shakes herself again and the sack goes to her back. Traveling another hour after the meal, we reached the place named Chalanko. This consisted of a very green plain covered by numerous trees, surrounded by hills, sloping meadows and pastures. Ato Muhibbi offered us treats here. Henceforth, the chill of the night was gaining in harshness day-to-day. I was having wood burnt outside and after it turned to ember, having it filled up in a saj and placing it in my tent on three stones like a brasier to reduce the dampness of my tent and for heating. Although wolves, hyenas again disturbed with their snarls, we were getting used to these, like getting used to the barks of dogs in the street.

Wednesday, June 1   Derru Base

Burka • The damage from the bovine plague • Telegraph, telephone • Our meals

The tents were taken down in the morning like always and the chests were handed over to the muleteers. We set out at half past twelve alaturca. We climbed a hill, then descended. We crossed a plain. The views are the same. As explained before, the sounds of the birds, the nice shades of big trees, meadows, pastures, planted slopes, domesticated animals, coming and going caravans follow each other. The land we passed is named Burka and it was more prosperous, more inhabited, more developed in the past. This district has lost its old prosperity and population due to the cow plague that caused a lot of damage in Ethiopia in the Gregorian year one thousand eight hundred and ninety.

The aforementioned plague had arisen in the Tigray state and with the exception of a few places invaded almost all of Ethiopia. Meanwhile, the people could not find animals to plow their fields because the cattle in Burka perished. They could not plant and harvest. Although the government had been able to give the required cereal to meet the essential needs of the people in the first year, it had not been able to do so the following year. The people had starved. In the meantime, contagious diseases such as small pox, typhoid and then cholera had arisen, decimating the population. It is rumored that the remaining hungry population had fallen so weak and powerless to defend themselves that wild animals such as tigers, wolves would attack their villages and eat the people they killed in front of everyone's eyes.

After continuing on the road for three hours, we ate and rested by spreading a rug in the shade under a group of trees and listened to the sounds of the birds as always. We continued travel again after one hour.

We arrived to Derru. The location of Derru is at the summit of a green hill like the other hills we passed. It is surrounded by numerous hills and crests that are adjacent to one another and piled one on top of another, level by level, some of which are higher, some lower, covered with trees and grass. There is a telephone center here. Just as Harar is linked to Djibouti with telegraph, there also exists a telegraph line from Addis Ababa to Harar and besides the telegraph communication machines, there is also a telephone machine in telegraph offices in Addis Ababa, Harar, Djibouti. Consequently, the people and especially merchants are communicating with each other between the mentioned centers at times the weather is suitable. There are no telegraph machines in the small centers in between which are only equipped with telephone devices. There is an official present at each telephone cabin. It is possible to speak for about ten minutes for a fee of one riyal. When there is telegraph communication between the three mentioned centers, the telephone officials in locations in between naturally give way. Communication is not being conducted that easily because of the remoteness of the distance and due to the persistent stormy weather around Addis Ababa. God willing, I will provide more detailed information later about telegraph by visiting the telegraph office once we arrive to Addis Ababa.

The telephone cabin here is a hut that is like other Ethiopian huts. It is two meters high, three-four meters wide, a round fence wall has been built and a long pole like a tent pole has been erected in the middle of the hut. Rods have been extended from the top of this pole to above the wall so as to pass it by one arşın. All of these have been tied with the vine strings that grow in the forest like rope. The roof rods have been covered with thin grass. The hut that is created is like a tent with long flaps, but additionally it has a metal sheet all around for the protection of the walls. The hut has a door that closes. The surface is covered with dry grass. There are two wooden chairs, with one for the person who is going to communicate and specifically for sitting across the machine, the other for the official. Spare wires have been piled to one side of the hut.

We retired to our tents after eating the evening meal and chatting a while. I will describe our dinners for a few days below based on the thought that esteemed readers who are epicures may wonder what kinds of things we are eating on the road. Our light breakfasts were being set aside in mess sets in the evening from the dinner. Our dinner today is lentil soup, grilled sheep cutlets with potato, fried chicken, the fried bulgur meatball that is referred to as 'kibbe' in Damascus, stewed plum. Olives, cheese are not included in these accounts.

Thursday, June 2   Tullo Base

The preservation of liquids on the road • Containers for provisions •Villages of this locality • Heavy rain • The movement of the ras from one place to another • Instant huts • Some lady hu • Neighboring lady hu

The chill of the night reminded us that we were at an altitude of more than two thousand meters from sea level. Such a mist had covered the surroundings when we woke up in the morning that it is not possible to make out twenty meters ahead of us. After the muleteers warmed their bodies by sprawling, tossing, turning, they started to load the baggages. With the surroundings a little more visible by the time the baggage was loaded, we set out. After descending from the mountain where Derru is located, we traveled for about two hours on the Burka Plain that was mentioned a day ago. All sides of the plain are covered with meadows, grasses, while the mountain, hills around it are covered with trees.

We came to the spring water named Burka Machalla at half past four o'clock. This is quite a nice location and a clear spring is gushing between the big trees on the skirts of the mountain and its shade. It is forming a natural pool. However, unfortunately a lot of cattle, cows had piled up when we arrived and since a lot of village women were washing all their things, we could not even stop there. The water had become murky, dirty and the place where the cattle were had taken the form of a swamp. We dismounted under the trees a few hundred meters' distance from there. The plain ahead of us is not entirely devoid of trees, some tree clusters can be seen here and there. The clusters have sometimes taken the form of a small forest. Huge eagles numbering twenty, thirty are resting on the tree under which we are. We ate and rested here. Haji Yusuf cooked for us a fresh omelet besides the meal from the evening. He is not going on foot like other servants, but follows on muleback behind us. He immediately lights up a fire to heat food, brew coffee when we dismount for lunch. He sees to his preparations. He sometimes also cooks things like omelets and grilled game cutlets that are prepared quickly. Our dessert is stewed fruit pulp[48] now. Besides the canned preserves we got in boxes from Port Said, we had also taken quite a lot of the dried apricots and apricot pulp of Damascus from Istanbul. We have jars with wide spouts and stoppers that shut firmly for the stewed fruit. Water, sugar, apricot or apricot pulp is placed in the jar from evening. It is wrapped in paper and placed in the food basket. Getting soaked and shaken over and over again, it becomes excellent compote by noontime. All that remains is to empty it in a clean mess bowl and eat it. Things like butter, strained yogurt, oily olives to be found in the basket have been procured from before and placed in vaseline jars that close quite tightly. Let alone pouring out, it would not even leak, even if the chests turn upside down.

Since there is not an inch where there is no grass on the land that we have passed until now, the saddles, bridles of our passenger mules are being removed when we dismount from the mules for lunch. These then graze abundantly. After a meal and rest within an hour, the mules were prepared and we continued on our way.

We arrived to another stream named Burka at six o'clock. It flows with a rustle since the location of this stream is quite steep. It is sufficient to turn a few millstones. After following the course of the stream for half an hour, we crossed to the other side and gave water to our mules. We started climbing the Tullo Hill that is the name of our base today. We arrived to Tullo, located at an altitude of two thousand two hundred meters, at half past seven o'clock. We occupied ourselves with observing the surroundings after our tents were pitched and we settled down.

Everywhere is a grassy meadow. The cattle of the surrounding villages are grazing on the meadows. The villages here do not consist of dwellings that are adjacent to one another and the huts are far apart from each other, scattered between the trees. Tullo huts, like the Quni huts, cannot be detected from afar since they are covered by trees and are not seen if one has not arrived beside them.

There was the gloominess of impending rain today. A heavy rain mixed with hail started at nine o'clock. Our tents, bought in Istanbul, have heavy linings.

---

48 *Pestil Hoşafı in Turkish

When bought, they gave them saying it is impermeable to water. However, it cannot hold back the rain here. Flowing in from the sides of the tent, this heavy rain turned the inside to a lake. We are watching this much of the beauty of nature. One must tolerate its whims a little, too. It can be seen that gazelles are roaming on the mountain ahead of us, but that they are timid. Ras Makonen had passed from here a week ago. Surrounding the mountain, those in his retinue drove the gazelle herds to the plain. They had hunted one hundred and fifty of them and the remaining ones had become timid because of this.

When a ras goes from one place to another in Ethiopia, a retinue in the thousands, a crowd results as the people of the places he passes join him with their family. The base of the ras becomes very crowded as those bringing durgu from villages and towns also come every evening with their cattle, sheep, and various provisions. Other than the principal men of the ras, these people do not have tents. Each family or just an individual builds himself a hut within a few minutes every day and shelters in it.

Construction of a hut consists of sharpening the lower parts of a few tree branches like a stake and erecting them on the ground around a small circle, then, joining the branches, upper tips to one another and affixing them together and covering the sides with dry grass. Construction is easy since there are forests everywhere. When the caravan departs the next day, they do not demolish their huts. Consequently, the road is full of bases, empty huts where the ras camped. The wood logs that are part burnt, part remaining are innumerable.

One of our muleteers is calling a person who is quite remote as much as his voice allows with bughaki, bughaki, bughaki hu. A hu definitely comes after every three bughaki. They always call each other here from afar in this way. After pouring for one and a half hours, the rain finally stopped and our kitchen could be set up. Our evening meal: Rice soup, chicken with peas, fried turtledove, potato with chicken liver, stewed fruit pulp. There was also sugar cane included in the durgu this evening. The tents were so damp, the inside, outside, the surface so wet that I reduced its chill and dampness by taking fire ember inside. Fire and guards were increased since there are a lot of wild animals here. The guards were checked upon waking up during the night.

Friday, June 3   Debbesu

Abu Shaear monkeys

In the morning, the tents were taken down and chests distributed to the muleteers and the baggages began to be loaded between the endless noises of the muleteers among each other. We set out on the road. Although villages, planted farms had begun to become sparser after Derru, the ruggedness of the land, its hills, streams, forests are continuing like before. At three o'clock as we were passing from a quite thick forest with tall trees, we came across numerous monkeys with strange figures on trees. Their hair is long like goat hair and multi-colored and they are the size of a dog. Ethiopians call them Abu Shaear[49] in Arabic since their hair is long. Their Ethiopian name is "Wani". Sergeant Yasin shot one of them with the Martini. It could not be acquired since it was not possible to go to where it had fallen due to the thickets. Breaking into a clamor when the shot was fired, the monkeys were uttering sounds, some threatening, some as though begging while they were getting further away from us by leaping from one tree to another. We came across caravans carrying ivory, coffee, beeswax, hides in the forest.

---

49 *Hair in Arabic

After covering four hours' way and climbing over many hills, streams, forests, we came to a plain named Hirna surrounded by hills with a variety of trees. A stream named Ayn with the power to turn a millstone as well as Hirna Lake at the edge of the hill are visible here. We had our lunch under a tree. The location of Hirna is at an altitude of one thousand eight hundred and thirty meters above sea level. We continued on the road after one hour's rest. After climbing a few hills, we arrived at Debbesu at eight o'clock, located at a quite high altitude.

The view of the place where we are is broad and nice. On our east side, the Kufa Mountain covered with green forests can be seen, while the Qoro pit plain full of hills, streams is on our west side and way below us. Mount Asabot, standing highest at the end of the horizon, is visible with great grandeur at a distance of a day and a half in that direction.

This evening's dinner consisted of rice soup, roastbeef with peas, turtledove burger, rice, and a quite nice dessert pastry called Süngeriye[50] made from egg, sugar, flour. A quite ferocious windstorm occurred at night and broke our tents like a sail. It demolished my tent. It disturbed the whole night. Fortunately, the rain that came with this storm was light, unlike the wind.

---

50 *Likely a reference to 'Sünger tatlısı' or 'Sponge desert' which is also known as Revani

Saturday, June 4   Quni Base

Lightning light like a whip • Rain, mud, damp and cold • We are located at an altitude of three thousand meters above the sea level

We set out on the road at twelve o'clock in the morning.[51] After descending from the hill where we were and climbing up another big hill, we rested and ate under a tree named jemiz or the fig of the pharaoh[52] at quarter to three o'clock.

The reason for the baggages to be tied fast as one piece with the mules becomes apparent; the descents, ascents are steep to a degree that it is difficult to go on foot. The wretched animals are languishing after traveling four, five hours a day. Sometimes they go up and down rocks more difficult than stairs.

After resting one and a half hours under a tree, we set out on the road. Descending, ascending hills again, we finally arrived to Quni Village, located at the summit of a high mountain. Although this place is at an altitude of about three thousand meters above sea level, we are protected from the effect of the wind to a degree because trees surround the place

---

51 * This is a reference to alaturca time and so if sunset the previous day was 7pm alafranga time, then 12 o'clock alaturca time would correspond to 7am alafranga time

52 *Sycamore fig

where we are camped. With the rain that started before we reached here continuing for about three hours, a fire could not be lit. Lightning is also striking abundantly. Struck by a quite mild lightning, like a fast whip, on my head, I was jolted with a violent shudder and I closed the umbrella. Our base livened up, fire was lit after the rain stopped. Everyone turned to his task. Our tents are soaking wet. The grass on which we are located took the form of a swamp. Albanian Şevket Efendi is laboring most. Walking around a bit without heeding the rain and mud, he shot a few birds.

There was golden oriole, quail, wild chicken meat at dinner. Our tents were so cold and damp that night that I filled a bottle with boiling water and put it in the bed in order to heat my bed. We are at an altitude close to three thousand meters above sea level tonight.

Sunday, June 5   Bedesa Base

The variance in sunrise • Birds are musicians • Monkeys are acrobats • The loyalty of slaves • Mules are cleansed by nature • Cauterization • Massage for animals • My physicianship • Variety of fans • The attack of predatory birds on wounded mules • The lightness of Ethiopians

Giving our belongings to the muleteers in the morning, we set out at twelve o'clock. As can be seen, we do not set out before twelve. Twelve o'clock appears like a late time to get on the road in June because the sun is rising at eight fifty-four in Istanbul today. However, it rises at half past eleven o'clock here. Night and day are almost equal to one another since we are really south. Following our departure, we started descending from Quni Mountain. We have been traveling for about two hours in a wild, high altitude forest consisting of a variety of trees. The thickness, size, height of the trees is preventing the penetration of the sun.

With no telegraph poles here, the insulators, in other words the porcelain cups to which the wire is tied, have been nailed to trees. We are hearing quite a nice harmony since a variety of birds are singing. The hairy, multi-colored monkeys mentioned before are plenty here, leaping from one tree to another. It is as though the birds are the musical band and the monkeys are playing gymnastics. The birds that are seen most here are parrot-like birds the size of a pigeon, with beaks and the sides of their eye red, while half their wing is pitch black, half is deep red like garnet. These are flying and leaping in flocks from one tree to the next. Şevket Efendi shot one of these. I warned him not to shoot again since its meat could not be eaten. He saved the wings. It really would make a nice decoration for women's hats.

At two o'clock, trees started to thin as we approached the skirt of the mountain. We arrived to a valley that had one side on this part of the mountain at three o'clock. There is a stream here named Burama that has sufficient power to turn two millstones and it is referred to with the name of this place. We came across a poor woman going from one village to another during the journey. The mule that she is riding was scared from something, not moving ahead no matter what. The woman keeps on saying something. It turns out that the woman was begging the mule!, saying "On the head of your father, on the head of your mother, do not torment me, move" She was assisted. Her mule was made to move.

We later came across a slave, who had run away from his master, tied to a chain. He had been captured. He is being taken to his master. Although slavery had been officially banned, it is mostly the export of slaves that is forbidden. Otherwise, a man, even with average means, who does not have a slave is rare in the country. It is all slaves who constitute the livelihood for farmers, merchants, muleteers. If slave labor is completely ended, there will be a lot of difficulty. They do not know employment of laborers for a wage.

Spreading our rug under a large, waterside sycamore fig tree, we ate and rested during almost an hour and grazed our mules. We set out on the road again. At five minutes' distance from the stream, we passed another stream of its size and same name. Crossing a third stream, we entered a plain surrounded by mountains and hills all around at five o'clock.

The border of Harar province ends from here on and Chercher territory starts. It can be seen from the abundance of the grass that the land is quite fertile and productive. While trees are not very thick here, occasionally quite a few wild, big and small trees can be seen here and there. The slopes of hills are full of villages, mostly Muslim and referred to as Agalla. There are also Amhara villages that are Christian.

At one time, there were more people residing in this vicinity, but their number has declined due to the aforementioned plague, local battles.

Crossing another stream, we camped ahead of Helfeta Mountain at six o'clock. The name of the location where we are is Bedesa. Since our way had quite a few descents and ascents, the people and animals became quite tired. As everyone who is not responsible for pitching a tent sprawls at full length under a tree as soon as we camp, the mules begin to rest as they always do by rolling and stretching as soon as their baggage is removed and those which are wounded raise their ears and, looking at the fire that was being lit, breathe as though saying ah! As I mentioned before, they do not give forage to their mules here. The mules are not shod. They do not know what grooming is. The animal feeds with grass. Its nails have been calloused, removed and anyway heavy rains wash the animal cleanly like a heavy shower or a water pump since it is without a pad, without a cover in the open and completely naked when it is not loaded. The harsh sun that rises afterwards dries it immediately. In this way, the animal is washed by the hand of God. However, there is a 'mountain' surgery for the wounded ones in the evening. A large fire is lit. Long, curved irons with wooden handles are put inside. Wounded mules are separated from the others. Belts are placed on front and back legs and pulled. The animal falls to the ground. Muleteers sit on its head, here and there and restrain it. One of them presses the iron that is glowing red from the fire to the wound. The hair and skin around it burn. The iron pretty much touches the flesh. The wretched animal brays loudly. Their friends that are waiting in line look fearfully, hopelessly. Foul smells emanate from the spot that was cauterized. Baggage is not loaded on animals that have been cauterized. They are left loose for a few days. Later, baggage is loaded again. So, you see the entire service that muleteers render to their mules consists of cauterization.

This operation always grieved me during the journey. For this reason, I advised them to have it done afar, opposite to the wind because it was creating foul smells. To make a long story short, the wretched animals are not well taken care of here. They are living on their own at the grace of God.

On the other side, in other words in Hejaz, animals are well taken care of. After giving forage to their mules, the wagoners in Medina also give them "takbis", alongside grooming in the evening. In other words, they massage them. Massage is quite accepted in Hejaz. They have massage done in hamams, houses even though there is no illness, most just for the comfort of the form, the rest of the body. A lot of people lie down on long wicker mat lounges even at coffee houses, coffee squares. They have massage done by masseurs. Most of the masseurs are Indian and for a fee of twenty para give a massage for about half an hour. So, you see, this principal is also prevailing with regards to animals. Camels, mules, donkeys are massaged. I was astounded when I first saw this operation.

I was going from the telegraph office in Manaha[53] Square to my house in Medina at night. A big donkey sprawled on the ground at full length, its owner sat on it, rubbing its body, shoulder. That the animal was being comforted could be understood from its groaning, stretching and from its extending of its other leg after the rubbing of one leg. I said to its owner, "Hey! What are you doing?" He said, "The poor animal became very tired today. I am doing takbis so that it relaxes". I continued on my way. Let us return to our subject:

The muleteers are treating their mules. When one of them becomes sick, they come beside me. They seek help from my, in their eyes, incontestable medical skills. I was giving medicine to the degree that these skills guided, in other words purgative, mint essence to those with excessive stomach pain, anti-dysentery sand to those with diarrhea, qasetin, antipyrine to those with headache.

Today, someone came limping. He extended his leg. He looked at my face pleadingly. The wretch's feet had swollen quite a bit from his toes until halfway on his sole. The wound between his toes had become so rotten that it is almost going to be infested with maggots. I am not a surgeon, there is no ointment, what do I do? Boric acid came to my mind. I told the guy, "I will heat some water in a clean container and give some powder. You will throw this inside. You will tie it with a clean linen. If you continue like this day and night, you will be better". The guy insisted through a translator saying, "in any case, put a medicine now". I remembered the cauterization operation in front of me. I immediately took out a cologne syringe from a pocket. I kept on applying the cologne between the guy's toes. It must have hurt so much that the guy's eyes popped out. He clenched his fists. He started rolling on the grass, straining himself. His pain subsided a little

---

53 *Near Masjid Al Ghamama

after half an hour. I took out some fabric. I took out some boric acid. I had him start rinsing. It started to heal in this way. I rubbed sai oil instead of ointment to soothe his foot. Let surgeons figure out whether I did well or not.

I am the surgeon for those here. They started looking at me with meaningful, suspicious eyes when they saw how much effect cologne had, in other words saw their friend rolling on the ground, wondering whether I gave the medicine with pure intent or whether it was something bad. I understood what they were thinking. Immediately turning the syringe to my face, I squirted it abundantly. I squirted it all over my face and rubbed it on my hands. Their doubts vanished. They became convinced that my medicine was not harmful, that the severe pain of their friend was from his wound.

Just as the surroundings of our base is rich with game birds, gazelle and rabbits, it is also full of ants, mosquitos, small insects, and various butterflies. If a person had the time to take from the variety of butterflies in this vicinity and stick these to papers, notebooks, a quite rich collection superior to a stamp collection would be gathered.

While our cook can prepare our meal with his apprentice, everybody wants to help the kitchen with a service. Some of us hunt birds. As for Şevket Efendi, he is preparing one of the desserts of his country almost every day since he likes food. Especially on account of three of us being from Syria, bulgur meatball, which is one of the Syrian dishes, was not absent even a single day. The cook learned this from the first day. Our meatball is not made from mutton every day, but mostly from game meat due to the abundance of chicks and chicken. Thank God, there is no complaint from food. Just as our mules are grazing on the green, fresh grass as much as they want, we are having our meals with a lot of game meat.

The soldiers and servants became used to eating in the open and overtly like us since most of them are Muslim and not quite bigoted. Meanwhile, the Christian muleteers, not giving up from eating privately, are continuing to eat under a big sheet. The muleteers' meals are mostly teff bread, plenty of coffee, red pepper, raw meat.

I could not yet discover where the evil eye might affect these foods. Wounded mules here are suffering the torment that some wounded camels in Arabia suffer. In Arabia, eagles, hawks, crows land on the wretched camels' backs and tear flesh from the back of the camel piece by piece. The camel would escape from this torment with much toil by snorting, rolling to the ground. This situation is now happening in the same way to our wounded mules.

As though the torment of the belt and cauterization that I described were not enough, the torment of the predatory birds is added to this. The bird grabs the flesh that it wants to tear and flies before the wretched mule turns its head and lashes a whip with its tail. One of the mules that was going to be cauterized escaped now. It is galloping all out in the plain without a saddle, bridle like a gazelle. Three muleteers are chasing the mule like a greyhound, in a manner with two of them holding a long strap from both ends and one with empty hands. They are running while keeping the distance between those stretching the strap. They are trying to get in front of the mule, while the lone man is trying to drive the mule towards the strap. This business went on for half an hour. The animal's power, strength were exhausted. It was caught with the strap that came to its chest. Meanwhile, the men showed no weariness. God knows the guys have been running for half an hour at the speed of the mule at full gallop during this maneuver. They maybe covered a distance of ten kilometers. There is no trace of fatigue. So, you see these people are like the desert Bedouin that I describe in the Journey in the Grand Sahara.

Atemi, one of our eskeris, got a really bad stomachache. His pain did not completely ease even though one of his friends rubbed his bare stomach to the utmost of his strength, so I soothed him with mint essence. It seems the massage (takbis) method is known by the people here, too.

Our dinner this evening consisted of soup with egg yolk and lemon sauce, grilled turtle dove, lamb liver, fried vegetables, meatball with bulgur, and lokma[54].

---

54 *A sweet with fried dough balls in syrup

Monday, June 6   Gelemso Base

Chercher Lake • Grass as tall as canes • Hanging bird nests • The tent collapsed

We set out at half past twelve in the morning. The land that we are crossing is rather flat compared to previous mountains, hills because it consists of terrain with a gentle slope and undulation. Although the capacity for farming is of the utmost level and birds and animals are abundant in the Chercher region, the population is very low relative to the size of the region.

At two o'clock, we started seeing Lake Chercher on our left side and from a distance of two kilometers. Since our path is going parallel to the lake, it is always visible on flat terrain, but concealed to the eye when there are obstacles between us, such as a hill or crest. In this way, the lake is appearing one moment, disappearing the next. This lake is about three times the size of the aforementioned Haramaya Lake and wild geese, ducks and various birds are found here in abundance. There are even hippopotamuses in it. These graze in the land around the lake at night. They go into the lake at daytime. After traveling for about two hours in parallel, the lake disappeared from the eye. This lake is at an altitude of one thousand seven hundred and fifty meters above sea level.

Coming alongside Chagha Inyani Village at five o'clock, we could only find place enough to spread the rug and sit under the shade of the trees in the lower part of the village. Fortunately, a caravan passing before us has plucked the grass of this much place and rested. The grass around us comes up to a person's shoulder. It gives the impression of being reeds from afar. Anyway, we have not yet found a dry place without grass to pitch our tent. The places without grass consist of fields that are ploughed and planted and the trail that we follow as a road.

After eating, resting here within an hour and also having our mules fill their bellies where they stood without the need to take a step, we continued on our way. Arriving at the Chagha Inyani Stream, we crossed to the other side with our animals. This stream is sweet, too, like the other streams that we came across and is strong enough to turn a millstone. While the land that we have been passing through since the morning is emerald green like others before, its trees are not dense and are sparse in the proportion of the trees in orchards on the Anatolian shore of Istanbul.

We thought these trees were orange or citron trees when we saw them from far because their branches are adorned with round spheres like orange. Upon approach beside them, we saw that these spheres were nests of small birds like canaries. Hundreds of nests like this are hanging from branches of trees. Each nest is moving like a swing with the effect of the wind because the grass cord with which they are tied is close to a hand span in length. The chicks are lying inside as though lying on a swing.

These nests have been woven with skill, from quite fine, strong grass and hung with a cord from the top of the thin branches, shoots on the outermost edges of the tree and are impervious to rain. Birds are coming and going from the side and near the bottom from a door made with quite some skill. The treetops are also full of other birds besides the nests. Leaping from one branch to another, they are all singing. One hour after our departure since lunch break, we passed a stream named Malqa Bellu and as big as the previous stream.

We came alongside Gelemso Village at half past seven o'clock. There is also a stream flowing here like previous streams. We camped with the intent to stay here this evening. The location of our base is on a small hill surrounded by green trees and few and sparse hills on all four sides. We had dry grass spread over the green grass since we could not find a dry surface on the hill and we covered its top with our rugs. We are cold since we are at an altitude of one thousand seven hundred and fifty meters altitude above the sea level. We passed some time shooting game a little. There was plenty of bird meat at our dinner. A violent rainstorm also broke out this evening, making us wet in the tent and demolishing my tent this time, too. Fortunately, I am under canvas, not brick.

Tuesday, June 7   Laga Hardim

The residence of Ras Makonen • The beverages named talla, tej, birz • Harsh punishment for a small offence • The inside of a local hut • Plant narghile

Although the muleteers wanted to stay here today, with the excuse of drying our tents that had been soaked wet, since the grass of the Gelemso base was quite soft and our mules really enjoyed it, we made do with drying the tents a little until one o'clock and set out with the intent to camp somewhere near. We left the muleteers, who were going to come from behind after one or two hours, there since our camp location was known.

We arrived to Laga Hardim at half past four o'clock by climbing a few hills, descending quite steep and difficult to walk slopes, slipping in the mud resulting from the rain and passing a few streams that had overflowed due to flood. Laga Hardim is a town consisting of some aggregation of huts located on top of a high hill. A small stream flows at the skirt of the hill. A big majority of the population here are Muslim like the people of the lands we passed, while Christians are few.

Daunted by the rain yesterday, we decided to spend the night at a place near huts for the first time, with the intent to take refuge from tents in the huts if we are caught under rain this time. There is a residence of Ras Makonen here of the style of the huts of locals, but big and oval shaped.

After the locals spread a few cattle hides in front of this residence under a tree, we spread our rugs on top of the hides and ate and rested. There were such thorns under the tree that if the hides were not there, it would not be possible to sit. I toured the residence of the ras after the meal. It is sixteen meters long, eight meters wide. Its roof is affixed on top of a few poles. It has a partition inside and the area behind this partition is being used as pantry. A canvas is stretched on its inner wall. It has an arşın wide local divan along the wall to sit on. Newspapers with pictures are hanging as decoration on the wall. The ras does not reside here, but stays if he happens to pass by, go hunting. Having almost turned it into a hotel for travelers here, the guard is even selling gourd pitchers, talla and tej in glass bottles. The vendor is a beautiful Christian Ethiopian girl. She possesses the speech to attract travelers.

The beverage called talla is a kind of local beer. It is made from barley or corn. As for the beverage called tej, it is a watery honey sherbet fermented with a kind of shrub called gesho. It becomes like a sharp wine and champagne as time passes. If it is drunk fresh, it has the taste of grape juice and does not inebriate a person. Muslims drink it without putting gesho in the honey sherbet, without fermenting. They refer to the sherbet without gesho as birz.

The location of our base today is nicer than the previous ones, overlooking a broad plain ahead. Our back, sides are surrounded by green, high hills.

The terrain that we passed until coming here is covered with trees, sometimes sparsely, sometimes densely. There are more than abundant kulkuval, or rubber trees. The streams that we passed do not allow passage in the heavy season of rains after one and a half, two months from now. Caravans wait on the sides of streams for days. They cross at a time when waters recede. One has to think of a different route to return from now on. The point where we are located is at an altitude of one thousand six hundred meters above sea level. While both this location where we are and its vicinity and the broad land starting from the Hirna Stream that we passed a few days ago until the shore of Awash River which we will arrive in a few days was under the rule of Fitaurari[55] Asfa until recently, Ras Makonen took this region from his hands and put him to shackles because this person beat a slave of the ras unjustly.

The shum (administrator) here, Ato Afti, and his clerk, Ato Sarti,

---

55 *Commander of the Vanguard. Fitaurari literally refers to the 'horn of the rhinoceros'

came to our side and we chatted quite a bit. Ato Afti had been in the retinue of Ras Makonen during the famous Battle of Adowa against the Italians and he gave me information about the battle. It will be included in the appropriate place.

Two Ethiopian youths are beating gesho with wooden pestles in a high mortar made from a tree log beside a hut near the hut of the ras. Saying "ainj! ainj! ainj!", the guys are raising and lowering the pestles at full speed. Around them women, girls, the whole family are all singing, matching a melody to the lifting and lowering of the pestles. In this way, the zeal of the men is increasing. I mentioned that the gesho shrub is the starter for the honey wine called tej. After we observed them oddly, and they us, I toured their huts.

A girl is grinding flour. The flat stone surface on which the flour is ground is affixed over a bed with a slope, at the height of a table. The girl is standing behind the high part of the stone. Placing the teff grains on the stone, she is crushing them with the stone press in her two hands. The teff that is crushed and becomes like flour flows to the hole below the lower part of the stone and accumulates there. It does not look like our handmills at all. Food is cooking on an earthen pot over a fire in the middle of the hut. The smoke of the fire is coming out from small slits close to the roof of the hut. An old woman is smoking narghile somewhere in the middle. The narghile consists of a gourd, a straw inserted into this, and an earthen top placed on the pointed end of the gourd. The long straw is put in like a pipe instead of the narghile pipe. The local bed frame named elga that is intended for the sleep and rest of the owner of the house is found on one side of the hut. The feet, the sides of this bed are from wood, the middle is from leather belts. Women are sorting grains like barley, wheat, teff on one side. Big slabs woven from cattle hide and grass are seen instead of trays. Oil, honey, and so on are stored in various gourds instead of jars, bottles in the pantry of the house. What a simple livelihood, what modest living. The wealth and capital of these people is the wealth and capital of nature.

Our caravan came. The tents were pitched. The meal was cooked. We ate. We settled the water that had become murky because of floods in containers. We were able to drink it like that. We are at an altitude of one thousand six hundred meters above the sea level.

Wednesday, June 8   Katyinwaha Base

Steep descents, ascents • The nature of the terrain is changing
• Abundant game • Gourd instead of a statue

The muleteers wanted the baggage quite early, saying our path is hard, our ascent is steep today. The tents were taken down at eleven o'clock, the baggage was handed over to them. The previously mentioned Shum Ato Afti, Ato Sarti, the police officer and others came while we were drinking our coffee and bid us farewell. We set out on the road at twelve o'clock.

The Altuki Mountain, the slopes of which we are on, is quite rugged and steep. Fortunately, the mules can climb since the road that we are following is snake-like. The wretched animals are exhausted from straining. After climbing an almost forty-five degree slope for exactly half an hour, we started crossing crests with gentle ascents, descents.

Upon arriving to the highest point of the summit at one o'clock, we discovered the quite wide Awash Basin and the Awash River inside it like a thin silver wire and the Kumi Mountain ahead of us in the direction we are heading. The trees of the mountain where we are located are relatively smaller than the previous ones we saw, all are wild and thinly spread out from each other. There are such beautiful umbrella trees among the trees that the branches had extended horizontally in a way to cover a circle with a ten, fifteen meter diameter even though the trees were three, four meters high. The view changed completely from this minute onwards compared to before. The Kumi Mountain is looking like a completely bare, large, monolithic rock devoid of plants.

Although the Awash plain appears like a flavescent and arid land, those next to me said that this yellowness was not the color of the surface, but the color of the dry grass. We descended the side of the Altuki Mountain towards Awash from half past one o'clock until three. This descent is rugged and steep, like the ascent. Pitying the mule, I wanted to travel on foot. Since my foot slipped and I tumbled twice within a quarter of an hour, I mounted again convinced that the mule was quite skilled here. Truly, the mule is going quite well since it is used to these roads. Coming to the bottom of the slope at three o'clock, we entered Argaga terrain. The trees here are relatively smaller, thinly spread out from each other, and have less shade than those before. The color of the surface changed from here onwards. Short, dry grass replaced green, long grass.

After searching, we found a tree with difficulty that could provide shelter under its shade for food and rest. Since the shade was not enough, Sergeant Abu Bakr, who was quite industrious, cut some branches from the trees and piled them on the branches above us. The muleteers desired to stay here this evening since the mules had become tired, but I did not permit them. I warned them to join us after resting for two hours since we had previously decided to stay at Katyinwaha. We watered the mules from the rain deposits that were there, some of us filled his flask. Our lunch break was quite hot since we were at a low point.

After resting from four o'clock until seven, we continued on our way again. Chickens the size of turkeys referred to as pej, gazelles, rabbits are roaming in abundance here. We shot seven, eight pej. A few of them hid between the shrubs. We captured the remainder. These were more than sufficient for our kitchen.

On the way, we saw a dried gourd, used instead of a pitcher, on top of a tree and a piece of cloth. These were the belongings of a quite brave and heroic Galla. He has hung these here upon the custom of the region to perpetuate his name. Passers-by are mentioning his name with benevolence and tribute. Those who do not know it, learn it in this way.

We reached "Katyinwaha" which means "little stream" at quarter to ten o'clock. Just as the plain we passed was hot, its trees were sparse, with small leaves, dry and without shade. The size of the trees on the two sides of this small stream, the thickness of the foliage, its extension alongside the stream as far as the eye can see, its canopy over the stream like a tunnel, the beauty of the grass under the trees, its coolness are so vitalizing that the traveler who covers this path counts himself as having reached heaven. We plucked fresh tamarind from the tamarind trees above our head. We drank with bowls. What a nice drink, what a cooling sherbet! A blessing more than this cannot be desired here.

The Katyinwaha Stream comes out of the Kumi Mountain Foothills. It flows cool inside a tree tunnel, in the shade, running without seeing the sun. However, it is also famous for its danger and hazard in the same proportion as its coolness and niceness. Wild animals such as tigers, wolves, hyenas in the plains rest in these shades during severe heats. Those that do not come during daytime definitely come at night to drink water. Consequently, we pitched our tents four, five hundred meters away from the stream and on a high crest according to the custom here.

After resting next to the stream for a while and washing our faces, we retired to our base. We filled up water before dark. A few rather large, abandoned huts are visible at a kilometer's distance before coming to the stream, on the crest of a somewhat high hill. When Emperor Menelik bought the Garra rifles from the French, they were stored here, then slowly brought and distributed around. We found quite a lot of dry grass, dry wood ready at our base since Ras Makonen had passed from here before us. Henceforth, we decided to depart very early since the path we were going to cover over the next few days was going to be hot.

Not having the big tent erected, I stayed in a small tent. The muleteers, eskeris slept in the open since the weather was hot. Our fires and guards are more in number tonight. A heavy windstorm that erupted at night drowned our eyes, faces in sand. The songs of some guards in Amharic, others in Galla are mixing with the ferocity of this wind. We passed the night in a strange harmony.

Thursday, June 9   Fantalle

Awash River • Economizing on the bridge • Karayus
• Volcanic terrain

Starting to load the baggage before sunrise to be able to depart while still cool, we set out on the road together with sunrise, in other words at half past eleven. After first passing the Katyinwaha Stream, then a few inclined, dry streams located in a rugged terrain and listening to the howling of the wolves, jackals, hyenas coming from our right and left, we reached the Awash River at quarter past one o'clock. This river flows in a very deep and big and quite steep valley relative to its own size. People, animals suffer quite a bit to be able to descend next to the water. It is crossed by climbing, slipping over huge rocks worse than stairs.

There is a bridge present over the river and at its narrowest spot, twenty-five, thirty meters in length, two meters wide, with stone piers and beams from a mix of iron and wood. When the waters of the river are low, travelers do not cross the bridge and instead go over the river. Brushwood is piled in front of the bridge at that time. Besides this, there is a guard's hut on the side that we came, overlooking the bridge so that when waters recede a guard sits here and oversees the bridge so that nobody crosses it. They said that this method was for thrift and out of respect to the administration. We sat next to the river for a while. We watched the burbling of the water between the rocks, its rapid flow. Those who wanted washed on one side. However, nobody really went too much inside the river because crocodiles are found here when the water is abundant.

This river is one of the principal rivers in Ethiopia and flows from the southwest to the northeast for about seven hundred kilometers and disappears in the lakes and swamps in the Osa terrain located to the west of the Gulf of Tadjoura, without reaching the sea. Since Awash is the lowest valley located in this vicinity, just as many rivers flow into it from its right and left, the rainwater from surrounding mountains and hills also gather in it. Although the Awash River is one of the natural ways to follow for the interior of Ethiopia from the Red Sea coast, it has not been followed.

We went over the bridge since it was not the season to cross the stream with animals. Climbing the quite rugged, steep, hard to pass opposite side of the valley, we emerged on to the plain. We decided to take a break here until mid-afternoon because daytime is excessively hot here and so not traveling a lot, we spread dry grass under the shade of a tree and then our rugs. After lowering their loads near us, the muleteers herded their animals naked to the stream to water them. We filled up the necessary water since there was not a stream at our base this evening. It really became very hot during the day. Some spermaceti candles inside the chest became like dough.

The land on this side of Awash is referred to as Gurusu. Henceforth, big trees are rare here. Meanwhile, the trees, which are sparse, consist of big shrubs. The grass on the ground is not green, but bone dry, sparse and yellow. In the nights we stayed on the mountains, we would find our tents, items left in the open soaking wet from the dew when we woke up in the morning even at times without rain whereas our surroundings were very dry this morning when we woke up. There was not even a trace of dew. The locals say that it rarely rains here since it is low-lying and has few trees.

A nomad community named Karayu camps on this land and then migrates. They do not know farming and agriculture. They also do not have interest in any religion. Their color is black. Their dress consists of a cloth on their waist. There is also a second cloth on the shoulders of some. They do not know to eat bread. They are nourished with the milk of animals like camels, cows, and sheep. They do not have tents. They only build huts that are a meter high from brushwood, grass, crawl inside and shelter. They come out from the inside by crawling.

It was not possible to shelter in the tent today due to the severity of the heat. Since the trees under which we were did not give that much shade, branches were cut from other trees and piled on the top, sides of these, increasing their shade. The Albanian Şevket Efendi who was very hardworking began to build a quite orderly shade as though we were going to reside here for days, months. He cut big branches from the trees at a distance. He lined them up on the side of a tree he picked. He covered the top of the tree with the other branches. Although it is quite hot, he is working under the sun tirelessly. He could not finish his shade even though it was nine o'clock. He was forced to look at his hut with longing and forced to leave it when we set out.

We saw the course of the Awash one more time after setting out on the road. The waters of the river had eroded black rocks over time and created a river basin with two sheer sides.

We came across a caravan as we were traveling. They had skinned a tiger that they had just shot and loaded it on a mule. We continued travel until half past two o'clock at night. We camped out in the open in the middle of the plain rather than pitching tent after crossing the Fantalle Mountain Pass. When we took our belongings from the muleteers, they returned the four canisters that we had filled at Awash River and handed over to them almost empty and apologized saying that it had spilled on the road. However, these fuel canisters had been prepared in Harar in a special way for water, placed in chests and lids were made for the spouts. The muleteers both drank these and spilled them in order to lighten the load of the mules that were carrying these. One should not take one's eyes off from these water canisters. Fortunately, our evening meal had been cooked from daytime and flasks had been filled.

We made a square from the chests and the gear in order not to be trampled on at night by the mules that were grazing around us and we moved inside. Such a heavy wind, storm erupted at night that we gave thanks that we did not pitch the tents because there was no doubt that it would swoop up the tents like balloons.

The baggages were loaded at eight o'clock since it was not possible to sleep due to the storm and we departed at quarter to nine o'clock, with lantern in front. Had there not been lanterns, a few of us could have fallen and split our heads because the land we crossed had so many rough rocks, holes, and ditches. Huge floods and volcanoes had turned the terrain here upside down and into a stone quarry. While going straight, sometimes the trail that is being followed suddenly ends in a sheer precipice. The trail is abandoned here. Another sloping trail is sought in order to descend. Sometimes it is necessary to go down one crest perpendicularly and climb another. In short, floods have turned this place to such a disorderly state that a person becomes confused how he should go.

I found myself at the mouth of a volcano, among coal piles at eleven o'clock while crossing the Abba Janber Pass. The smell of gas was obvious to such a degree that Sergeant Yasin asked whether this was a gashouse. It appears that the volcano here is not extinct yet. The smell of smoke is coming to our nose. Since a famous person in Ethiopia named Abba Janber had been ambushed and killed by the Karayus in this pass, the pass is named after him. We came across a tired mule left on the way here. The caravan that we came across must have left it. The wretch has exhausted his strength to walk and it is far from water. If wild animals do not tear it to pieces at night, it will perish from thirst.

Our travel tonight was not only with the help of the lantern, there was also the help of the weak moonlight which came out at eight thirty. After walking three and a half hours properly, we took a break both for some rest and to drink coffee. It had now become morning.

Friday, June 10   Tadecha Malka

Dik, dik • Pej • Argobba • Harsh heat • Fire smoke • Terrifying flies • Beautiful animals

Taking out the teapot from the saddle, the cook heated water with shrubs. Besides coffee, we prepared some meat broth from some marrow and had breakfast with rusk and after three quarters of an hour we continued on our way. Now, Mount Fantalle can be seen well. It has embraced the land we are in all around, like a bow. After going a while, we climbed its slopes consisting of rugged terrain and rocks when the tip of the mountain ahead of us came across our path. When we arrived at the summit, Ferhan Mountain and the green Tadecha Malka Valley at the base of this mountain, trees, and its stream appeared. We started descending from this naked, waterless mountain that we were on with great happiness since we wanted to reach this nice valley as soon as possible. At this moment, Şevket Efendi shot two little gazelles referred to as "dik dik". These gazelles are dwarves and are the size of a large rabbit. It does not grow more than this.

The number of houses began to increase as we approached Tadecha Malka. Since pej and common wild chicken are plenty, and turtle dove and sparrow especially abundant, not even spending one round on them is seen as warranted.

We reached Tadecha Malka after covering a distance of six hours today. The Kasam River that is a tributary of the Awash River passes from this valley. The Kasam River is born on the foothills of the Mefrez Mountain and, after flowing about two hundred kilometers from west to east, joins the Awash River at the place named Sadi Malka. This stream is the size of the Kağıthane[56] Stream that we have and its water is sweet, its currents rapid. The course of the stream in Tadecha Malka overflows part of the land, covers it when it floods from rains since it is not much lower than the surrounding terrain. Many trees grow around it due to this.

---

56 *Flows into the Golden Horn In Istanbul, Turkey

I see the water canal method here for the first time. A canal has been opened a little beyond Tadecha Malka and channeled to the land above the stream, and a kind of farm has been established. Eight, ten huts have also been built for agriculture. We see the mountain named Ferhan across from the Tadecha Malka location. While there are not tall trees here like in the mountains we passed, there are enough trees for wood. An Islamic community named Argobba inhabits this mountain and makes a living with farming and agriculture. They have animals like cattle, sheep, goat.

Today, the weather is excessively hot. We became happy as though having reached heaven when we saw the stream, trees since the land that we passed was mountainous and relatively arid. Our biggest desire is to spread a rug on the grass under the shade of a tree beside the stream and rest and eat. We crossed the stream when we came next to it, saying that perhaps there is a better place on the other side. An Ethiopian person whom we had met on the road a few days ago was resting under the biggest tree there. He greeted us the moment he saw us. He entreated us [to join], took us to his place. He took out soda bottles from his saddlebag. He brewed coffee, offered it. After chatting with him for a while, we crossed to the other side of the stream again and rested under a distant tree, next to the cornfield of the farm that I had mentioned.

Insects such as ants, flies were plenty here. So, we retreated to a secluded place. Our kitchen was set up here and the gazelles, pej chicken were cooked. Our lunch and dinner were prepared together. The heat was quite harsh and the blowing wind was raining dust, dirt over us. We could not find the freshness and coolness that we expected when we saw the valley from afar.

The people on the other side of the stream are burning dry grass together with trees as is their habit. The crackle, smoke of the fire is coming all the way to us. The habit of burning forests to make farms is prevalent in Ethiopia. They burn the dry grass every year, too so that the earth is nourished from its ash and gives more grass.

The heat today even affected our local servants and soldiers. These people are all sprawled under trees, here and there at full length, none of them wanted to move. I would have liked to record the temperature. However, I had placed the thermometer at the bottom of the chest upon seeing the normal weather in Harar. How can it not be hot? We descended from mountain tops, from an altitude of two thousand five hundred, two thousand seven hundred meters to nine hundred meters or so. Tadecha Malka is at an altitude of nine hundred and twenty-two meters. The flies are the size of bees here and green colored and hurt like a bee when they sting.

Two quite nice cattle herds came to the stream while writing these lines. One of the herds consists of sheep with only jet black heads, necks, while the remainder of their bodies is all white like cotton, the other are cattle calves the size of a goat.

Since the Chercher road joins the Adal road in the Tadecha Malka locality, the numerous caravans that rest here converge on each other. A number of abandoned Karayu huts are standing near us. I thought these were ant nests from a distance of two hundred meters. I could not discern that these were Karayu huts until coming next to them. The hut consisted of a few tree branches, covered with dry grass. Its construction would not take more than half an hour.

The caravans on the two sides of the stream started to load their mules when the heat of the sun cooled in mid-afternoon. It is the custom in Ethiopia that if a caravan is to come next to a water source and camp, if the place to pass is a stream, the caravan will only camp after crossing to the side of intended travel. Consequently, there will be caravans on both sides of the stream. Everyone would have crossed to the side that they were going to in time just in case it rains during rest and the stream floods and turns to an impassable state.

The place where we are located is next to a stream. We were feeling a lot of heaviness since the wet fields were creating humidity. Our bodies were worn out with the effect of the hour-long sleep or rather blackout that had befallen us with difficulty during the day. Consequently, we had our baggage loaded, filled our water. After climbing the crest ahead of us, we set out from there with the intent to camp at a higher point. After traveling about an hour and a half, we arrived to the plateau. The coolness, lightness of the air here really revived us. After camping in the open and having our dinner with great appetite, we fell unto a sleep of rest. The heaviness, fatigue that fell during the day disappeared.

Saturday, June 11   Choba

Macadam roads thanks to a road roller • A terrifyingly large fire • We camped in the open

We all woke up in an agile, vigorous shape and full of joy in the morning before sunrise. Our two servants who had gone to look for the mule that was lost in Tadecha Malka had not reached us yet. We judged that they had not found the mule. We postponed our departure to afternoon both to wait for them and to fill water from the Kasam Stream that we would need during the day, rest our mules and graze them.

Although it was nice to stay in the open at night since there was no cold and dampness, we pitched our big tent and, raising the flaps, sheltered underneath given that it was not possible to stay under the sun until evening.

I had warned the soldiers and servants to bake enough bread for two days so that there would not be need to consume too much water since we had been informed that there were no streams in the Choba and Menabella stops ahead of us.

Although we were next to the stream yesterday and today, they did not prepare their bread there and asked for water from us after we camped at night to bake their bread. Despite their own accounts of a lot of people perishing from thirst between Awash and Tadecha Malka and Tadecha

Malka and beyond, none of them had either a flask or a water gourd. Each trusted the other, none carried a water container.

Our muleteers did not pitch tent, [and instead] made shade from tree branches. Although we were at a high elevation, the heat discomforted us quite a bit today. We drank water all the time during the day. The canisters came from and went to the stream a few times. The weather cooled at ten o'clock.

We headed towards Choba. Nearby, His Imperial Majesty Emperor Menelik has brought a road roller from Europe that moves with steam. A few thousand people brought this, taking turns over the straight Adal road, pulling, rolling it with ropes until Tadecha Malka. However, it had not been possible to roll it from here and a winding macadam-like road over crests, mountains had been constructed beyond here until Addis Ababa. Thousands of people had worked on this, too. Thus, the road roller had been transported to Addis Ababa. In short, either the roller was brought to make the road or a road was made to transport the roller. Thus, we are at times following the road and at others taking short cuts in places that are not that rugged.

When darkness fell, we saw a quite big fire on our right side at a far away mountain in the vicinity of Belga Castle. Obviously, a forest had been burnt to make a farm as always.

By lighting a lantern and continuing on our way until two o'clock at night, we reached the location of Choba. All the land from Tadecha Malka to Balchi is referred to with the name of Menjar.

Choba is a village, like other villages in the region, consisting of a collection of some huts. Since there is no stream and spring water, wretched women are bringing water from far streams, rainwater deposits. As our baggages did not catch up today, we camped in the open and our rug served as bed, cloaks as blanket, and saddlebags as pillow.

Sunday, June 12   Menabella

Drudgery of women • Talla

Although our baggages had not reached us, we set out on the road at half past eleven in the morning, saying that we will meet at the next stop, since we did not want to stay at this waterless place. After an hour, we passed a cemetery and the ruin of a mosque belonging to the Muslim Argobba tribe. We saw the salt lake named Galule on our left side and at a distance of five, six kilometers.

We reached the locality of Menabella after traveling four hours. The people of the village here carry accumulated rainwater with leather bags and pitchers from a quite deep and terrifyingly steep valley. They drink this. I went to the edge of the valley. I looked down, may God protect us! It is a precipice like a vortex from hell. One feels sick to one's stomach just by looking. Completely devoid of vegetation, it consists of rocks, black stones. Wretched women are climbing winding trails, ascending with water, some with a large jar on her back, some with a large leather container on her shoulder.

We camped under a tree with a light shade. Sergeant Abu Bakr and our other servant, the most hardworking, cut tree branches from here and there and set these on the branches of the tree we were under. They increased the shade as much as possible.

A guy from the community came and sold us a container of water. Then, an old woman came and sold thirty-forty kıyye[57] jar of talla. Our soldiers and servants surrounded the jar since they were quite thirsty for this beverage. By filling the gourd that served as both bowl and jar lid, they drank in turns. They emptied the jar in five minutes. Seeing the appetite and desire of the servants, the village girls are continuously bringing talla and walking around us. However, since the cheer of those who drank talla exceeded the limit, I absolutely forbade talla today.

Since our muleteers desired to graze, comfort their mules more than covering distance, they did not come today, either. Fortunately, we have enough provisions in our saddlebags, water in our flasks. The weather is suitable to camp in the open, too.

Since the grass is dry and roads have not seen rain from Tadecha Malka onwards, the way is dusty and dirty. The dust, sands in the plain are being scattered around as the wind blows. We rested under the tree until evening, with our umbrellas in our hands. We slept under the tree at night, taking advantage of the coolness. We spread some dry grass under the rug instead of a mattress.

---

57 *1 kıyye or okka = 1,283 grams

Monday, June 13   Balchi

Abundant game • Harerti • Agayas Woldu • Burka Stream • Monkey cavalries • Live sun shield • European salt • Dangerous goat path • Overnight stay in the hut

Even though it was morning and the sun had risen, nobody came from our muleteers except for Ayalla. With the company of three soldiers under the charge of Osman, one of our soldiers, we left them to find the muleteers and meet us at the Burka Stream ahead of us. We set out, too.

We are sometimes moving on rugged, sometimes flat terrain. The pej, wild chicken are grazing in flocks. There are also gazelles, rabbits abundantly. We shot what was needed for the evening. We had them loaded by the servants.

At half past three o'clock, we arrived to Harerti, the marketplace of the Menjar region. This is a quite developed town. Its huts are rather orderly. A lot of people from surrounding villages gather here every Saturday. They buy and sell things.

During the journey, we came across a person named Agayas Woldu who is the shum, in other words the governor, of the vicinity of Chercher. The aforementioned, who is a Muslim, had accompanied Ras Makonen to Addis Ababa and is returning. After greetings and words, explaining that he was very saddened that he was not present when we passed through his lands, he highly requested that we definitely be his guest on our return and inform him when we set out. Declaring that we would accept his invitation if we returned from this way and thanking, we parted. Our soldiers spoke very highly of this person. They said he was quite rich and generous, brave and heroic and that he had killed eight, ten elephants, quite a few tigers in hunting and game hunting and killed many enemies in battles and combat. Going awhile further, we reached the Burka Stream that is flowing in a valley. We became extremely happy considering we had not seen running water since Tadecha Malka. A tributary of the previously mentioned Kasam Stream that we passed in Tadecha Malka, this stream does not appear to be flowing since the slope of its course is gentle, generating pool like deposits between rocks here and there, and it can probably turn one mill.

The Balchi Village is seen like an eagle's nest on our west side at the top of a quite high and steep hill. Both the people of this village and the people in the surrounding area carry water from this river. Besides this, they have dug big and small holes on the flood bed. They also use the rainwater that accumulates. However, it almost takes the form of a swamp when the water in the holes is finished. We came across a few before coming to Burka. Reeds had grown inside them. We spread our rug under a tree twenty, thirty meters from the stream. Stretching a few branches over the tree and the ikhram of the soldiers, in other words the shemma that they wrap themselves in, we sheltered underneath.

Hundreds of monkeys have drunk water and are returning. Şevket Efendi fired on them once. They were startled. They started running, chattering. Since the little babies could not run, they climbed on the backs of their mothers, fathers, clung to their necks with their hands and could escape in that manner. The view of those mounted rather than those on foot was quite strange, quite funny. There were such large ones among the monkeys that Şevket Efendi was convinced that these were definitely bears. I would have agreed with him, had I not seen big monkeys in zoos.

With clouds coming out, lightning striking at this moment, a heavy rain began. We did not get wet with the help of our boots, canvas, and umbrella. The rain stopped at half past eight o'clock. The clouds dispersed. The sun appeared with its full strength and heat. Our bodies had become dirty and uncomfortable since we had been under a lot of dust and dirt since crossing the Awash River and sweated a lot. Those who wanted stepped aside at the river and bathed. Finding water between two appropriate rocks in the river, I bathed, too, with the loofah and soap that I always carried in my saddlebag.

There was nobody around me when I started bathing. After rubbing the soap to my face, head with my eyes shut, I poured water with the mess tin and opened my eyes. Suddenly, what do I see? A shadow like a cloud has descended over my head. I raised my head up. A quite strange scene! A dark colored Ethiopian was standing over the jagged stone behind me! But standing how! He has worn the hood of his oilskin on his head. Holding the two ends of his oilskin with his two hands, he has spread it like wings, bent forward by doubling over. He has covered me completely with the cloak like a tent. He is dressed below waist, naked above and does not have any clothes other than his oilskin. He is laughing when I look at his face with surprise. I asked what he wanted. He pointed to the sun, then at my head with his finger. Understanding that he had taken this position with his oilskin to protect me from the sun, I thanked him and pledged and decided not to bathe under the sun from now on because, in truth, just as the sun of this place can easily cause sunstroke in white people in little time, it is also not quite nice to suddenly come across live umbrellas like this.

After withdrawing under the tree, a few children who were watching our clothes, dress from afar came beside us slowly. Yasin Efendi gave the one who came closest a coffee candy. He showed the piece of candy to his friends. They turned it over and over. They first tasted it with the tip of their tongues. They decided that it was salt because it was white, but then decided it was European salt because its taste was different. A servant who listened to their debate translated their debate, decisions. They ate it. They asked for European salt in turns. Yasin Efendi gave them one, two pieces of candy each. They left from our side satisfied.

After reaching Burka, Bekir Efendi went to the telegraph center in Balchi. Informing the shum there and Addis Ababa of the laziness of the muleteers, he complained. Mounting his mule, the shum went from here to gather them. At half past ten o'clock, we set out towards Balchi, located at the summit of the hill, since we did not have much hope that our baggages would reach us this evening, either. The slope is quite steep and rugged.

One side is a precipitous valley that is a few hundred meters deep, while the other side is a steep mountain and the trail is narrow and rugged. We are traveling one by one. Although the mules are climbing with strain, a number of Ethiopian girls, some carrying water, some wood, and so on as their loads are climbing this slope with enthusiasm, merriness, singing a song, laughing as though returning from a stroll.

We arrived in Balchi within an hour. This village is high up, on the skirts of a plateau dominating the Burka Valley we passed, overlooking a cliff. Since they had swept and prepared the hut of the shum, we entered there. High up is not like below and the wind is strong, the weather cold. Having a fire lit outside, we brought it into the hut. You see, we are now cold after complaining of heat during the day.

The hut that we are in is round in the shape of a tent with flaps, like the other buildings of the region. The beams of the roof have leaned on the pole in the middle and spread around it like the irons of the umbrella and leaned on the wall of the hut. The door of the hut is wooden, while its frame and cover are not from wood, but from stretched cattle hide. I had written that hides were also being used instead of carpets due to their abundance. Although the shape and construction style of the huts I have seen so far since entering Ethiopia more or less resemble one another, in places that are in depressions and so are hot for this reason, the fence walls of the huts have been cast at the height of a person, the top has been left exposed so that air circulates. Meanwhile, in huts located in cool and cold places, holes have been left relative to the coolness of the location. Consequently, we are in semi-darkness when the door of the hut that we are in closes.

Tuesday, June 14 Tchefe Donsa

High plateau • Beautiful cattle • Chankura Stream • Laga Dubi Stream • The noise of wild animals • Severe cold

Upon the appeal of our fellow traveler Bekir Efendi to Addis Ababa with telegraph, the shum who was assigned to find the muleteers yesterday gathered them and drove them ahead of him. They came in twos, threes. They gathered. Giving the excuse of the fatigue, exhaustion from the road of their animals, they apologized. We explained that we would not lose sight of them again in order not to camp without belongings and we would not set out on the road until their last mule was ahead of us.

In truth, the animals had become hungry since the grass has not been green and plenty like before, but dry and sparse for several days and they had become tired since they had been traveling on the road every day for quite a few days. Finding barley, corn here, we had them fed. We filled their belly. Nonetheless, it appears that the muleteers are not desirous of departing from here today. They declared that their animals were very tired because of the slopes that they climbed and that if they did not stay here for a day or two, they would not be able to continue the way. A few of them even disappeared from sight assuming that their mules would not be loaded if they were not there.

Despite their evasion, we had some mules loaded by their owners and those whose owners had slipped away loaded by our servants so that we set out on the road at half past six o'clock. This highland that we are passing is quite fertile and productive, highly populated so that we are coming across a village once every five, ten minutes.

Their cattles are quite well fed, nice and fat like the cattle we came across until now. The most beautiful cattle that I saw in my life are Ethiopian cattle. I had mentioned the lightness, elegance, gracefulness of their goats like gazelles, the whiteness of their sheep like cotton. Especially their cattles are without peer. They are worth seeing. Their height is tall, their back is humped, and their horns are quite long and symmetrical. One does not get enough of watching it. Their prices are very reasonable. A cow valued at ten, twelve lira in Istanbul is bought here for one, one and a half lira. The reason for this is the strength of the vegetation of the land. Anyway, I had mentioned that meat is the most abundant food in Ethiopia. It is evident from the dung piles that the people are burning dung since trees are thin and sparse in the land we are passing.

We arrived to the Chankura Stream after traveling an hour and a half. This stream does not have trees around it, flows on bare terrain. Since the current speed is more than the Burka Stream, it is cleaner and sufficient to turn two millstones. We did not stop here. Watering our mules, filling our flasks, we continued on our way. We passed a flat terrain after this. Although all of this land is suitable for agriculture, a part of it is planted, while the remainder is empty. Trees are beginning to become more rare as one comes across a tree only once an hour. Shrubs also cannot be found in the land that is not planted, being covered full of wild weed.

We arrived at the Laga Dubbi Stream at eleven o'clock. Flowing slowly like the Burka Stream, this stream has generated deposits between rocks, here and there. We shot two big wild ducks here.

We arrived to the Tchefe Donsa Stream at half past eleven o'clock. This stream flows very slowly. After half an hour, we came to another stream with the same name, but more rapid flow. Passing this too, we continued on our way. We camped in the desert at half past one o'clock.

We took to pieces one of our provision chests and burned it with the dung to cook our dinner this evening. Since the night fires were only lit with dung and the flames were weak, wolves, hyenas came quite close and disturbed us with their howls. It became very cold tonight. We shook like a leaf in the tent. Our water became chilled with ice.

Wednesday, June 15   Akaki

Successive crests • We became guests of Haji Ahmad Efendi
• Gramophone • Buffet

Rising at half past eleven, the sun began to warm the surroundings a little. Nonetheless, we drank a tea each to warm up. Since the grass of the location we had camped was plenty, we could only get the muleteers to load the baggage at half past one o'clock. We are traveling continuously higher on a gentle incline since Balchi. The land that we are covering today consists of at times rather flat terrain, at others undulating, gentle sloped hills and streams.

While the valley named Akaki, where we would rest, began to be seen from afar, after climbing each hill another hill that we had not seen hitherto is confronting us. Exactly the same situation that occurs when coming from Medina to Rabigh can be seen here, too. The town of Rabigh is seen from afar. One assumes that after passing the crest in between, one will arrive there. The crest ends, another crest appears. In short, we could finally reach Akaki Valley at seven o'clock after passing many crests. While this valley is big and deep, the stream that flows in it is hardly the size of the Kasam Stream that we passed in Tadecha Malka. During periods of rain, the abundant floods that come from the surroundings join here and since its course is steep and deep, there is a thirty meter long rather proper wooden bridge over two meter wide stone piers here.

The surroundings of the valley are devoid of trees just like the terrain we passed. We found a little shrub with difficulty to heat our food here. Although we had told the muleteers that today we would supposedly spend the night at Chula located an hour and a half's distance from Addis Ababa, only some of them joined us even though hours had passed since our arrival here. And they said that they could not go forward another step from here and proposed that we stay at the river.

A farm and a house exist on the top side of this valley. The owner of this is one of the respected merchants of Addis Ababa, Al Haj Ahmad Efendi Bin Abdulqadir from Jeddah and when we were in Balchi the aforementioned had invited us both to his house here and in Addis Ababa. While we were eating and resting along the river, the head jeweler of His Imperial Majesty the Emperor Hanefi Efendi from Daghistan, his tailor Albanian Zakaria Efendi and others, the representative and slaves that Ahmad Efendi had sent especially came and requested us to climb to the house above. Mounting our mules, we climbed the slope of the valley together with those who came to greet us. We came up to the plateau within half an hour. We entered the farm of the aforementioned.

Many slaves and concubines were busy with cooking food in the house that consisted of a big hut. A quite nice, decorated, two winged, large tent was pitched outside, in the middle of the field and a big and excellent gramophone, playing quite beautiful Istanbul tunes, was set up in front of this.

We found a quite nice buffet arranged inside the tent with a variety of biscuits, sweets, pineapple, apple, pear compotes and almond, pomegranate, lemon syrups, and various cigarettes over a table covered with clean linen. I really thought that I was in the dining lounge of an excellent hotel. We drank coffee, tea. We ate from the desserts.

The servants and soldiers were left in amazement and astonishment in front of the gramophone. Saying, "How does the person inside this fit in? He is so small, his voice is so loud!", they are debating with each other. They cannot believe in any way that there is not a person inside it. They are obviously seeing a machine like this for the first time. Frankly, it also did not even come to my mind that a gramophone would be found in Addis Ababa. Silencing the phonograph, we started chatting with those who came to the reception. The representative of Haji Ahmad Efendi declared that he was busy with arranging and decorating his residence in Addis Ababa and so had not been able to come yet. The Muslim community was so happy by the arrival of our humble delegation here that some of them are shedding tears of joy. They stated that all Muslims located in Addis Ababa are quite pleased and that they would all come to greet tomorrow. With the muleteers bringing our belongings, our tents were pitched.

Haji Ahmad Efendi of Jeddah came from Addis Ababa. That the aforementioned is quite well mannered, polite, generous, hospitable, and charitable became evident both from his behavior and the testimony of everyone about him during our journey here. Even though he has so many slaves and servants, he cannot stay still and wants to do everything himself. Having requested from His Imperial Majesty the Emperor that we stay at his residence during the period of our humble delegation's stay in Addis Ababa, he submitted to us the paper, containing the permission given to him regarding this matter, from the Emperor's palace chamberlain. The satisfaction stated by both him and all those who came to greet and the prayers for His Imperial Majesty, our master, the mighty Padishah are without limit and innumerable.

After dinner and chat in the evening, everyone dispersed to his proper place. They informed us that the reception ceremony that would be performed by the government would be held at a place named Chula located an hour's distance from the capital.

Thursday, June 16   Chula

Sincere bonds and prayers to our mighty master, His Majesty
•Lavender flower welcome • Interview with Monsieur Ilg • The greetings
of the Emperor • Heavy hale and rain • The cheapness of livestock
•Sheep, goats are not milked • A silver set is a reward • Wild animals
again

In the morning, everyone shaved, wore his new clothes and prepared to go to the capital. After having an excellent breakfast, we headed towards Chula at quarter to two o'clock, forming a big group with those who came to greet. During the journey, a lot of people came before us, firing shots. They were about thirty, forty individuals from among the notables of Arab, Indian and local Muslims who had worn their best clothes, mounted their most decorated mules. When they approached our humble delegation, they all dismounted from their animals and showed extraordinary respect and deference to our delegation out of respect to His Highness, the mighty Imperial Majesty, the supreme benefactor and said a lot of prayers for the prosperity of His Imperial Majesty, our master, the Padishah.

We continued on the road with extraordinary revelry, with a bouquet of flowers presented to each member of the delegation, having a variety of colognes sprinkled upon us, handkerchiefs with cologne and silk thrusted into the hands of each of us, and a garland of flowers that they had prepared previously fitted on the head of the animal I was riding. After advancing a little, a delegation appeared. After a while, another delegation appeared and increasing, multiplying in number in this way, we approached Chula.

This time the Swiss Monsieur Ilg, who is in the position of prime minister of His Imperial Majesty the Emperor as it were, appeared on muleback with about thirty of his retinue. When near us, he dismounted from his animal at a distance of thirty, forty meters and our humble delegation also dismounted and we came together on foot. Declaring his arrival at the direction of His Imperial Majesty the Emperor and communicating the greetings, compliments of His Imperial Majesty the Emperor and inquiring after our health quite a bit, the aforementioned stated that our entrance to Addis Ababa would be in an official manner, other persons and a lot of soldiers had been assigned for this at the direction of the emperor and consequently, they would come here tomorrow for this and welcome and accompany us from here. After chatting with the aforementioned for about half an hour, he parted from us to present our respect and thanks to His Imperial Majesty the Emperor by telephone and to receive other commands for tomorrow. We resided in the tent here today, too. Besides the waves of visitors and Muslims, many Greeks, Armenians also came from Addis Ababa.

At eight o'clock daytime, hail mixed with quite heavy rain poured as usual here every day in this season and the pits in the meadow we were located on became like a lake and the inside of our tents became soaking wet like before. One of the Ethiopians, who hesitated entering the tent during rain, sent his new hat to my side for safeguarding. He stayed bare headed while it rained. After a while, the sun came out and began to dry the surroundings. Quite a few cattle are grazing in the meadow ahead of us. There are also quite beautiful horses among them. The price of horses that I guessed at forty, fifty lira is six, seven lira. The most beautiful animals here are the Adal horses. While their neck, front side are quite spectacular, their rumps are low. They do not raise tail. However, how much would it cost to take these animals to Istanbul? It is nothing to take them from here to Dire Dawa. The railway fare from Dire Dawa to Djibouti is expensive, the fee for the Messageries ships from Djibouti to Suez is even more expensive. The Egyptian Khedivate is not letting animals be taken out even by transfer from the coast under the pretext of disease.

There were about ten Circassian gendarmes from Syria accompanying me when I was supervising the construction of the Hejaz telegraph line.

Since their company was in the Karak[58] Sanjak, their animals were all superb and beautiful Arabian breed horses. The cheapest cannot be bought for less than twenty-five liras in Istanbul because it had been bought for ten, fifteen liras in Maan, or rather Karak.

On our return from Hejaz to Syria via the sea route, the gendarmes had sold their beautiful animals in Jeddah for three, or at most four liras each due to the freight, railway costs, transfer and so on expenses. This is because the people of Jeddah are not very keen on horses and use camels.

Due to the cheapness and abundance of cattle in Ethiopia, the best way to commercially benefit is to establish big dairy farms, a soujouk, pastrami, meat stock factory in Dire Dawa, which is the current terminus of the railroad, or the nearby Harar. Despite the abundance of cattle and while there are so many cows, sheep, goats in the places that I passed until now, they do not know how to produce cheese anywhere. They only make ghee and butter from cow milk. They never make use of the milk of sheep, goats. To milk them is allegedly almost shameful because it is the right of the calves. Sheep, goat are said to be small creatures. What would come of its milk! I am telling the locals here at the appropriate time that most of the butter that we eat abundantly in Aleppo, Syria and even Istanbul are from the milk of the sheeps of desert Arabs, that the the sum of the milk little by little from each sheep generates a lot in total; they are astonished. You see, if factories of cheese, soujouk and other such easy products are established in the mentioned places, the products that are easy to transport can come out significantly cheaper relative to the prices of Europe because pastures are quite ample and abundant here. There is almost no other cost than hiring shepherds for the cattle to be obtained. Their hides, bones can also easily be dispatched to Europe.

There are persons riding animals with silver tacks among the people who came to greet us today. These tacks are a gift of the emperor to them. They cannot make silver gear with their own money and use them. Silver animal tacks, sword, shield and so on are respected here in terms of awards and ranks and can be used when gifted by His Imperial Majesty the Emperor.

---

58 *In Jordan

Our base turned to a fairground from the coming and going visitors. Since Ahmad Efendi has set up the gramophone here, too, a lot of people have gathered around it and they are listening to all the songs in full attention and astonishment. Occasionally there is conversation and talk of a conjuror, too. When the sound of laughter also comes out from the machine following talk, the locals are left in amazement while laughing wholeheartedly. The picture of a person was depicted on the machine. Some of the naive ones claimed that this person made these noises and even that he was hiding. The smarter ones corrected the others' view by declaring that this false notion was invalid and that the Europeans (the French) had locked in a devil inside the machine. The wretched people are quite intelligent and savvy. However, they had not seen schools.

The visitors started to withdraw slowly when darkness fell. Those who brought their tents stayed at our base. Big fires could not be lit around the base at night because only enough wood to heat coffee and food had been brought from Addis Ababa to here. Jackals, wolves disturbed a lot due to this reason. They cleared off after they were fired on several times.

Friday, June 17   Addis Ababa I

The effort for a mosque • Joy of the Muslim community
• Greeting ceremony • Our entrance to Addis Ababa • The durgu of the emperor • Our residence • A brief history of Ethiopia • A description of Ethiopia's geography • Types of people and administrative division

In the morning, they came again, first an Indian merchant, with flower bouquets, colognes, perfumed handkerchiefs. We sat in my tent. We drank coffee. Since it was Friday, Friday prayer was discussed. They stated that there was not a mosque in Addis Ababa and that they even performed prayers during religious holidays in the plains, outdoors.

The Christians of nations other than the Ethiopian nation such as Greek Catholics, Armenians had wanted to build a church purposely for themselves in Addis Ababa. The local government had responded along the lines of, "You are Christians. We are Christians. You can worship in our churches". Due to this, the Muslims had not applied saying that perhaps their attempt would be fruitless. They even said that while there were about two thousand Muslims in Addis Ababa, they did not yet have a place for a cemetery and that they were burying their dead in their houses, gardens. I promised them that finding an occasion, I would demand both a license for a mosque and a place for a cemetery from His Imperial Majesty the Emperor. With this occasion, they all raised their hands towards the heavens and prayed for our benefactor, His Imperial Majesty, our master, the mighty Padishah. They were all shedding tears of joy. They related that the Muslim community had been gathering for a few days at night to pray for His Imperial Majesty, our mighty master and were busy with debating the reception they would do upon the arrival of the Ottoman delegation.

At half past three o'clock, Monsieur Ilg and others assigned to greet besides him, with the company of the soldiers of the emperor and empress present in Addis Ababa, came to Chula. Monsieur Ilg introduced the notables of the persons one by one. These were the old Heru ruler, Ras Wolde, Imperial Chamberlain Azaj Kazu, the commander of the soldiers of the empress Fitaurari Irdi, his deputy Dejaj Abata, Abdullah Aqeel from the Arabs, Abdullah Sadik, Jerah the representative of Indian Gulam Ali, Yusuf Ali the representative of Mohammad Ali, Haji Salih of Massawa, Sheikh Said Aba Zar'a, Al Haj Mohammed Abu Bakr.

After introduction, we mounted our animals and set out towards Addis Ababa with the emperor's soldiers in our front, back, and sides. At this moment, the military attaché of the French embassy Captain Monsieur Martin de Cain came, wearing his official uniform. He stated that he had come to greet and welcome us on behalf of Ambassador Monsieur Lagarde. We are traveling on the road sometimes talking with Monsieur Ilg, sometimes the aforementioned, and sometimes through an intermediary with His Excellency the Ras. The view was quite nice, beautiful. The ground, hills, rivers are all green like emerald. Addis Ababa looks like a big military camp from afar. The imperial palace on a high hill is attracting the attention most. The persons and soldiers who are accompanying are all in official clothes, in other words they have worn their military uniforms. Some had rings on their ear, some bracelets in their arms, some were wearing a helmet on their head from which thin chains, rings, beads dangled to their cheeks, chest. Each of these is a sign of distinction, equivalent to a medal.

All of the soldiers are barefeet. I paid attention to the feet of the ras and the notables. They have worn shoes. The shoes of the ras were from thick felt and to be able to fit his big toe in the stirrup, the big toe had been separated in the shoe from the other toes like a glove finger. He has fit his foot in the stirrup in that way.

The people have jammed the roads, squares, and roofs at our entrance to Addis Ababa and want to see the Turkish "Jennar".[59] Receiving greetings,

---

59 *Possibly referring to the word general

respect from all sides, we came with this crowd until the front of the residence where we would be guests. Shaking hands with the greeters here, I requested them to offer my respect and thanks to their majesties the emperor and empress and everyone dispersed to his place.

His Imperial Majesty the Emperor is not in Addis Ababa and has been busy with some construction for quite a while at his summerhouses in Addis Alem and Holeta located at four, five hours' distance from here. Upon checking through Monsieur Ilg whether our humble delegation should go there to to fulfil its assignment, he declared based on the statements of His Imperial Majesty that since we were tired and in need of rest His Imperial Majesty the Emperor would come to Addis Ababa especially for the meeting a few days later. While Haji Ahmad Efendi has prepared his residence for us with the permission of the emperor, our provisions started to come raw daily from the imperial palace from today onwards since we were guests of His Imperial Majesty the Emperor.

The durgu that came today consisted of things like a big and nice cow, three sheep, three lambs, one hundred pieces of bread, five jars of honey, five pitchers of tej, one jar ghee, one jar boiled berberi (red pepper paste). Mohammed Abu Bakr also sent a large cow, three sheep, two bottles of sherbet in other gifts. Since the cow was unruly, our soldiers could in no way catch it. They butchered it after cutting its leg with a sword. In proportion with the abundance of our provisions, our soldiers and servants also have a good appetite. Since the top beams of the hut where they are located are quite sparse, I can see them from the living room where I am. They eat the whole day. They drink plenty of tej.

Although most houses of Addis Ababa consist of a single storey, the residence where we are has two storeys, a big living room and a wide balcony all around it. All sides can be seen since the location is high and the big marketplace square is right in front of us. Our living room is furnished with the most beautiful carpets. The doors, windows are decorated with the embroidered curtains that the Istanbul antique dealers sell to the Europeans. The living room is about fifteen meters long, eight meters wide. Haji Ahmad Efendi had done whatever was possible to do for our comfort. His joy due to the presence of the delegation with him is extraordinary. The others are congratulating him. He greets those who come and go, supervises those brewing coffee, cooks, and butlers. He is running from one side to the other. He wants to do everything with his own hands. I have been to many places. Hospitality and hospitableness can only be this much.

Since it is not the custom to make courtesy visits to anyone before His Imperial Majesty the Emperor returns to Addis Ababa and the meeting with him is held, the time until then will be occupied with the recording of information on the situation here that has been collected.

A Summary of the History of Ethiopia

When the twelfth dynasty of the pharaohs turned the land between the first and second waterfalls of the Nile to the state of a province subject and belonging to Egypt, its soldiers, advancing until the foothills of Ethiopian mountains, were marauding. The border had advanced to Dangali during the thirteenth dynasty and to the point of the convergence of the Nile with the Takaze River during the eighteenth dynasty and in this way Ethiopia had virtually been annexed to the country of Egypt. The religion and language in Egypt had also spread here. Its rule was as a distinct province and mostly given to the children of the pharaohs.

They built certain monuments in some places like the ancient monuments in Egypt and erected obelisks. Nine hundred and thirty years before Christ, this province gained the form of an independent government. One of the pharaohs who was ruling independently in Ethiopia, a person named Piankhi Meriamen, captured the country of Egypt between the years of seven hundred and forty before Christ and seven hundred and thirty. After fifteen years, the Ethiopian pharaoh named Sabasun expanded his country until the shores of the Mediterranean and became one of the great rulers of that century and established a new ruling dynasty. Due to the intervention of the Ethiopian pharaohs in the affairs of the Syrians and Judah, there had been battles between themselves and the Assyrian rulers and the Assyrian ruler Assar had entered Egypt in six hundred and seventy before Christ and arrived to the city of Memphis and captured it with his army.

Although Sabasun's son Tanu Anamanu had invaded the Egyptian border again in the year six hundred and sixty six before Christ, he was defeated by Assur Banibal, of the Assyrians, in Teb (Tayiba) in the year six hundred and sixty three and from that date onwards Ethiopia had remained separate from the governments of other civilizations of the time. At that time, capital of Ethiopia was the city of Napata and ruled by the pharaoh named Amon (Aemur) and a spiritual committee from his retinue.

During the era of Ptolemy I in Egypt, the Ethiopian rulers tried to expand their border to the north. In brief, Argaman captured Philae.

After Egypt was annexed by the Roman Gaius[60] Augustus two centuries before Christ, Ethiopian pharaohs wanted to enter into friendly relations with Rome, but the Roman Petronius had battled the Ethiopians twenty three years before Christ and burnt Napata which was the capital. The mentioned city had not been rebuilt after this date and the city of Baruwa further to the south, which the Greeks called Meroë, was adopted as the capital. The Ethiopians have old monuments such as temples, ruins, cemeteries from the third waterfall of the Nile to the west of where the White Nile and the Blue Nile join and their language at this time was the Egyptian language, their script was hieroglyphs which was also the ancient Egyptian script. They later adopted other hieroglyphs that experts of antiquities could not decipher and understand.

Just as the Ethiopian northern border in ancient times had exceeded the present border by quite a lot, it had reached beyond the equator in the south and been bounded in the east by the Red Sea which is the natural border, and in the west supposedly passed the White Nile and its tributaries and extended to Senegal, Niger basins via Chad. Consequently, a lot of Sudani people and kinds were included in ancient Ethiopia besides the current Ethiopian kinds. However, the mentioned area had slowly lost in breadth and size, withdrawing to between the Red Sea and White Nile and Egyptian Sudan and Zanzibar and later losing the Red Sea coast and shrinking on four sides, it has been limited to its current border that will be described later.

Since the actual Ethiopia region is difficult to pass and like a fortification dominating the surroundings, the Egyptian pharaohs had not

---

60 *Roman control of Egypt is dated to 30BC in alternate sources

dared enter the interior of the region and satisfied themselves with driving their marauding soldiers along the Blue Nile and Takaze Rivers till the foothills of this aforementioned fortification and harrying the Massawa, Djibouti coasts from the sea.

The color of the population of Ethiopia at the time was a reddish color people similar to the Egyptian population and the people living in the south of the Arabian Peninsula. Various people had migrated there over centuries before Christ from the Arabian Peninsula by crossing the Bab Al Mandab Straits.

When Greeks came to explore and survey this region for the first time from Red Sea coasts, they found a community living the customs and speaking the language of the Himyar and Saba Arabs who were in the south of the Arabian Peninsula.

Most of the parts that had been occupied by Egyptian Tabata and Meroë Pharaohs were invaded by the old Arab Emirs and had come under their direct subjugation or protection in the third century before Christ and had stayed in their hands until the fourth century after Christ. At that time, Aksum was the most important administrative center of Ethiopia. In ancient times, Ethiopians established relations through trade with Romans in Egypt and the Greeks who had come there. The Israelite religion came in from Yemen before Islam and Christianity. However, Christianity came in at the hands of the Priest Frumentius who was sent by the empress, the wife of Constantine, the Emperor of Byzantine. This religion did not spread in Ethiopian regions until two centuries afterwards at the hands of the priests who were sent by Justinian from Egypt and who taught the Ethiopian people the Orthodox order of Christianity.

Ethiopian priests and men of religion state that dates and records, which were kept in churches and monasteries, claim that the existing royal family descends from the line of Menelik, the son of Solomon, son of David, from his wife Balqis, the Queen of Saba[61] and the kings from this family used to make Aksum the capital of their kingdom in old times. This is what the Ethiopian gentlefolk believe. This administration in Aksum could not maintain its strength and continued to decline until its weakness

---

61 *Queen of Sheba

prompted the Jews, who were living in the lands of Simien located in the north of Ethiopia to the east, to covet it. A girl named Iodit or Esther arose among them and marched at the head of Jewish revolutionaries and was the cause for them to annex the territories until the border of Shewa under the rule of of these Jews. Of the eleven kings who ruled after Esther, the most famous was Lalibella who ruled and lived in the middle of the twelfth century. It is said that this Israelite king has many surviving monuments in those regions until our day. In the Gregorian year one thousand two hundred and fifty-five, Yigon Amlak, King of Shewa, who was from the ancient ruling dynasty from the line of Menelik the first, arose and returned peace and calm to the country, but all the coasts fell in the hands of Muslims who were always attacking with the Jews on the Ethiopian regions. At the beginning of the fourteenth century, Amda Seyon took back the city of Zeila. This ruling dynasty reached its highest potency in power and strength at the time of Ishaq. However, its power started to wane after that because of the wars of Muslims and due to internal strife. Mohammad Gorani attacked these countries and conquered a large part and left its government on the verge of extinction and it was not rescued from this devastation except for the help of the Portuguese who made an agreement with the aforementioned government to permit them to introduce the Catholic Church to Ethiopia in regards to helping with the Muslims.

In the year one thousand five hundred and thirty-three, Muslims attacked Ethiopian regions under the command of the Emir of Zeila and Massawa, Amhara and Tigray with their horses and men and struck Aksum, the capital of the Ethiopian country, then retreated in front of Portuguese soldiers who were united with the Ethopians. Strife started after that in Ethiopian regions because the Portuguese were busy spreading Catholicism in Ethiopia. So, the Ethiopian clergy became angry and bloody incidents erupted between the followers of the Orthodox sect and the followers of the Catholic sect. These religious wars continued a full century and, at the end, the Ethiopians were able to expel the Catholic clegy from their country in the seventeenth century and they moved the capital of their government to Gondar. After this date, Ethiopian regions stayed closed to the Europeans for a century and a half. In the year one thousand seven hundred and fifty, a Catholic priest sent missionaries among the Ethiopians to spread their doctrine and from that revolutions arose and led to the Faliyin attack on Ethiopia and the capture of Tekla Haymanot, the Ethiopian king. In the year one thousand eight hundred, the King of Tigray succeeded in subduing the country and restored security, but strife and revolutions returned after his death and lasted until the nineteenth century, rendering European endeavors to discover Ethiopia and civilize its inhabitants futile.

At that time, Ethiopian regions were divided into three administrations subject to the name of one king and these governments were Shewa and Tigray and Amhara. In the year one thousand eight hundred and fifty, the administrator of the palace of the ruler of the Shewa Palace named Kassa arose and seized government by force from Ras Ali, the original ruler. Then, he attacked the Amhara government in the year one thousand eight hundred and fifty-two and occupied it and he attacked the government of Tigray in the year one thousand eight hundred and fifty-five and conquered it and proclaimed himself king in Ankober, with the name of Tewodros. He triumphed over the Faliyin, then made an army of one hundred and fifty thousand soldiers and wanted to arrange them in the new European style, all this to return ancient Ethiopia's power and to raise her glory.

His relationship with the English state was good, but those good relations soured afterwards and changed from friendship to animosity. Thus, England sent a military expedition under the command of General Napier in the year one thousand eight hundred and sixty-five and defeated Tewodros in the Battle of Magdala. So, he committed suicide. However, General Napier and his troops retreated from Ethiopia in the year one thousand eight hundred and sixty-nine after he made a truce with Ras Kassa, the Prince of Tigray. In the year one thousand eight hundred and seventy-one, Ras Kassa forced Ras Gobeze the Prince of Amhara and Ras Menelik (who is the current emperor), the Prince of Shewa, into obedience to him and to accept his being king to all of Ethiopia. He wore the imperial crown under the name of Yohannes. During that time Ismail Pasha, the former Egyptian Khedive, annexed Ethiopian regions to the Egyptian Khedivate and occupied the territory of Bogos and the town of Karate in the year one thousand eight hundred and seventy-two. However, the Egyptian expeditions to occupy Tigray which were sent in the year one thousand eight hundred and seventy-four and in the year one thousand eight hundred and seventy-six were defeated in the face of the Ethiopian soldiers, so they went back whence they came. Numerous important events such as the removal of Ismail Pasha, then the Orabi[62] revolt and the appearance of the Mutemahdi occurred at that time and those events saved Yohannes from the expeditions of the Egyptians. However, he fell between the populist Italian ambitions from one side and the attack of the Shiites of the Mutemahdi from the other side. The Italians entered Massawa in the month of September in the year one thousand eight hundred and eighty-five. So, Yohannes sent an expedition on them, commanded by Ras Alula, and triumphed in Dogali against a small party of Italian soldiers. In the year one thousand eight hundred and eighty-nine, Yohannes accepted the advice of the English and their incitement and attacked the Shiites of the Mutemahdi in Qallabat where his soldiers were defeated and he was killed in the same battle. After that Menelik, the Prince of Shewa, succeeded him in the empire. Italy benefited from the death of Yohannes and the defeat of his soldiers, but wanted more and so announced war on Ethiopia. This backfired on it in the Battle of Adowa where it suffered a bad defeat and was obliged to enter a truce with His Imperial Majesty Menelik whose position became stronger. He became a king to all the kings of Ethiopia after that and he is now ruling his country in full peace and calm.

Brief Description of the Geography of Ethiopia

The region of Ethiopia is bordered in the north by Egyptian Sudan and the colony of Eritrea, in the east again Eritrea, Somalia, in the south Ogaden and by Egyptian Sudan in the west. Not just consisting of mountainous terrain, the mentioned region includes terrains of various structure, with differing formations and climates.

In short, the towns located in plateaus over high mountains and hills, like Addis Ababa where we are located, are fairly cold. The large and broad highland of Harar, which we passed, is a plateau with mild weather. The

---

62 *Ahmed Orabi led a revolt to end the English and French influence in Egypt

area named Samhara, which is parallel to the Red Sea coast, is a depression and quite hot. Meanwhile, the land around Sobat River, a tributary of the White Nile in the south, consists of swamps created by the flooding of this river.

A mountain range above Samhara is steep in the direction of the Red Sea. Its other side spreads gently towards the plateau with the sweet Nile, with the average altitude of this plateau at one thousand five hundred meters above sea level. There are a range of mountains of various features and heights above this, with those known as Amba among these almost the shape of a steep prism. Some can be climbed with only a lot of difficulty, while some can almost not be climbed at all. The backs of these mountains consist of fertile and developed plateaus and the Simien and Gojjam Plateaus are at an altitude of two thousand four hundred meters above sea level, Sauira Plateau three thousand, Ras Dashan four thousand six hundred and twenty, and Kollu Mountain four thousand three hundred meters. The most famous and largest lake in Ethiopia is the Tesana (Tana) Lake, which is the source of the Blue Nile, and there are numerous lakes in various places, especially in the southeast.

The Ethiopia region is considered to be one of the hot regions in the world. While lower locations are hot, some places are temperate, some places cold due to the high altitude. Consequently, the region is divided into three different sections, hot zone, temperate zone, and cold zone:

The first zone is lower terrain, in other words the section that is up to eight hundred meters in altitude, that has high vegetation capacity thanks to the heat, humidity and heavy rains. Tamarind, bamboo and similar such plants grow here in the form of a forest. In the second zone, which is from eight hundred meters to two thousand four hundred meters, besides the trees and plants, in short crops like olives, grapes, corn, that grow in the south of Europe, coffee and tobacco are grown. Although the third zone that is above two thousand four hundred meters is cold, its weather is the most refreshing and this zone brings to mind sceneries of Switzerland, Balkans, and the Alps. The night chill freezes a person.

While a lot of valleys take the form of rivers that end in the Red Sea during periods of rain in Ethiopia, they stay dry most of the year. Meanwhile, on the western side, besides the rain floods that end in the

Nile Valley, big rivers such as the Blue Nile, Omo, Sobat, Mareb, Takaze, Atbarah become tributaries of the mentioned valley. The Awash River is famous and its direction of flow is opposite the others'. Besides these, one always comes across smaller creeks such as the streams that I came across and described while going to Addis Ababa. Travelers are rarely forced to carry water for a long distance.

Types of People and the Administrative Division

There are twelve million people living in Ethiopia and eight million of these are Muslim, four million are Christian. There are about two hundred and fifty Jews residing in the direction of Semien. Ethiopians are principally divided into two kinds named Ethiopian and Galla. Ethiopians are a people derived from the marriage and mixture of ancient Egyptians and the Semites, who migrated there from the coast of the Arabian Peninsula, with the local population. One of these kinds looks like the Arabs, the other a little like the Sudanis.

Those from the first kind are more beautiful. In terms of feature and stature, they are distinguished from the other kind by the lighter color, thinness of their lips, beauty of their faces, eyes, moderation and symmetry of their height. Those who live on the Semien Plateau, Tesana Lake shores are of this kind. Ethiopians are not considered black, but members of a Semitic people and the original Ethiopians live in the high plateaus and high parts that dominate the surroundings like a fortification.

Gallas live in the southern parts of the country. Although they have an actual religion of their own, most are Muslim, some are Christian, and have originated from the mixture of Ethiopians, Somalis and blacks. Not all Gallas live in Ethiopia. They have spread in the south of Ethiopia, Somalia, Ogaden and even in the Bahir region. The overall population of Gallas is estimated at around six, eight million. These people had established a strong administration in Qitar in the past and had become a part of Ethiopia from the sixteenth century.

Gallas do not have one color, some look Ethiopian, some Sudani. They are generally tall and strong people. I had witnessed their diligence with my own eyes and recounted it. Just as there are those who engage in agriculture, there are those who practice animal husbandry as nomads, and those that make looting and plundering their business. They are brave and warlike. Gallas are very intelligent and very suitable for education. Galla children used to translate when I spoke to Somalis who did not know Arabic. Besides their own Galla language, there are also those who speak Arabic and Somali languages. They are divided into about sixty tribes. They have a lot of respect and obedience to tribal leaders. The Muslims among them engage in farming and agriculture and animal husbandry.

The Ethiopians are brave and intelligent and they are most enthusiastic about war and fighting, carrying weapons. While their principal employment and source of livelihood is their cattle, they do not completely neglect farming and agriculture and they plough with quite basic, mostly wooden tools. Only about one in twenty-five of the suitable part for agriculture in the country of Ethiopia is being exploited, according to my humble estimate and what I have heard from knowledgable persons. As we see, it has mostly been left in its natural form. Ethiopians live on the domestic agricultural crops that they grow, and the milk and meat of their cattle. Only the richest and the few demand food and beverages from outside. Their principal crafts consist of softening tanning leather through curing, making cutting blades, and weaving thick fabrics from cotton, wool. They make basic things required for their own needs. In the past, they were making do with the cloth that they were weaving within the country. American fabric[63] is now used most because it has outcompeted domestic textiles due to its cheapness.

The Ethiopia region is divided to states, provinces and each of these is being governed independently. These comprise big and small numerous governments subject to annual tax by the emperor. The big ones among these are the following: Shewa, Amhara, Tigray, Harar, Gojjam, Jimma Bajghar. The smaller ones are the cities of Hemaren or Hamasen in the north, Ghame (Agame), Sararwi, Shiri and their famous cities are Aksum, Adowa, and Enderta. The ones in the middle are the regions of Waggaro, Semen, Wehe, Lasha and Mebea. Their famous cities are the townships of Gondar and Alaka. In the south, Damot, Kaffa, Guwarge. Their famous cities are

---

63 *Possibly a reference to calico

Ankober and Addis Ababa, which took its place and where we are located.

The big states communicate and deal directly with the emperor. The smaller ones among these deal with the state that they are subject to. Big states are ruled by ras, the smaller ones by those in lower ranks. This arrangement resembles the type of old government that is referred to as feudalism because each subject does not know except for the ras who appointed him in his post. He can take away this post from him any time he wants. So, the ras is like a sovereign ruler in his domain of government such that he manages the royal and military matters of the country, as he desires. The ras can wage war against foreigners and the ras also frequently fight among themselves. The rights of the ras include obliging people to pay some taxes as he wishes and purchase weapons. Altogether, although the ras is subject to the emperor, he is an absolute ruler. The ras are obliged to pay the tribute that they are liable for to the emperor and transfer their soldiers to battle at the command of the aforementioned. Sometimes the negus, in other words, the title of ruler or the king is given to some big ras. The title of the emperor is negusa negast or the king of kings and these high titles are only used in correspondences. His Imperial Majesty the Emperor is referred to with the title of Janhoy (Emperor). Since the Shewa government is the domain of the aforementioned, he is the Emperor of Ethiopia and King of Shewa. The ras often attack each other when one of them finds that he has enough strength to occupy the lands of the others, to take it from his hand. They may also stage a revolution against the emperor himself because the princes, in other words, the ras do not care except to increase their military power and might in wars and conflict instead of working to increase the wealth of the country and improve agricultural and commerce and provide causes of happiness for the people. Peace and security now exists inside Ethiopia and all ras and princes are under the command of the emperor and completely at his service and obeying orders, so they do not have any relations with the outside or foreigners. Some respected Ethiopians who the Ethiopian government does not trust and suspects their sincerity are distanced in far and different places and they are always under strict control. Ras Sebat and Mengesha, the son of Yohannes, are among these, with the first one exiled in Harar and the second in Ankober.

Saturday, June 18   Addis Ababa II

Funeral, burial • Crying for a fee • Grieving, inheritance • Fondness towards superiors • Muslims and Christians do not eat at the same table • Jimma Abba Jifar princes • Imperial seal • Some Ethiopian dishes • Tej production • Birz • Honey in its natural form • Founding of Addis Ababa

Someone came early in the morning on behalf of His Excellency Ras Wolde and asked after my health, comfort. I heard a noise from the outside while I was in my room. A lot of women are shouting altogether saying, "Wih! Wih! Wih!" I went out to the balcony. Apparently, it was a Christian funeral. A few priests with white turbans -priests in Ethiopia wrap a white turban lengthwise, over a high felt cone- are walking in front of it. Many women are both leaping and wailing rhythmically "Wih! Wih! Wih!" behind the funeral. When leaping, their arms, which are rising like a soldier in quick march, are moving back and forth. The funeral is covered in white, four people are carrying it on their shoulders.

Muslims prepare and bury their dead in the manner we know. Meanwhile, Christian Ethiopians wrap their deceased tightly with white fabrics like the old mummies of Egyptians. Besides the female kin, relatives, women are hired for a fee to cry and wail if the deceased is a great man. Men walk behind the women. After the placement of the remains in the grave, the relatives and the relations of the deceased leap and wail for an hour around the grave, then cover it with earth. The rich are buried with a coffin. The poor are without coffin.

Those following the funeral go to the house of the deceased after the burial. Wailing and crying continues there for about a week. The grieving sometimes continues for longer depending on the status and renown of the deceased. The relatives and relations of the deceased, friends, those crying for a fee eat nice dishes during this period. They drink plenty of tej. These receptions for the deceased are as good as the prestige of the deceased. A ceremony that is almost like wedding ceremonies takes place. They go to great expense and however much the deceased is respected, the expense increases in that proportion. They also have a reception on the fortieth day of death and the following year. The women of the deceased shave the hair on their heads for mourning and also brand their forehead, cheeks with hot iron.

Wife and husband are the heirs of each other. With the death of one, the property passes to the other. Property passes to the offspring after the death of both. However, they are obligated to settle funeral and reception expenses. Sometimes, they even supplement the inheritance because there is nothing left. They fulfill the custom. They refer to the reception of the deceased that is given after forty days and one year as tezkar. If the deceased has not left a will, the wishes he told the priest he confessed last prior to death takes the place of a will. The priest declares this after death.

After obtaining details about funerals of the deceased, the translator of the Russian Ambassador Monsieur Lishin came and asked after our health and welcomed us on behalf of the aforementioned excellency the ambassador. Ato Basha Balanij, whom we had met in Tadecha Malka and who treated and honored us and even offered to gift mules at the time, came to visit us.

When I had seen the aforementioned in Tadecha Malka, his clothes were excellent, clean and he wore shoes on his feet, a hat on his head, and a black broadcloth cloak with atlas silk on the inside on his shoulder. While he was like this on the road, now in the capital he was barefooted, bareheaded, his oilskin was from rough felt, his underwear, undershirt was from common American cloth. I extended the required courtesy to the aforementioned. I chatted with him through the host, but I asked our translator during the talk the reason for his previous attire and present attire without letting on. He said that it is a sign of humility and obedience for him to wear common clothes since he will be in front of a lot of superiors in the capital. Sometimes owners of wealth and capital even feigned poverty against their superiors, apparently. This is both humility and safety. The aforementioned had not taken the servants and mules in his retinue to Addis Ababa and left them in Chula. The conversation turned to the strength of vegetation in Ethiopia during our chat. The land gives crops twice a year here, sometimes three times. Grapes give fruit twice a year. Apparently, cows, sheep give birth twice a year. What a fertile place.

It was time to eat. The table was set. Ato wanted to go. I did not let him. I invited him to the meal. He stayed hesitatingly. They set up a separate table for the aforementioned than the one for us. I asked the reason. Apparently, Muslims and Christians in Ethiopia did not eat at one table, from the meat that the other has cut, from each other's bowl. Consequently, as cooked dishes came to us, cans that had come from Europe were opened at the Ato's table. This custom of the Ethiopians must have passed from the Israilites.

In the afternoon, Suleiman the brother of the ruler of Jimma Abba Jifar Mohammad bin Dawoud, the ruler's son Abdul Rahman and his other son came before my humble self and following prayers for the health of the protector and the longevity and welfare of His Imperial Majesty the Guardian of the Caliphate on behalf of both the aforementioned and themselves, they welcomed us. They had been informed that I was on the road. They had especially come from their country to meet. I guessed Suleiman was thirty-two – thirty-five, Abdul Rahman twenty – twenty-two, and the other seventeen. Although their attire is plain, signs of nobility are on their face. They asked in Arabic the distance from Istanbul to here, from Damascus to Mecca, and whether I went to haj. All three speak Arabic well. They asked questions regarding the size and orderliness of Istanbul, and about Mecca, and Medina. I saw the overwhelming desire in them to see Baitullah[64], the shrine of His Holiness the Prophet and the capital of the supreme caliphate[65]. They have been educated in Arabic and are literate. Opening their watches, they showed the brands on the crystal. They asked what this was. I told them they were factory brands. One of the watches had a small illustrious cipher[66]. When I told them what this was, they kissed and put it on their head. They rubbed it to their face. The value of the watch rose quite a bit in their eyes. I wish I had brought some small plaques with the illustrious cipher; what a great gift it would have been. When I was on the Grand Sahara journey, one of the respected merchants had told me that he had earned quite a bit of money due to

---

64   *Mecca

65   *Istanbul

66   *Seal or emblem of the Sultan

the printed ciphers that he had imported to the middle of Africa. The famous Hungarian orientalist Vambery[67] had related to me that while he was traveling in Central Asia, Turkistan, there was a passport from Istanbul with him. Some people would come from a few days' road to visit and see the illustrious cipher on its top and perform ablution before visiting. May God keep that sacred name, that glorious name eternal, high and mighty until the end of time.

The visitors liked my fez a lot. They ordered fez from the Albanian Zakaria Efendi to wrap a turban on the fez or to wear the fez from now on. My fez are big and do not fit their head. I would have presented it to them. I strolled a little on the balcony with them.

There are more than ten thousand people in the marketplace in front of us due to the fact that it is Saturday. Live, inanimate, whatever is sellable is being sold here. The surroundings are full of all kinds of animal and cattle, all kinds of grain, roosters, chickens, piles of red peppers. The aforementioned visitors left after saying prayers for His Imperial Majesty our master, our mighty Padishah again. Although I took their photos, the plate did not come out well since the weather was quite cloudy.

Ethiopian cuisine was discussed during the meal today. While Ethiopian dishes are very diverse, the foremost dish that the gentlefolks eat daily is the meat that they call zini, which is fried in oil after being diced. Plenty of red pepper is put in it, such that one seeing it would think it is cooked with tomato. The second is what they call tesmi, which is cooked on cinders. It is meat and a kind of grilled cutlet. The third is the raw meat that they call berundu, which they eat by dipping in red pepper without bread.

Their most consumed and national dish is named siru and consists of dough cooked in water over which oil, red pepper have been poured and it is a type of asida[68] to which our sisters have gotten us accustomed. The asida flour of the nobles is made from chickpea or lentil flour. That of the poor is made from broad beans and it has been rumored that the poor eat from flaxseed flour in some places. Ambasha is made from fermented wheat dough and is cooked in the oven. Dabbu is made from fermented

---

67 *Arminius Vámbéry-professor of oriental languages and a Foreign Office agent

68 *Made from wheat four, sometimes with butter or honey

wheat dough and is cooked in steam. Gutnefu is fried with plain oil and has minced meat in dough. Kikel is a kind of meat stew. Ethiopians put red pepper into the unfermented, yeastless yogurt I described before and eat it.

The primary item eaten with bread by the poor here, in other words instead of olives, cheese, is red pepper paste. Each household stashes red pepper in okkas[69], large quantities. They make a paste like tomato paste from that. They dip the bread they refer to as 'injira'. If the poor finds this food all the time, he is satisfied.

With a few pitchers of red pepper paste in the imperial durgu that came yesterday, our servants, soldiers ate the raw meat with a big appetite by dipping it into this. They also cook asidas from corn, beans, another kind of corn flour they refer to as dra, teff, wheat, and also barley. They put so much red pepper into these dishes that if those like us were to dip a finger into that dish, let alone take a bite into our mouth, it would take the place of mustard burn. They also bake a pastry named injira like the way they bake teff bread that I described before. However, they ferment its dough. Before pouring it on the saj, they rub the saj with plain oil. This pastry is a kind of salted pastry. They also make a kind of lokma[70] from dough named dabgalu that is suitable to eat during travel. These lokmas are the size of hazelnuts and the inside is not empty, but filled. They make the dough into strips. They cut it into pieces. After making them round, they do not fry them, but roast them on saj and sell these like roasted chickpeas. I bought some from a woman on the road for our servants. I could not even eat one because this, too, has a lot of red pepper.

They also make pastrami to eat on the road that takes the place of meat when there is none. I saw our muleteers make it several times. After cutting and separating the meat, they cut each piece like a strap, long, without width. They hang these on a rope like hanging laundry and dry them. They collect them when we set out on the road. They open them again when we camp. They then eat this by dipping into red pepper. The poor do not seek salt that much since salt is precious. Salt does not even come to their mind as long as there is red pepper.

---

69 *1 okka = 1,283 grams

70 *Lokma is a fried, round Turkish pastry

Tej and birz pitchers that come on behalf of His Imperial Majesty the Emperor stand both on our table during meals and on the table after meals. I asked how these are made since birz is quite delicious and healthy. A sherbet blended with one measure of honey, five measures of water is filled into earthen jars they refer to as gombo. They sprinkle a type of pounded shrub they refer to as gesho that looks like a cherry laurel so that the fermentation is accelerated. They also put inside one-two pieces of a kind of tree root so that it renders its color bright yellow and transparent like champagne. After the jar is filled in this way, its lid is closed. Its mouth is sealed with mud so that air and ants do not enter. The jar is left under the sun in hot places. When there is no sun and in cold places, the jars are placed on hot cinder, near a furnace so that fermentation takes place. The lid of the jar is opened after five, six days. The gesho shrub that is floating at the top of the sherbet, beeswax, the bees that have mixed in the honey and so on are gathered. Then, the sherbet is filtered by pouring it through a thin reed. Tej that is ready to drink is created. If tej stays in a container that has not been sealed tightly for a few days, it becomes quite sour vinegar. On the other hand, birz is the drink of the Muslims and gesho is not put in this and it is not fermented much. It is more delicious and superb than grape juice. We are drinking it instead of water.

The national beer of Ethiopians is talla, their national wine is tej. Gentlefolks drink tej every day. It is consumed a lot in wedding receptions. Their cheer exceeds limits to a degree to make Bacchus satisfied. At the same level as the satisfaction of His Majesty Bacchus, it will be hinted when the time comes that Her Majesty Venus is also quite pleased with Ethiopia. The Ethiopians generally drink tej with a horn instead of a bottle and glass. The gentlefolk began to drink with pitchers and glasses since loads of bottles, loads of pitchers, glasses, chalices began to come with European civilization. However, Europeans are making iron horns that are enameled inside and out just like the shape of a horn to compete and are sending them here. They have good sales. Caravans are carrying their water with big horns. Gilded, ornamental pitchers from diamond cutters can be seen in the households of the ras. Tigray people call tej miyaz.

Honey is quite abundant in Ethiopia and the produce is collected after the rainy season. Ethiopians are not obliged to feed bees, setting up hives since honey is produced naturally. The bees grow their produce in the cavities of rotten trees in forests. The people search and find this. A type of bird renders the service of guiding people.[71] Since this bird loves honey a lot, it is always busy searching for it. When it finds a hive, unable to hide its happiness it goes up to the top of the tree and announces its success, happiness with beautiful songs from there. Those who are looking for honey surround the hives with this foolish bird's guidance. They scare the bees with smoke, fire, take the honey. Evidently, explorers who cannot benefit from their discoveries are not just in Europe, but also Africa.

Women supervise household management in Ethiopia. The wives of even the most notable persons do not shy from cooking. Would that the wives of our gentlemen with modest means, themselves knew how to cook so that they are freed off the grief of cooks!

Since the residence that we are in is in the middle of Addis Ababa at an elevated location, I am observing the surroundings as I am receiving information about the country.

While the center of Shewa government had been Ankober before, His Imperial Majesty Menelik had transferred the capital twenty years ago to Entoto located on the top of the high mountain in front of us, and currently in a state of ruin. It is cold and frequently covered with clouds there because it is at an altitude of three thousand two hundred meters and the top of the mountain.

Her Imperial Majesty Empress Taytu had liked the plateau that was on the foothills of the mountain and three hours' distance from there, in other words Addis Ababa's location, and constructed a mansion there and with the emperor's retinue, commanders, high officials, and so on also going down there upon this, the capital also descended from Entoto. Since the empress gave the name Addis Ababa to the new mansion that she had had built, the capital that came into existence was also referred to with this name. Addis Ababa means new flower because the meaning of 'addis' in the Amhara language is hadith in Arabic, in other words new; the meaning of 'ababa' is flower. The region is on an undulating terrain and numerous crests. The houses, quarters of the city are scattered and far from each

---

71 *Honeyguides lead humans and eat the larvae and wax after the honey is removed

other since each of the imperial dynasty, the ras, commanders and high officials like a crest or a hill and build at its center, while their subjects and retinue and servants build their houses around it and so it almost looks more like a big military base than a city. This is because when the ras and commanders who do not permanently reside in the capital come, the tents of those who do not have houses, their subjects and their soldiers are pitched. The caravans that come for trade from the surroundings and from the seaside also reside in tents. As a result, the capital is almost composed of residences and tents.

The population of Addis Ababa is about fifty thousand at present. His Imperial Majesty the Emperor first built a new mansion named Addis Alem (Alam Hadith), in other words new world, at five hours' distance from here, then another mansion named Cennet[72] between this and Addis Ababa, turning those places into retreats and since roads have been built from the capital to there, roads are now being constructed in the capital, too. The engineers are French and the people are working as forced labor. These people are forced to see through the task that has been set to the degree of their power and ability. For example, since there are no crowbars to remove stones, they remove stones with canes that have iron nailed to their tip. They carry the stones on their heads since barrows and crates are not available. He who cannot find a crate carries the earth on his lap. The work performed by five persons in Istanbul is being done by forty, fifty of these people because tools, instruments, and so on, let alone being insufficient, are extremely limited. The hardest tasks are given to prisoners in chains. These people work under the surveillance of persons with whips in their hands.

We are cold despite our winter clothes since Addis Ababa is at an altitude of two thousand seven hundred and fifty meters above sea level and we are in the rainy season and it definitely rains every afternoon. The buildings of Addis Ababa consist of the ground floor only. However, the imperial office and some of the newly constructed embassies, and the houses of some of the merchants from abroad are two storeys.

---

72 *Cennet in Turkish means paradise. This could be present day Holeta Genet

Sunday, June 19   Addis Ababa III

The Emergence of the infidel • The sects in Ethiopia • Greetings of the emperor • Visit of the Armenians

In the morning, the Sheikh of the Jeberti, Sheikh Mohammed Said Yahya came to visit my humble self. The aforementioned is from the city of Gondar, which is the old capital of Ethiopia, and was among the people who migrated to Sudan because of the persecution that occurred to Muslims during the time of the Emperor Yohannes to oblige them to change their Islamic religion. Sheikh Said stayed with the followers of Mahdi for almost twenty years. He told us stories of the war that occurred between the Ethiopians and disciples of the Mahdi. We shall tell this story at the end of this chapter.

He arrived to Addis Ababa a while ago to file his complaint to the government against a heretic named Zakaria who appeared in Shukula near Gondar. He told me that Zakaria declared himself prophet and he interpreted the Qur'an as he wanted and changed the rules of religion the way ignorant people, who followed him, like it. He made the fast until noon and allowed the use of intoxicants and debauchery and immoral relations with women and the number of his subjects reached four thousand. Sheikh Mohammad Said is afraid that there will be strife between the Muslims because of him like the strife of the Mahdists and he came to Addis Ababa due to this to raise his complaint to Ras Gugsa, ruler of of the region that includes Gondar. During the conversation, the aforementioned sheikh said that the Jebertis had spread Islam in Ethiopia and that the famous historian Jeberti was from Argobba. He explained that Ethiopian Muslims were of the Hanefi or Shafi schools and that the Qadiriyya order was most prevalent in Ethiopia, then Khatmiyya and Shadhiliyya. In fact, I had heard while coming on the road that most of the Islamic community here commemorated His Holiness Abdul Qadir Gilani by saying chants.

The weather is quite cold and damp today. Anyway, I cannot get warm no matter what since I arrived in Addis Ababa. Besides the rain, a lot of lightning is falling around. Lightning strikes cause harm here. Striking three children in the plain three days ago, it has killed two, while one is continuosly shaking his head as though afflicted by epilepsy.

After Sheikh Said Efendi left, Monsieur Ilg came to my side and, based on the commands he received with telegraph, presented His Imperial Majesty the Emperor's greetings and asked after our comfort and health and stated that the aforementioned, His Imperial Majesty would return to Addis Ababa in a few days and receive us since his mourning would be ending. Since one of the emperor's grandchildren, whom he loved a lot, had recently passed away, the emperor, and the dynasty, and notables and the people are in mourning.

The gentlefolk of the Greek and Armenian communities here came to visit in the afternoon. Armenians migrated to Ethiopia after the known events. More than three hundred of them arrived to Addis Ababa and some brought their women, while others migrated without their women. A lot of them regretted what happened and they are angry at those who cheated them. I found them homesick and they lamented whenever I mentioned the names of Anatolia and Istanbul. They admitted that they were mistaken and the state showed patience and compassion. But what use after what has happened (baad harab-ul Basra).[73] I learned that the Armenians living here wanted to create their own society that would have separate governance. However, the emperor told them that he sees malice in these requests. "Your state expelled you because you were not loyal. Bring us a reference from the Ottoman state or other countries, otherwise go out of my country". They were obliged to ask his majesty for several months to write to the patriarch to ask for sponsorship.

---

73 *An expression literally meaning 'after Basra is destroyed', referring to 'what good is regret after damage has been done'

The marketplace in front of us is empty today since it is Sunday and the scenery is the opposite of yesterday's. Apparently, this is a public square. Convicts are hung from trees in front of us. God willing, this square does not serve this function until we leave.

Types of Penalty and Trials of Afa Negus

Penalties in Ethiopia are organized based on misdemeanor, felony, and murder like everywhere else. However, the penalties here are very bitter like their red peppers. Misdemeanors: It is punished by whipping, according to the degree of misdemeanor. There are brave fellows who receive a hundred whips here. The hands, feet of the person sentenced to whipping are tied with huge straps or ropes, and he is laid face down. One or two persons pull each of the four straps to such a degree that the guy's arms, legs almost separate from his body. His face, chest no longer touch the ground due to being stretched and he remains suspended. The executioner whips the wretch's naked bottom, back, calves with a long whip.

The felonies of theft, treason, insulting religious sanctity, and rebellion are punished with the cutting of the hand or foot, sometimes cross-amputation, in other words, right hand and left foot. This punishment is also executed in the public square. The relative of the felon or good samaritans would heat an iron plate in fire until red hot, or alternatively, boil plain or olive oil in a pan before the hand cutting operation so that as soon as the hand is cut, the location of the wound is either soaked in oil, or branded with hot iron so that the blood stops. If nobody is found to perform this kindness to the felon, he dies with his blood gushing. There are plenty who die.

In the war with Italy, the Italians had a lot of local soldiers from around Massawa and the native population enlisted. Thousands of these who fell captive in the hands of the Ethiopians were declared traitors after the war and they had each had one hand and one foot cut and most of these had died from blood loss.

As for the punishment for a murderer, it is reprisal. In other words, it is execution. If the heirs do not accept blood money, they deliver the murderer to the executioner, or if the heirs want, to the heirs. One of the heirs usually kills him in the way that the act of murder was committed, in other words, if he had slaughtered with a gun, he shoots him. If he cut with a sword, he cuts him with a sword. If dagger, he kills him with a dagger. In this regard, heirs sometimes, and even often, exceed the humanitarian boundary. For example, not killing the convict immediately and after making him sit tied in the square, he lunges at him as though to cut his neck at one stroke. He makes do with only the threat and, thus, torments the murderer spiritually. Then, before striking, he cuts his nose, ears. Later, he cuts his neck very slowly. They torture him physically.

If the heirs accept blood money, the guy pays blood money for the killing. If he does not have money, he provides a hostage or guarantor and sets, with the heirs, a period of time and starts procuring, collecting the money during this period. He is forced to give his life instead of the money if he cannot pay the money in the specified period. However, this situation only occurs rarely because everyone helps a person who is collecting blood money. If the murderer does not have money, he takes a drum with a strange sound in his hands. He wraps himself from head to toe in a burqa. He goes from village to village. He plays the tambour, begs. Those passing on the road, the village community help, knowing what his intention is from the tambour and his attire.

There was a lot of torture as punishment at the time of the previous emperor, but it is cancelled now. They say they used to punish people and soldiers by putting them all, one one by one in a hut. They would then burn the hut with those incarcerated inside. Those angry with him used to undress his body naked, then wrap his legs and calves and hands with thin strings tightly so that blood came out from the fingers of his feet and they did not leave him until he paid a big ransom. Most who are put to this punishment die and they throw their bodies to wild animals outside, but all these punishments have now been cancelled thanks to His Majesty the current emperor and the ras. However, the punishment for spies and liars to rulers is the cutting of the tongue.

Courts

The judge in Ethiopian regions and cities is a senior man who is present in the city. He adjudicates cases such as the cases of tribal chiefs. However, in the capital, the judge is the emperor himself. At the time of Tewodros and Yohannes, the kings sat to judge and adjudicate cases by themselves, but His Imperial Majesty Menelik does not. He only sees important cases and sometimes judges these himself. In his place, there is an important official called "Afa Negus" in seeing the cases. It means the tongue of the king or the person who talks on his behalf. Accordingly, he announces his order in the name of the emperor and shows dangerous cases to the emperor to take his opinion. It used to be that Tewodros would sit on a throne on an open square at a certain time every day and twelve would stand on his right side and twelve on his left from the men of the elders and the head of the priests. One priest carries the Ethiopian law called "fata negus". They open an umbrella above the head of the emperor and stand behind or around him and they surround him and the litigants approach until there are three meters between them and the emperor where they stand. The plaintiff calls with a high voice saying: "Janhyo Janhyo" which means His Majesty the Emperor and repeats this cry seven times asking for his case to be seen so that the Afa Negus approaches the litigants to hear the case of the plaintiff and the defendant and witnesses. Then, he returns to the emperor and he announces what he heard clearly. If the case is simple, the verdict is announced immediately, otherwise memoranda will be issued back and forth as follows:

One of the senior elders sitting on the right side of the emperor presents his opinion in this case and then, the one on the left also gives his opinion about this case until they take the opinion of all advisors and the clerk of the case sitting on the left side writes all opinions in a notebook especially for this. When they have taken all opinions, the emperor orders the priest who is carrying the law to loudly read the section that applies to the case and after that passes judgement and Afa Negus communicates this to the litigants. Sometimes Afa Negus hears four or five such light cases by taking together the statements of plaintiffs and defendants and witnesses at one time and communicates the verdicts to their owners all at one time.

For this reason, they always select men who are brilliant and smart and with a strong memory for this position. The verdicts are executed immediately. At present, Afa Negus stands on behalf of the emperor in capital cases, but in other cities and villages, the ras and dejazmach or the administrator or the shum (the mayor of the city) separate these cases depending on the situation. There are members in proportion to the size of the city or the village and they help judges in separating cases and stand as members of the court.

The Ethiopian Law Called Fata Negus

Fata negus is the law of Ethiopia in force. It was gathered and written down in the middle of the thirteenth century in the Gregorian calendar by one of the Christian scholars of Egyptian Copts named Asaad bin Asal and it has two parts. The first is about the church and religion and worship and it was copied from the Copt sect and the religion of Israel. The second specializes on rules and procedures taken from the Shaafi sect, especially from the book of Tanbih by Ishaq Al Shirazi. Three hundred years ago, the minister was ordered by the Ethiopian negus at the time to work with this law called "fata negus". The word "fata" is abbreviated from Arabic "fatawa" and it is the plural of fatwa and negus means najashi, so the sentence means "fatawa najashi".[74]

"La Basha", or the Detective Exposing the Thief [75]

They look for the thief here through hypnosis, which is called "spiritism" and "hypnotism" in Europe and mandal in some places in Arabic regions, instead of search and investigation. This is the way of search:

The shum (mayor) specialized in search comes with a little plant powder which looks like dried jute mallow and casts it in milk, then they have this drunk by a juvenile boy. The boy starts trembling after drinking

---

74 *Fatwa is a non-binding legal opinion by a Muslim scholar. Asmaha, the ruler of the Kingdom of Aksum in the 7th century, was referred to as najashi (negus) by Arabs, or king.

75 *Arabic text has 'La basha, or the Investigator of the Thief, and Exposing the Thief'

this milk. Then, they give the boy a narghile. He smokes it and the state of the boy changes from trembling to fainting. He starts walking as though in sleep and starts describing the place of the theft and the thief with signs and gestures and the mayor holds a belt tied to the waist of the boy with his hand, and he walks behind "la basha", which is the name of the doped boy, wherever he walks. Everyone who meets the boy on his way immediately kowtows. The sleeping boy can enter any home he wants and if the door of the home is locked, they immediately open it for him. If the owner of the house is not present, they break the door altogether. All paths in front of the "la basha" must be open and if perhaps la basha does not know the location of the theft and the thief in signs and gestures, then they wait until he lies down at a place and stays there. They then judge that the stolen money is present at that place.

Ishi - Beru Hatyu, Aftun Hatyu – Three Brides and a Groom

A person going to Ethiopia hears these words a lot. I asked, "I am hearing this a lot, what does it mean?" They said, "The meaning of ishi is alright sir, ready sir". However, the needful of ishi is being performed very late. For example, we tell muleteers on the road: "Kindly pack. Let us get on the way". They then say ishi. Hours pass, they do not load the baggage, say ishi again. They were amazed at our hurry. Time never has value here.

Meanwhile, "Beru hatyu, aftun hatyu" is "God willing tomorrow, God willing the day after". This, too, does not have a limit. It is along the lines of "inşallah, maşallah" [76]. One of the visitors told a story regarding this. A merchant had given merchandise to a respected Ethiopian person. After a while, he started asking for his due. The person would respond by saying beru hatyu to each request since he was not in a hurry. The merchant has his baggages loaded. He passes by the person before getting under way. When the person asks, "Where are you going? We did not give your money yet. How did you load the merchandise?" He says, "Half of the containers are beru hatyu, the other half aftun hatyu. I will trade with these". Sensing that the matter is very urgent now, the man is embarrassed and settles the merchant's money.

---

76   *'God willing, great' in Turkish adopted from Arabic

Zakaria Efendi, one of the visitors, had gone back and forth on the Adal road while going to the coast. He has actually seen that the period of ishi, beru hatyu was longer there. The wretch was only able to go from Addis Ababa to Djibouti in forty-five days. However, he had learned a lot of the attributes of the Adal during this period. The aforementioned had stayed as a guest at Mohammed Tenbagu of the Adal Sheikhs during the journey and attended his wedding. Sheikh Tenbagu is both lame and his hand on the side of the lame leg is missing. He got engaged with three virgins at the same time and had his nuptial night with the three on the same night. What a practical man! Since polygamous marriages are so prevalent there, he had escaped with one expense rather than spending on a wedding each time he took a girl. There must be some customs that have stayed with Adalis from before Islam. According to the statement of Zakaria Efendi, they open a vein in fat cows. They take some quantity of blood. They drink it. As the cow grows fatter, the operation is repeated. In this way, part of their nourishment is the blood of their cattle. Mind you, during my journey in the Grand Sahara of Africa, I had mentioned that they would take blood from the vein of a camel and drink it. However, they do this there when they do not find food. On the other hand, for Adalis, it is their custom. The bravery and mastery of weapons of Adalis is also famed here. They recount that an Adali attacks three tigers at one time and gets the better of all three of them with [a] shield [and] spear. After presenting some Ethiopian affairs and customs above, it is necessary for us to narrate the wars that occurred between them and the disciples of the Mutemahdi. [77]

Some Words on the Development of Wars Between the Disciples of the Mutemahdi and Ethiopians [78]

The city of Qallabat, which we are going to talk about as follows, is located south of the Gadaref region and is on the shores of the Atbara River and delimits the border of Ethiopia and Egyptian Sudan. The origin of the community of this city is Western Sudan and the Tekro

---

77 *One who claims to be savior

78 Translated by Amina Sanaa Al Muayad Al Azm and Nouwar Muayad Al Azem

people who used to pay tribute to the Ethiopian government. When the Egyptian government took over Sudan, they fortified the city of Qallabat and prepared it to defend itself and used the notables of the region as administrators even though they used to pay tribute to Ethiopia. The region of Gadaref is located north of Qallabat and surrounded by the Atbara River from the east and south and its soil is very rich and fertile and its trade is extensive. The capital of Gadaref is Abu Sin. This city expanded and has high-rise buildings with many floors built in brick or stones, and other than its original inhabitants, it has many Syrian, Egyptian, French, Greek, and Armenian merchants. The city is surrounded by many orchards. There are plenty of fruits like grapes, figs, custard apple, bananas, pomegranates, and oranges. The lands of Gadaref are fertile and productive so that even grapes and dates bear fruit twice a year. Its big cities consist of Azar and Doka and these are two commercial cities.

Battles Between the Ethiopians and Disciples of the Mutemahdi

After the fall of the city of Kasalla at the hands of Dervishes at the time of Emperor Yohannes in the Gregorian year 1885, Osman Digna rose from Suakin and had twenty thousand Dervishes with him and gathered thirty thousand on the road and headed towards the place called Kufit located on the Egyptian-Sudanese border. He sent a threatening correspondence to the famous Ras Alula, the Ethiopian. The ras responded that he would meet him on a certain day. The ras came on that designated day and had eighty thousand Ethiopian soldiers with him. He surrounded Osman Digna's camp from every side and attacked and routed him. Osman could not survive except with difficulty. So, he took refuge in Kasalla and had five hundred people with him.

In the Gregorian year 1886, Abdullah Al Taaishi, Khalifa Mutemahdi who resided in Oum Durman, sent a correspondence to the Shukria tribe residing in the Ribra Desert and ordered them all to come to Oum Durman. They knew from what they learned about the oppression of Al Taaishi that he intended to maltreat and rob them, so they migrated to Ethiopia. Awad Al Karim used to be the sheikh of the tribe at that time and several hundred of the men of the tribe and its notables were present in Oum Durman. When Al Taaishi learned about the emigration of the tribe, he imprisoned Awad Al Karim and two hundred of his men and put them in irons and, then killed them all. As for those who migrated to Ethiopia, poverty spread among them after a while because the weather did not suit their cattle and so they all died after a short time. This tribe was counted as one of the largest tribes in Sudan and wealthiest.

Awad al Karim, who was killed by Al Taaishi, had a son named Abdullah and his mother was Jaaliya. For this reason, he preferred the side of his uncles and submitted to the rule of Al Taaishi who made him Governor of Gadaref. He was able to bring these regions under the rule of this new gang. At that time, there was a man who taught children the holy Qur'an in the city of Qallabat named Mohammad Arbab who followed people and mixed with them. Al Taaishi made him a preacher from one of the preachers of Mahdi and had Abdullah followed. He forbade the people from paying tribute to Ethiopia. The Ethiopians were busy at that time fighting the Italians who attacked the Ethiopian hinterlands of Massawa.

There was a man with the Mutemahdi from the notables of Ethiopia called Mohammad Jibril who came to the Mutemahdi and followed him. He sent him to Ethiopia to call on all Christians in Ethiopia to follow the religion of Islam and to call on all Muslims to believe in the Mahdi and submit to him, so proclaimed Mohammad Jibril with the order of the Mutemahdi. When Negus Yohannes saw their attempts and invitation, this situation occupied his mind and he became extremely sad. He was maltreating Muslims during this period contrary to the customs before him. He treated them with harshness and cruelty despite the freedom of religion in the country such that even the sister of the negus followed the Islamic religion without any hindrance and married one of the Muslim princes. Yet, the negus was tormenting a lot of people to force them to be Christian. When the ras and princes advised him at this time, especially His Imperial Majesty Menelik, they blamed him for his deeds and asked him to abandon this unpleasant and savage way. I saw with my own eyes some Muslims whose hands and legs Yohannes had had cut. The oppression of Yohannes led many of them to emigrate and take refuge with the disciples of the Mutemahdi. They made a place like a camp to stay in at a location called Aradib north of Qallabat and they named this place Tabarak Allah.

Al Taaishi installed one of his men, named Mohammad Faqra, as governor. At the end of the year one thousand eight hundred and eight-two when the Emir of Qallabat visited Al Taaishi, he gave him a lot of weapons and horses and ordered him to alter the direction of his horses and men towards the country of Ethiopia.

So, this emir turned back and started attacking the cities of Ethiopia and ruined many villages and cities. Mohammad Faqra the Emir of Tabarak Allah also started to march on and loot the villages near Tabarak Allah. When the Ethiopians saw this, they brought a man named Ajeel Al Hamrani who was originally from East Sudan. He and many of his tribe had taken refuge in Ethiopia and escaped from the oppression of Al Taaishi. They gave him weapons and military supplies and made him guardian of their border in the place named Atabeh. This man did not dare to attack the Mahdist camp, but used to attack the people of villages and camps on the shores of the Athbara River of the people who followed Mutemahdi by force.

In December in the year 1886, Ras Azar attacked the city of Qallabat and killed Emir Mohammad Arbab and most of his soldiers, and the rest escaped to Gadaref. Another Ethiopian regiment also attacked the camp of Mohammad Faqra and obliged them to retreat to Gadaref. When the news of this defeat reached Oum Durman, Al Taaishi immediately prepared twenty thousand Dervishes under the command of Yunus bin Al Dikam and sent them to help the ones who retreated. This army arrived to Qallabat in April and occupied it. The Ethiopians retreated in front of them. After the occupation of the city, he arranged his affairs and declared complete freedom to merchants in coming and going to Qallabat and announced this among the people. So, Ethiopian merchants started to come to the city with their goods and when there were a lot of Ethiopian merchants in the city, the aforementioned Yunus started to show the malice in his conscience and disposition toward oppression and arrested all Ethiopian merchants and confiscated their assets and goods and put them under irons and sent them all to Al Taaishi in Oum Durman. When these wretches arrived to Oum Durman, Al Taaishi spread the rumor that Yunus had won in Jihad and these were all slaves of war, but the truth was known to everyone. Yunus was from the tribe of Al Taaishi and Al

Taaishi was the husband of his mother who married many times. Yunus was a poor vagabond when Al Taaishi, who became a bad successor for the Mahdi who was also a bad predecessor, gave him the leadership and command of over twenty thousand men. He is a very cowardly man with ludicrous judgment who keeps praising himself and has broad claims and strange allegations.[79]

In the Gregorian year 1886, Al Taaishi sent forty thousand troops and cavalry with several cannons to Qallabat under the command of Hamdan Abu Anja, one of his commanders, to take revenge from the Ethiopians. When Hamdan arrived to Qallabat, he took charge of command from Yunus Al Dikam and Yunus returned to Oum Durman. After he arranged his soldiers and the situation, he approached Gondar, the capital of ancient Ethiopia, with two thousand troops armed with Remington rifles and two thousand cavalry. When he arrived near the city, ten thousand Ethiopians suddenly appeared in front of him and clashes broke between the two sides. After a few hours, the Ethiopians were routed, leaving six thousand dead and wounded on the battlefield, and the rest fled.

Abu Anja entered Gondar and pillaged the city and burnt it and destroyed churches and killed the priests. Then, he returned to Qallabat, with a lot of bounty like silver, gold, ten thousand horses and mules, and

---

79 Among his claims this story: One day he heard that one of his slaves was slaughtered by a crocodile while he was taking a bath in the Nile. Yunus became very angry and told his men he wanted to take revenge from the Nile by drinking all the water and not leave even one drop and that he wanted to go to the Nile shore. When this news spread, some people who wanted to please him told him "Lord, your good deeds are enough to finish all the water of the seas including the rivers, but if you drink the water of the Nile, we and our children will die from lack of water. So, pity us and do not do it". He insisted on taking revenge from the Nile and the more he insisted, the more the sycophancy and ignorance of the people increased. They kept on begging until they collected more than the price of a slave by multiples and gave it to him, so that he desisted from drinking the water of the Nile!! This story is very famous among the people there. This man was found alive among the dead people in the last battle that occurred between the Dervishes and Egyptian soldiers in the opening of Sudan. He lay on his face so that everyone who saw him would think that he has been killed. When they caught him, they offered him a bucket of water from the Nile for him to drink accordingly! He was drinking eagerly until his belly was full and his eyes popped out. He could not finish the water in the bucket and he is now in prison in Tagir Rashid in the region of Egypt with Osman Digna and the rest of the Dervish prisoners.

three thousand girls and boys captured. The girls of these areas do not look like the Ethiopians, but are very beautiful and dark-skinned resembling the Egyptians.

Abu Anja sent an appropriate number from the concubines and boys and one thousand mules and fifty donkeys from this loot to Al Taaishi and distributed the rest to his men according to their fittingness and stature. After he kept some of it for himself, he also sent some of these loots to Yaqoub, the brother of Al Taaishi. Hamdan Abu Anja announced the freedom of trade on the condition that the merchants pay him one fifth. He stuck to his word and did not do what Yunus did as mentioned before. Consequently, Ethiopian merchants came to Qallabat. He used to take one fifth from merchants in goods and dairy products and honey and butter and other things and all these were enough for the army that was under his command.

Hamdan Abu Anja died in Qallabat in the year 1889, so Al Taaishi put in his place Al Zaki Tamal as the emir of this city and he sent with him four persons from his men to declare his rule on behalf of Al Taaishi. Al Zaki is an infamous man for oppression and harshness and surpassed peers in oppressing people and seizing their assets.

The Death of Negus Yohannes in the Battle of Qallabat[80]

When the news of the rout of Gondar reached the ears of the Negus Yohannes, he was very sad and started preparing to take revenge. However, the news of his preparations was reaching Al Taaishi through his spies.[81] Al Taaishi was also very cautious and busy strengthening Qallabat with soldiers and fortifying the city. He built a fence around the city that was difficult to pass from tree trunks, blackberries, and plants with thorns, with a perimeter of ten thousand meters.

In the year 1889, Negus Yohannes marched towards Qallabat with two hundred thousand, mostly cavalry, fighters. He surrounded the city and ordered his soldiers to attack the city from all sides. He was standing in

---

80 Translated by Maria Saseh

81 *Abdullah Al Taaishi, successor to Mohammad Ahmad Abdullah who declared himself Mahdi, or the person who would appear at the end of times to fight evil

front of his tent with his princes and officers, tracking the movements of soldiers and watching the war. The Ethiopians burned the fence tree trunks, then they attacked the Dervishes with great bravery and beat them back. When the Ethiopians saw their victory, they dispersed to loot and entered the Dervishes' houses. While they were busy capturing women, girls and boys, and looting houses, the Dervishes received large reinforcements from the north from men who used to be in the regular Egyptian Army and who joined the Dervishes when Sudan fell under the rule of the Mutemahdi. Their leader Faraj Allah approached with his men, attacked the Ethiopians and directed his fire towards the location of Yohannes. A bullet hit the aforementioned negus and killed him on the spot.[82] When the Ethiopians saw the death of their great leader, terror entered their hearts and broke the strength of their hearts, so they marched with the booty. They started retreating and the Dervishes followed them steadily and methodically. They attacked their camp suddenly at night and killed most of them while sleeping, like dead from fatigue.

The Dervishes recovered everything that the Ethiopians took in booty and all the imprisoned women and men. They also gained the possessions of the negus and his studded crown. They took his body, which was inside a wooden coffin, and went back to Qallabat with their booty. Loot and plunder after victory seems really harmful to the victor as well, and the sudden arrival of supplies brings a great benefit to the loser.

Al Zaki Tamal sent the head of Yohannes, his studded crown, and his personal belongings to Al Taaishi in Oum Durman[83]. Khalifa Mutemahdi's joy and the happiness of his men from this victory exceeded description. So, Al Taaishi held feasts for the people for forty days and slaughtered thousands of sheep and calves to thank them for nailing his enemy.

---

82 *Other sources indicate that the negus died after a few hours and after nominating Ras Mengesha Yohannes as his successor. Ras Mengesha was believed to be his nephew, but Negus Yohannes revealed before his death that Ras Mengesha was, in fact, his natural son

83 *Omdurman in modern day Sudan

Monday, June 20   Addis Ababa IV
Miscellaneous

Many visitors came today and most of our conversation was about various subjects, with one having nothing to do with the other.[84] Each one of the visitors talked about his job or what he knows. The jeweler of the emperor told us: "the emperor presents his commanders and subjects with horses instead of medals with their tack and sword and spear and so on. Consequently, there are a hundred craftsmen being supervised by master craftsmen in the palace. The citizens do not receive fixed wages instead they receive lands and fields in reward". There are a lot of female slaves who make candles from beeswax and oil in the palace of the negus and the empress herself supervises them.

Christian Ethiopians -excluding their gentlefolk- do not wash their bodies or their clothes, so it is not difficult for a person after communicating with them to differentiate between Christians and Muslims because the Muslim renews his ablution every day several times this shows on them and the lethal infectious diseases like venereal diseases and other infectious diseases among the public for Christian Amharans are because there is a lot

---

84 Translated by Amina Sanaa Al Muayad Al Azm

of mingling between women and men and these diseases are rarely found in Muslims. Slaves here are allowed in fact although officially forbidden and the price of concubines and slaves is very low. The price of slaves is between ten and twenty riyal and the price of beautiful concubines from Quragi or Jamalka people is only equal to forty-fifty riyal.

The employees in Ethiopia avoid showing their wealth in front of their superiors. Some of them bury their money in the ground and they may die without anybody knowing where the wealth is hidden and buried.

The emperor gives lowest ranking employees columns of salt instead of wages. This takes the place of money in Ethiopian regions. Each five or six of these columns equal one riyal. Each column is sculpted in the shape of a prism with square sides and weighs one kilogram. This salt is exported from the Welo region, which is a part of the Tigray Province, and it is under the government's monopoly and ownership.

A lot of this salt is presented, among other things, by Tigray's ruler every year to the negus, instead of royalty. The employees who receive salt instead of wages can exchange the salt with money or can buy whatever they want to take in commodities and food.

The most popular currency is the Maria Theresa coin as in most Arab and Sudani countries. This currency has the value of two francs and twenty-five centimes. There is also the Ethiopian riyal that Emperor Menelik minted with his face on one side and the picture of the Lion of Judah on the other which is the national symbol of Ethiopia. This riyal has halves and four quarters. The riyal is equal to sixteen Ottoman kuruş. There are not what we call brokers in our countries to exchange currency in these countries and instead there are merchants who earn much more in exchanging money than the currency broker earns. It was necessary to change a little money for the road when we were in Harar. The merchant deducted three kuruş from each riyal. It means he took one riyal for thirteen kuruş. They exchange money for rifle cartridges, especially Garra cartridges and exchange every eleven cartridges for one riyal. We saw some men and women vendors on our way who preferred to take cartridges instead of currency and kuruş. When a person buys something, they include in the price some of the cartridges and if you ask the price of something the seller will say one riyal and one cartridge or one kuruş and two cartridges.

Empty cartridges are also included in purchases and sales because they can fill and sell them again. The emperor used to lend some money to some merchants from his own pocket to facilitate trade.

Today, the Greek gardener of the negus sent us some delicious vegetables and Zakaria Efendi sent us some kind of nice beans. Vegetables such as gourd, beans, tomato, cauliflower, cucumber, cabbage, spinach, purslane, parsley, onion, potato, garlic and radish and other varieties grow here abundantly. Uma berberi, which is red pepper, is the most abundant. There is a place which has mild weather called "Leban" which is seven hours' distance from the capital and all kinds of fruits and vegetables grow there abundantly and quickly like bananas, plums, lemon, figs, grapes, watermelons, and melons.

I have mentioned Zakaria Efendi gave us some kind of green beans. I found this vegetable strange. He told me that some Indians gave them the seeds and they planted it and it grew a lot. It now yields large quantities without interruption in the summer and winter and it is not similar to the beans we know in our countries that give single pods yield while this one yields bundles of pods.

Its owner does not know whether this unusual proliferation is from the strength of the soil or is inherent in the plant and he also does not know how many years it will give this yield along these lines.

Amharans are circumcised when they are born and do not eat pork at all. They abide by this custom even if they are Christians. I heard from some Frenchmen that they do not like Europeans, but they respect Europeans because they are afraid of the emperor and the reason for this hatred was the war with the English and Italians and the French searched in Ethiopian regions for mines and treasure so that they had the belief that the French want to invade their country. They hated the engineers because they were employing the Ethiopians to break stones and to build bridges. A European person told me that "I ask God to preserve Emperor Menelik for us, if this man dies I am afraid the things that happened to Europeans in China may happen in this country". I told him the ras and commanders do not let the people to do awful things like this. He said yes but the hate and envy between the ras for the seat of the emperor and disagreement between them is such that who knows what will happen.

Every year a military gathering occurs in the capital called Salaf and it takes the place of the maneuvers done in Europe. The ras come from every corner of the country with their soldiers and a large army is formed and they train in military skills and war games and some speeches are given and they read some inspiring. It is allowed for every employee to complain of his circumstances to his leader freely and recount his virtues and bravery in war and bravery in hunting wild animals and he asks for a reward from his leader. I learned that from Europeans whom I talked with that in the previous military gathering, they showed what their feelings were towards Europeans by waving swords in the face of Europeans present at the base and pointed rifles in their face even though in jest.

Ato Haile Mariam, the translator of Ras Makonen, came to visit me today. He was new to the French language. This person is erudite and used to answer everything that I asked him. He answered me briefly.

History of the Calendar[85]

The start date of the year for Ethiopians is the birth of Jesus, peace be upon him, and the difference between their calendar and the European calendar is eight years. They start the year at the beginning of September and there are five or six extra days that are called "Bagumah" at the end of every year.[86] These do not enter the count in the former year or the actual year. Regarding the days of "Bagumah", these are five days every five years and six days of Bagumah on the sixth year. Since these days are not counted as parts of the days of the year, it will become different so they put a date that they call as the next "Bagumah" from such and such year.

The use of these years and months is confined to government and for recording in the country only. However, most of the public do not use it and if you ask one of them about his age for example, he tells you "I

---

85 The sections that follow have been translated by Amina Sanaa Al Muayad Azem

86 *The solar year, or one rotation of the earth around the sun, takes 365.24 days. Since a calendar year must have whole days, epagomenal days, which are not part of a month, are added so that the calendar year is reconciled with the solar year

was born in the year the English entered Magdala", or he says "My older son was born at the time the ras attacked such and such place". It means they pay heed to incidents as the start and do not consider time in hours, but they know the time from sunrise and the rise or setting of some stars.

I asked Ato Haile Mariam about Negus Ashama, who was a contemporary of the Prophet, peace be upon him. He answered that the "name of this negus in Amharan is Ajha and he was the ruler in the vicinity of Tabhafi Dansa and his brother Abraha used to rule in Aksum". I asked him about Mohammad Gorani, who is famous for his conquests there.[87] He said that "this man was from the forces of the ruler of Harar four centuries ago and then he became stronger and conquered all of Ethiopia for fifteen years during which time the negus retreated to Gowandar. Then, the country was taken from him and returned to its owners with the help of the Portuguese". The aforementioned are the ones who brought firearms during this period to Ethiopian regions for the first time.

The Religious Order

The Copt sect entered from Christianity to Ethiopia in the fourth century in the Gregorian calendar. The negus commanded all Christian people must put blue ribbons on their neck so they can be distinguished and this custom is continuing to this day in Ethiopian regions. You will find all Ethiopian Christians put a blue collar around their neck and they hang a small cross from silver, or something else from metal, and they call this collar and cross "mateb" and these are the product of Syria. The Muslims also put these ribbons around their neck today, but instead of the cross they hang leather amulets that have some verses from the Qur'an, or prayers instead of the cross. They call these Ethiopians here "Jeberti" which means Muslim Ethiopian. The Jebertians are pious and hold on to their ethnic and religious customs. They possess ardor and courage and they work in commerce and industry.

The Christian Ethiopian monasteries and convents have a lot of priests and nuns. They permit themselves to marry only once in a lifetime.

---

87 *Gorani meaning left-handed. The Arabic text may have an error and could be referring to Ahmad ibn Ibrahim Al Ghazi nicknamed Gragn in Amharan

If a priest's wife passes away or divorces, he cannot marry a second time. These priests are exempt from royal levies and taxes and they take gifts from the people and commanders according to their financial ability. Everybody wants to enter these seminaries and convents and it is a great thing in Ethiopian regions because men of religion are very important in the eyes of the people. A priest's son usually also becomes a priest like his father. Nobody can oppose a priest whatever the political case and situation. If a war breaks out between two ras, the priest is allowed to move from the camp of one ras to the camp of the other ras and they can communicate whatever ideas they want. Nobody can object to that.

The most important spiritual leader in Ethiopia is the Copt archbishop and they call him "Abuna Laala Al Anba". He is elected and sent by the Copt Patriarch from Egypt and after this bishop there is a priest named "Issagiya". He is responsible for the religious rules of churches and punishment of the priests who contravene religion and its methods. The third leader is a priest who lives in the city of Aksum (the old capital) and he is called "Nirabeyt". Aksum stayed the capital of religion and source of churches and it is now like Rome for the Catholics. The biggest church in Ethiopia is located in Aksum and all works are preserved there, all the records and religious sect histories. Based on Ethiopian customs, when the emperor is going to be crowned in the mentioned city, the Nirabeyt puts the crown on his head and the others among these three envy him.

In churches, there are benches for women with distance between them. These churches have no bells, but various size stones tied with rope instead of the bells. These stones make a sound like a bell when they touch.

If anybody comes as an immigrant to the city of Aksum, nobody can touch him. Many murderers running from justice and political offenders all take refuge because nobody can touch them.

If there is a local war in the region, he who does not want to take part in this war will come to this city and take with him everything, all the precious things he owns. However, they have broken this custom repeatedly. No wonder because there are sometimes exceptions to rules. In this regard, when a war happened sixty years ago in the region and the enemies of one of the combatants (Ras Adbiya) gathered in Aksum and gathered a lot of weapons and military provisions there and started making preparations to attack him, he entered Aksum and captured all his enemies and put them in shackles and took all the weapons and provisions from them, protesting that these people took shelter in the holy city with the objective to arrange their military preparations without intervention in the holy city. Priests were against what he did and threatened him. When he saw this, he threatened to hang them all if they prevented him. The priests then decided that the commander was right and gave up threats.

Most of the nuns in Ethiopia become nuns in their houses and do not go to monasteries. They do not get married and spend all their times in worship. There are three types of weddings in Ethiopia. Priests officiate only one of these weddings.

Types of Wedding

The first way is the natural way and they call it "rumuz". If the man wants to marry a woman according to this way, he asks her to accept him as a husband. If she accepts, she becomes his wife without celebration, or conditions, or religious ceremonies. The man is responsible for the livelihood of his wife and offering her all that she needs for maintenance and the woman is responsible for all house chores and she must go with her husband wherever her husband goes. They can be separated if one of the spouses wants to be separated. If there are children under three years of age, they stay with their mother and the man is obliged to provide alimony, but when the child is three years old, the father has the right to take him.

The second type of wedding is the civil marriage and this happens with the consent of the two sides, under the watch of witnesses and the mayor of the city who must be present. They record everything that they own from their assets. If divorce occurs, what they own must be divided equally among them according to their agreement, but if only one side wants the divorce then that party has no right at all to take from the joint assets. The woman can marry again after the divorce occurs. They celebrate again when she remarries and has a civil marriage. The relatives and kin of the two sides send presents and all gifts that come must be shown to everyone. Girls from Ethiopian regions marry at young ages. They must be under thirteen.

The third type of marriage is the religious wedding conducted by priests in churches. There is no divorce in this marriage. If one of the spouses passes away, the other cannot marry again and because of this, demand to have this type of marriage is very little. Some of the people who married under civil marriage and lived with their wives for a long time and did not have any hope to marry again have changed their civil marriage to religious marriage.

The mothers suckle their offspring for four years and midwives deliver pregnant women in Ethiopia exactly like they do in other regions. After birth all the women neighbors celebrate the birth of the baby. On the seventh day, the woman gets up from her bed. A feast is given to relations and friends on this day. If the woman gets sick, old women and midwives treat her because there are no doctors and they may ask the priest for some medicine to treat her because priests claim they know treatment. The manner of their treatment is in only two ways. They read the bible or make them drink roots of some herbs that they have squashed. They have great belief this can heal them.

Diseases and Treatments

Ethiopians generally become afflicted with tapeworm and its complications in the intestines. The reason for catching these diseases is consumption of raw meat and for this reason they dry the leaves of the tree named "qusu", crush it and then put in water and drink it when required. They then drink coffee so that the worms in the intestines die. If a person takes too much of this paste, he will immediately die because it is a strong poison. Such occurrences are commonplace.

They treat trachoma, headache, high fever, indigestion by bleeding the brow and the patient sits on their knees and they put their hands on his neck, one on top of the other and they bring him a belt and handkerchief and stretch his hands and neck with a firm pull so that he must bow his head to the front and so all the blood goes up to his head. At that moment, they cut the middle of his brow with a knife or horn and blood comes. Then, they tie his brow and it stops bleeding. Cupping is very widespread in this region and so they do not even need a doctor, in other words, a priest. They treat severe cold (bronchitis) and joint pains (rheumatism) with heated iron and those people have patience to endure the pain of branding. Other diseases are treated by boiling some herbs and plants.

Music

The Ethiopians like to beat on musical instruments and to sing and dance. They have the best amusement centers and enjoy themselves a lot and are very happy when they find a skilled person who can use musical instruments. These musicians are very simple and their instruments are tambour, which has one string only made from reed cane, and reed flute and drum and naqarat[88] and long flute. They sing with tambour in their weddings and when they bury their deceased and mourn them. Tambour players earn a lot of money. Men and women dance together during festive celebrations. Ethiopians love dancing very much. They beat on a big drum during battle and the songs they have are all about wars and heros and hunting and bravery, and [they have] some love songs, too.

Their dancing is like shaking and jumping with light leaps. In wedding banquets they make circles and a girl enters inside this circle and a young man stands in front of her and starts singing love songs and dancing, explaining to her what love and passion is in his heart. After a while, a rival comes out and starts dancing and singing like him and does his utmost to be better than the first. Then, a third and a fourth one show up until the girl prefers one of their songs and the beautiful love jokes that he used in describing his love and passion (in truth, she prefers the one her heart was leaning towards before dancing). She starts to sing and describes her passion by singing and gestures and signs. Quarrels frequently occur between the people in the crowd and participants that develop into fights and the people around them look and bet over who will be victorious as if in a cockfight until one of the fighters loses his strength and that moment

---

88 *A type of rounded drum with hide on top, played in pairs

is the end of the dance. Sometimes the fight ends with the death of one of them, but, after the end of the dance and the conclusion of fighting, the two rival fighters who clashed together return as if nothing happened between them because the fight is an obligation of the dance such that the dance consists of a struggle with the girl as the subject and it is no secret that this increases the strength of the participants and raises their energy level, agility and stamina.

War and duel performances must be represented in all Ethiopian amusement parks and their meetings such that hundreds of the relatives of the groom and his friends come armed to the village or the city where the bride lives and stand in an attack posture and relatives of the bride gather armed and stand in a defensive posture in front of the community of the groom. When the gathering is complete, the groom gives a signal to attack the relatives of the bride between the loud sounds of rifles and play of horns and drums and the noise of horses and the event ends with the triumph of the groom's community. With the preservation of these national customs, the Ethiopians maintain their strength and energy and even increase it.

Tuesday, June 21   Addis Ababa V

Al Haj Mohammad from the Bani Aqeel clan came to visit me this morning, along with scholars of Dellu who arrived from their own town to lodge a complaint against a heretic named Zakaria who was mentioned before.[89]

I asked about Negus Asmaha who was the contemporary of our Prophet Mohammad, peace be upon him, and the correspondence that went back and forth between them and the companions who migrated to Ethiopia. He responded, "Asmaha means 'Attiyah'[90] in Arabic and this negus is buried in a place called 'Moukatel Al Alameh' in a province called Tigray and our master Jaafar Bin Abu Taleb, God bless him, met the aforementioned negus in Moutakel Al Alameh which is close to Agame. A big souk takes place there every year to which thousands of Muslims and Christians arrive to visit the tomb of the negus".

---

89 Translated by Omar Khoja and Samia Azem Aidi
90 *Grant or present

The Cordial Relations Between Ethiopians and Muslims

During the Rise of Islam

At the onset of the Islamic message, Qureish pagans caused the Prophet and his esteemed companions a lot of harm. As their transgression increased, the Prophet, peace be upon him, gave his leave for the companions to migrate to Ethiopia. The companions who took this route by themselves without the company of their wives and children were Abdul Rahman bin Awf, Al Zubeir bin Al Awam, Misaab bin Omar and Hatab bin Amr. Others who were accompanied by their families were Othman bin Affan with his wife the daughter of the Prophet and her slave Baraka the Ethiopian, Abdullah bin Abi Salma and his wife Hind, Hashem bin Abi Huzeifa and his wife Sahla, Amer bin Abi Rabiah and his wife Leila Al Adawiya, Abu Sira and his wife Um Kalthoum. They all left Mecca incognito during the month of Rajab in the fifth year of the prophetic message. They sailed on a rented boat off of the Shuba harbor on the Red Sea coast towards the African coast where they landed in Ethiopia. They were well received and welcomed by the negus.

These expatriates returned to their homeland upon learning of the news that the Qureish had embraced the message of the Prophet only to find out that the news was incorrect as they were approaching Mecca. At that point, they decided not to enter Mecca and instead sought refuge with the elders of Qureish. Thereafter, the Qureish pagans intensified their assault on Muslims at which point the Prophet, peace be upon him, permitted those who wanted to emigrate to Ethiopia for a second time to leave and hence many have, including Jaafar bin Abi Taleb, the Prophet's cousin, with his wife Asmaa, Khaled bin Saeed with his wife Fatima, Abdullah bin Jahsh with his brother Oubeid bin Jahsh along with his wife Oum Habiba, Qeiss bin Abdullah with his wife Baraka, Tlaib bin Omar, Amer bin Abi Waqqas, Abdullah bib Massoud, Miqdad bin Amr, Omar bin Othman, Shammas bin Abdul Sharid, Hubar bin Shaaban, Abdullah bin Sufian, Hisham bin Huzeifa, Salma bin Hisham, Abbas bin Abi Rabiaa, Mutab bin Awf, Qudama bin Mazoun, Abdullah bin Mazoun, Hatab bin Al Harith with his wife Bint Al Mujallel, Khattab bin Al Harith with his wife Fakha bint Yassar, Sufian bin Mouammar with his wife Hasna, Khatn bin Huzafa, Abdullah bi Al Harith, Abdullah bin Huzafa, Al Harith bin Al Harith as well as Mouammar bin Al Harith totaling one hundred and thirty two in all with their children and their next of kin.

Upon learning of the Prophet's migration to Madina, Abu Mousa Al Ashaari along with fifty migrants set sail crossing the sea towards Madina but they were faced with waves that threw them off course to the dryland of Ethiopia in the African continent where they met their migrant brethren.

The Qureish pagans were not satisfied with just persecuting Muslims, so they had also sent envoys loaded with gifts ranging from Arabian horses, silk, and much more to the negus and the clergymen urging them to oust Muslim migrants from Ethiopia. The delegation was headed by both Amr bin Al Aas and Oumara bin Al Walid. They met with Ethiopian officials upon their arrival and presented the gifts to their intended recipients and disclosed the objective of the visit. Arabs and Ethiopians were aware of each other's traditions and customs due to the close proximity of both states to one another and the extensive trade traffic across the Red Sea.

Once the delegates met with the negus, they informed him that a citizen of Mecca alleged prophecy and founded a new religion that many people had embraced and some of whom had sought refuge in Ethiopia to ignite sedition and corruption in this land. So, the wise and fair thing to do was to oust these newcomers and deport them to their homeland.

Nevertheless, the negus was a rational, fair and level headed man. He was well cognizant of the migrant's morals, ethics, correctness and peacefulness during their residency in Ethiopia. Out of courtesy to the visiting delegates and the king's shrewd diplomacy, the negus asked Jaafar bin Abi Taleb in front of the visiting Arab delegates to explain why they had to migrate to Ethiopia. Jaafar answered with a declaration of the annulment of paganism they used to practice and the correctness of the religion they had embraced while reciting some verses from the Qu'ran. It is also said that the negus had a huge compassion and affinity for the clear religion of Islam. Jaafar's argument hence refuted the delegates' claims and prompted the negus to return the gifts that they brought along to the delegates and stated that it was neither fair, nor noble harming these neighbors who were full of honesty and dignity. As a result, the delegates left in disappointment.

Right after the defeat of pagans in the Battle of Badr in the month of Ramadan of the second year of the prophetic migration, another delegation, headed by Amr Al Aas and Abdullah bin Rabiaa and loaded with gifts, went to Ethiopia again lobbying to oust the migrants in retaliation. The delegation's campaign failed again and they returned empty handed. The negus personally informed his Muslim guests of the news of the Badr victory over the pagans.

The Correspondence of the Prophet, Peace Be Upon Him, with Negus Ashama[91]

In the sixth year of the prophetic Hijra, the Prophet sent Negus Ashama a correspondence with Amr bin Omaiyah Al Zhamari, one of the esteemed companions, calling negus to Islam and to look after the migrants who were present in Ethiopia. The negus was a really religious man of conviction so kissed the correspondence with great pleasure and believed in it and sent the response with the aforementioned Amr bin Omaiyah.

The Prophet sent another correspondence with the aforementioned Amr bin Omaiyah to the negus on the seventh year and, in that correspondence, he mandated him to perform a wedding between the Prophet and Ramla Oum Habiba, the wife of Abdullah bin Jahsh who died in Ethiopia. So, the negus sent one of his concubines to tell Ramla Oum Habiba that the Prophet wanted to wed her. She accepted and gave the concubine a bracelet and a ring for this news and gave representation to Khaled bin Said bin Al Aas. Negus Ashama invited Jaafar bin Abi Taleb and the emigrant companions to him and they solemnized [the wedlock]. After the solemnization, the negus gave a big reception to the emigrants to show his pleasure and sent four hundred dinars to Oum Habiba as dowry in the name of the Prophet and Oum Habiba, the daughter of Abi Sufian, departed, God bless her, from Ethiopia to Medina. The negus provided her dowry and ordered Sharjil bin Hasana to be in her service. The Prophet asked in his last letter to the negus to send all the emigrants

---

91 The sections that follow have been translated by Amina Sanaa Al Muayad Al Azm

in Ethiopia to Medina. So, the negus rented several boats for them and he sent them to Medina.

The Negus Ashama gifted to the prophet robes, shirts, underwear, shoes, a ring, three arrows, a bottle of musk and jellabiyas[92] and sent these gifts with Oum Habiba. The Prophet gave one of those arrows to Omar bin Khattab and the second to our master Ali bin Abi Taleb and he kept the third for himself.

In the ninth year from Hijra, the Prophet sent presents to the negus, but Ashama died before the arrival of the delegation carrying the gifts. When news of his death reached the Prophet, he gathered all the esteemed companions and they prayed for his soul.

Various

One of the men of Ras Wolde visited me today and informed me of the greetings of the ras and that he apologized for not being able to come today due to feeling unwell and that he would come to visit tomorrow or after tomorrow. Then, in the afternoon, Bulos Ilyas Baghdadi Efendi came to visit me. He has lived in Damascus for twenty years, but came temporarily to Ethiopia to look for gold mines in these regions with the permission of the negus. I learned that he traveled to the regions of Wolloga and Baru and Jangali and Transvaal. He showed me samples of gold ore and told me that the Ethiopians in these regions take the gold from rivers and floodbeds in the simplest way and filter the sand. Since the gold particles come from mountains with rain and floods, Bulos Efendi looked in many places and streams and found gold mines in eleven places in different environments: he first found gold mixed with marble and stone and the second way he found gold in nature was in arteries and veins between rocks on the ground and of twenty-three carat. I have seen the samples and so verified the veracity of his words.

Bulos Efendi used to work in gold mines in Transvaal. He said that the carat of gold there is only sixteen carats. He extracted one thousand dirhams worth of pure gold here from the direction of Baru and Jangali

---

92 *Loose fitting body length garment

despite shortfalls in the amount of required instruments for these works and lack of smelters and presened it to Emperor Menelik as a sample. The people mining gold give a percentage from what they find heads of government. A lot of gold comes to the emperor every year among the goods that are presented to his majesty as tribute. It is now conserved in sacks at the treasury. It is said that the emperor is planning to mint Ethiopian currency from this gold in his name. Bulos Efendi told me a few things about weights. He said that the basis of weight here is rial that weighs nine dirham less two quarters. Each rial is equal to one "nuki" and every six hundred nuki is called "farasalla". The weight used among merchants is farasalla and each one of the frasalla is sixteen and a half kilos.

The gentlewomen walk veiled here and ride mules when they come out of their houses. Men ride [horses, but] not like the European women ride horses. A female slave walks in front of her, [while] she has a cane in her hand and several of the servants behind.

I used to find a taste of salt in the coffee, whether it was with sugar or without sugar, since the day I arrived to Addis Ababa and I did not know the cause of this. I learned today that they put salt in the coffee as an extra treat to guests because salt is very expensive here. It so happened today that the guy who brews the coffee put in our coffee salt, then the servant also put a big quantity of salt, so we could not drink it. When I learned this I forbade the servants who are responsible for making coffee from putting salt in the coffee. The servants were shocked by this request and started apologizing, showing us the necessity of putting salt, insisting on putting salt in the coffee since if they do not put salt in the coffee they are insulting us in their opinion. We could not stop them from doing this except through the owner of the house to whom I explained that we are not used to putting salt in our coffee.

Wednesday, June 22   Addis Ababa VI

Ras Wolde came to visit us in the morning today. He was appointed as our guide by the emperor.[93] There were forty servants and slaves behind him. In Ethiopia, every person is followed by servants and entourage depending on his status and worth. The higher he is designated, the more he adds to his entourage and slaves who follow him when he walks from one place to another even inside the city. I mentioned earlier that thousands of slaves followed Ras Makonen when he came to Addis Ababa where the people do not see the worth of the person who has no servants and slaves. When the person is rich, he brings a servant to his house right away and starts to have him walk from behind all the time and calls him an askari because servants and slaves obey their masters like soldiers obey their officers and leaders.

Two of his slaves entered the hall with him and stood behind him. The rest stayed outside. One of the slaves held his hat and the other waved a fan for the flies. Ras Wolde is very kind. He is past sixty and has gone to

---

93 Translated by Nouwar Muayad Al Azem and Amina Sanaa Al Muayad Al Azm

France and Italy many times on missions for the emperor. This ras built a house in Jerusalem and made it a trust for charities. He told me that he went to Jerusalem and government officials honored him a lot there. He likes the Ottomans and asked me to offer his respect and great reverence to the Sublime Porte of the Sultanate when I am back at the capital. It appears to me from talking to the aforementioned that he is not inattentive [to the fact] that this world is fleeting and the afterworld is more lasting and that is why he has no tendency to adornment and has a tendency to help the miserable and the poor of all people and religions without distinction.

We stayed for a while to have a conversation. Then, he asked permission for himself and his entourage to leave after promising to come again. After he left, Haji Ahmad Efendi, the owner of the residence, came. He was at the customs office to clear some goods and baggage consigned to him.

There are two places for customs. One inside the palace of the negus and the other outside it. The merchandise that passes through Harar on the way to the capital arrives to the customs office outside because normally those goods have been through the Harar customs office that selects nice things and takes them instead of the custom fees. As for the merchandise that comes from the coast directly to Addis Ababa, these enter the customs office inside the palace directly and will be opened there. If the negus finds anything he likes, he keeps it instead of custom fees. The estimated fee for customs is three percent from the merchandise that passes through Harar because the merchandise owner has already paid ten percent in the mentioned city. The fee on directly imported merchandise from the coast to Addis Ababa is thirteen percent. There is not an appraiser for the merchandise at customs, but the fee is taken following a price declaration by the goods' owner and the merchants have to certify those prices and nobody exceeds moderation because if he raises the price, he will pay extra fees for this on top.

We were informed yesterday that the negus is coming to Addis Ababa today. At five o'clock alaturca, the emperor's cortege appeared at a distance of approximately one kilometer and we could see it from our balcony. His Imperial Majesty the Emperor was riding a mule and was accompanied by more than a thousand people, most of them riding mules. One of the servants was holding a big and red umbrella above the head of emperor.

The road leading to the emperor's palace was visible from our house. When the cortege arrived to the palace, the edges of palace crowded with people. Some of them were from his retinue and some had come to greet the negus. After two hours, Monsieur Ilg came to us with greetings from emperor and to ask about our health and comfort and informed us that the duration of mourning for his granddaughter would end on this coming Friday and that our meeting with His Majesty would be delayed to after the mentioned day and the emperor apologized for this delay. We thanked His Imperial Majesty the Emperor and then kept on talking with the aforementioned. During the conversation, I informed him that His Imperial Majesty the Sultan would be pleased if the Muslims were given a piece of land to build a mosque on and another piece of land for a cemetery to bury their deceased in. Monsieur Ilg promised to submit this to His Imperial Majesty the Emperor.

The deceased princess, granddaughter of the emperor, was ten years old and the wife of one of the sons of Tekla Haymanot, the ruler of Gojjam Province. After the death of Tekla, his son was appointed ruler of the aforementioned province. The people used to talk among themselves that the princess died from the evil eye because the people here have great belief in affliction from the evil eye. They are used to eating food under veil and cover, fearing from an affliction of the evil eye.

Buda - Affliction of the Evil Eye -

Tfu Tfu Means the Evil Eye is Warded off

If one of the Ethiopians is afflicted here by hysterics or a light madness they say that the eye has touched them and they call a priest specialized in such sicknesses. When the priest comes near the patient the ailment increases, in other words the patient becomes excited, until his relatives have to hold and calm him. At that time, the priest takes a piece of plant in his hand and puts it on the nose of the patient and the patient smells it and, after a few seconds, says "such and such person cast an [evil] eye on me". He mentions the name of a person and someone is immediately sent to bring this person. They order him to spit on the sick person and he immediately gets better from his illness. They call the person who has cast the eye "buda" and the punishment for the buda is the removal of an eye, although they now settle for beating or scolding him. The wretched buda begs the patient, or his relatives, or the priest for them not to complain about him to the government. In the Hejaz region, there is a sickness, or custom, that is similar to the affliction of the evil eye here which they call "zar".[94] It only happens with women and I do not believe the affliction of the eye which is present in Ethiopia is the same as the zar present in Hejaz because the person suffering from zar does not heal from the affliction with inhalation of plants or something else, but the owner of the house, or husband, or the father, or mother must spend several thousand kuruş to set up a table at her house for women and neighbors. They dance and sing until the zar comes out from the afflicted person's body. There are cases among the Sudani concubines in the capital[95] that resemble the Ethiopian buda. It passed to Istanbul women, [so] when they show their affection towards their children they spit on them lightly and they say "tfu tfu tfu, let my eye not be cast on you" and this custom has passed from Ethiopian slaves.

Monsieur Ilg

All who go to Ethiopia, or read something about it, will definitely hear the name of Monsieur Ilg because this man has a high position at the court of the Negus Menelik who appointed him special advisor and prime minister and minister of foreign affairs. When the emperor was the ruler of the region of Shewa before he became emperor, he wrote to a Swiss merchant in Aden to send him a few Western educated persons who have knowledge and virtue to employ them in his government.[96] A few young people came to Ethiopia after a year, each with a speciality in industry and science and among them was the aforementioned. He had finished

---

94   Haqqi and Rafiq Al Azm's note: Zar is known in Egypt and it is a sickness of devils possessing ignorant women, hurting their relatives and neighbors

95   *Referring to Istanbul

96   *A Swiss coffee trader named Conrad Furrer.

his education at a famous engineering school in Switzerland. Later, these young people had returned to their country except for Monsieur Ilg who stayed there and won an important position at the court of His Imperial Majesty the Negus with maturity, perseverance, diligence, trustworthiness and honesty so that he became his best friend. He now resides in Ethiopia with his family. He sometimes goes to Europe, then returns to Ethiopia. He became rich and an owner of assets and property because of his position and friendship with His Imperial Majesty the Emperor. He served Ethiopia well and was hard working. This diligent man is now fifty years old and knows French, German and Arabic and he can talk in the Amharic language and can read and write it like one of them. He is the one who translates the letters that come from abroad.

The Swiss Monsieur Ilg, Advisor to Emperor Menelik

Thursday, June 23   Addis Ababa VII

In the morning, a visitor named Nagadras[97] Haile Giyorgis, one of the close companions of His Imperial Majesty the Emperor, arrived and there were many slaves and soldiers behind him.[98] He conveyed the greetings of the emperor and told me that His Imperial Majesty had wanted to spend a few more days at the palace named Cennet located in Holeta, but had to return and come to the capital especially to meet the official delegation of the sultan and he sent a messenger to ask the prince of the state of Jimma Jafer, who was here a few days before and then traveled to his work location, to come back to meet us. I asked him to give our thanks to His Imperial Majesty the Emperor, and then he left with his retinue.

On this day, we heard a lot of cries and screaming from the direction of the imperial palace and when we asked what the cause of these noises was, they answered us that the belongings of the late princess who had died were placed on a mule and the mule had arrived to the capital and, for this reason, the grief of the people was immense. I believe they have many citizens who were crying because of sadness and grief and some were paid to cry.

---

97 'Head of merchants' supervising markets, customs, taxes
98 Translated by Samia Azem Aidi

At two o'clock in the afternoon, Monsieur Ilg informed me that His Imperial Majesty ordered a piece of land to be bestowed to build a mosque for Muslims and for another to become their cemetery and that they decided that His Majesty the Emperor would meet the delegation of the sultan on the coming Saturday on an official basis. I was very pleased to hear about the bestowal of the land that is necessary to build the mosque and cemetery. So, I requested Monsieur Ilg to extend my thanks to His Majesty the Emperor and we decided to name the mosque Hamidiye.

After Monsieur Ilg departed, I went out to the balcony like always, and I looked upon the marketplace that was very crowded with people, with men and women. The notables among them were wearing azar[99] so that men looked like women. When you look upon them you cannot distinguish between a man and a woman because they cover their faces up to their eye like a woman, but one will recognize women by a servant walking in front of a mule and she will be holding a cane. One also recognizes the gentlefolk by the European made socks they wear without shoes. The women here wear socks not to protect against the cold, but as adornment. Sometimes a woman also mounts a mule with her husband seated in front or behind her. One will frequently see a wife, husband, and their child on one mule. Some Ethiopians came while I was writing these lines and requested from one of the servants of Ahmad Efendi a sample of glass. I learned from him that glass panels are of the window type that are sold for a kuruş in Istanbul and for one riyal here. A drinking glass is also not more than a kuruş, but is sold here for a riyal. The reason for this dearness is because fragile goods often cannot be brought from the coast to Addis Ababa except after losing three fourths or four fifths of the goods because muleteers do not pay attention to the boxes when they unload and load them and however much you explain or tell them of the necessity for care when unloading and loading, they will not change their way of loading. During our journey, I saw muleteers were careless in loading because each day they were loading our chests upside down and every time I spoke to them in this regard they told me "ishi ishi", but they still do as they please. Other goods are also expensive here. A canister of gas is equivalent to

---

99   *Broadcloth

eight to nine riyals and a sugar container is one riyal. In the rainy season, prices will go up a lot if the arrival of caravans is late from the coast. The people here drink coffee with honey and so have no need for sugar in this instance. They do not need European goods. We sometimes used honey for dessert when we were on the road before and found it to be delicious. I mentioned before that honey in these regions is abundant and very cheap. In the Jimma Jaffar district, there is a type of bee that makes nests under the ground and nobody can know its place except for a small hole through which the bees enter and exit. They take out a lot of honey from this hole, but the taste is not like the taste of the honey made by bees making honey from trees.

The Language of the Ethiopians[100]

The current Language of the Ethiopians is the original Ethiopian language, also called the Geʿez language. This language is from Semitic languages like Arabic, Hebrew and Syriac. The mentioned language entered Ethiopia through Tigray and Massawa by people who emigrated in ancient times from Yemen. From there, it spread inland until it became the most common language. Throughout generations, changes occurred to it as incurred by any language due to the incorporation of the nations next to them. Therefore, foreign words and commercial Greek expressions came into it and it branched into many languages, with each called in the name of the Ethiopian nations based upon the different regions where they lived. The most famous languages are Amharic, Tigray, Gondar, and the language of Jimma Abba Jaffar, Somalia, Shewa, Dangala, Adal, and Harar.

Ethiopia consists of autonomous governments with its internal directorates under the leadership of the empire that is mostly in the hands of the strongest prince of the provincial governors, and the seat of the prince is considered the capital of the empire that will be relocated from government to government and from region to region. The Geʿez language mentioned before was the official language of the country as well as the religious language when the leadership was in the hands of

---

100   Translated by Hassana Almuayad Al Azem

Tigray governors, and when the king's capital moved to the southwest, the Amharic language became the official language of Ethiopia and the Geʿez language remained the religious, scientific, and the historical language, as it were. The people of Massawa and its vicinity and the people of Tigray used the language of Geʿez in their writing and it is akin to the classical Arabic "Fusha's" relation with regards to the colloquial Arabic languages spoken by the people in Yemen, Hijaz, Syria and Egypt that differ in dialect when spoken, but not in writing. It is said that the attacks of the Galla tribes and their continuous raids on Ethiopia and the Muslims' conquest and takeover are among the reasons that left the Geʿez language and the Amharic language almost neglected. Even if it has completely changed due to the infiltration of foreign languages from external peoples and tribes, it is still written with Geʿez language letters. The letters of this language look like Himyarite letters. It is known that the Himyarite language is the language of the people of ancient Yemen, and this confirms the opinion that says the entrance of the Geʿez language to Ethiopia came along with the entry of Yemeni immigrants, as well as the lineage of some Yemeni tribes to "Koch", to whom the Ethiopians are affiliated with in the Torah, confirms their linguistic interrelation with the Yemenis. The Geʿez language was written like in Arabic from right to left before, but the Ethiopians imitated the Westerners and wrote it from left to right. As for the numbers, they adopted them from Greek and modified it to properly correspond to their language. Let us bring some examples from each of the Geʿez and Amharic languages to compare with Arabic.

Arabic	Geʿez	Amharic	English	
ANA	ANA	ANAHU	I	
ANTA	ANTA	ANTA	YOU	(Male)
ANTY	ANTY	ANTY	YOU	(Female)
ANTUM	ANTUM	ALANTA	YOU	(Plural)

When contemplating the people's conversation, a lot of Arabic words are heard in the Ethiopians' languages, and here is another example from their prayers. When the Ethiopians invoke a recognized prayer[101] by the

---

101 *Lord's prayer

Christians, we hear them praying in the Arabic language. Note that the letter (B) in the Geʿez language is pronounced like the letter (V) of the French.

Arabic	Geʿez
Abuna al'lathy	Avunatha
Belsamawat	Bis'smyat
Yatakadasu Ismak	Yatakadasu Ismak
Kama Bis'sama	Bikama Bis'smay
Kama Huwa Alard	Kay Huwa Yahder
Egh'fer Lana Sayi'atina	Hibdj Lana Aysana

Certain European linguists studied Amharic and the Geʿez languages and they wrote many books. The most famous authors in Latin were Rudowive from Frankfurt, and in English Isenberg from London, and in French Le Mondon from Paris, and in Italian La Guidi from Rome, and in German Praetorius from Halle.

Besides these, there are other books on Ethiopian languages written by Dilmann and Frans. The French Geographical Society printed a large book in four volumes written by Konig that contains clarification regarding the Ethiopian languages.

Friday, June 24   Addis Ababa VIII

Monsieur Ilg paid me a visit this morning and, after he conveyed the greetings of the emperor, he explained to me the way the reception was going to be celebrated the following day.[102]

While sitting in the balcony today, I could not but notice how the Amharis wore their head covers. The notables wore a hat, while the rest did not. Some left their hair as it was, while others shaved all of it. I have seen some who shaved their hair from the middle and left it on the sides, as if wearing a hat. Some wore a small turban on top of their heads, while others wrapped their head with a piece of tape called "qurdala".

Some of our chests needed to be repaired, and so we found fittings to wrap these chests with cowhide. We already had hide from cows butchered by a Muslim. The Christian carpenter refused to use this hide, or even touch it. This strange bigotry in [Addis A]baba, despite the fact that Christians and Muslims in Ethiopia lived together in peace and harmony, where religious conflicts did not take place, took me by surprise.

---

102   Translated by Hassana Almuayad Al-Azem and Ghaith Almuayad Al-Azem

That afternoon a man who served one of the ras came by and asked how we were doing and conveyed greetings from his ras. In the evening, the pantryman of the negus paid me a visit as well as the head of the butlers who goes by the name of Iseslaqi Mashasha. The duties of this man did not share resemblance to the rest of the butlers so that on occasion he was charged with feeding the negus with his own hands. I have seen several times the servants of some of the ras bringing a glass of water with their hands to the mouth of their ras and after his master quenched his thirst he would wipe his mouth with the side of his gown taking into account that I have not seen the servants feeding their ras or the emperor with their own hands, but I heard that story from a few men of the emperor's entourage.

Our servant called Juma'a understood little Arabic and he was very much inclined to learn it so that you would find him repeating everything that had been said in front of him. So, for instance, if one of us ordered some water he would not bring it until he repeated what had been said by the letter, and if you laughed in front of him he would also laugh, and if you frowned he would frown as well. If by chance you have some guests, and for some reason you called upon him to run some errand and you asked him to wait for a while, he will turn his back on you and your guests and stand still in the middle of the room like a statue. That is because he is too shy to stand facing you.

The weather that day was cold, so we had to start a fire in our room for warmth. Juma'a came with the fire within the teak and placed it on top of the carpet without placing anything underneath it to prevent the fire from reaching the carpet. One of my visitors saw that and talked to him in Arabic saying "what have you done Juma'a, you are going to burn the carpet" and cursed him in colloquial Arabic "may your house be in ruins". Juma'a did not hesitate in repeating the last sentence. So, we all burst into laughter and when Juma'a saw us, he started staring at us and laughing with us.

It is no secret that we are Istanbul city dwellers where winter is extremely cold. However, in spite of that and in the middle of June, we had to put on the fire to heat our room in Addis Ababa, situated in Africa, because the city is situated at a very high altitude and it is the rainy season.

Military Service in Ethiopia

Besides the special troops of the emperor, each ras supports a quantity of soldiers proportionate to the size and wealth of the region and state that he rules so that their aggregation makes up the Ethiopian army. Besides these active soldiers, freehold lands such as villages, farms are required to give a sufficient quantity of redif[103] proportionate to their size and wealth without weapons, but with each individual bringing an animal, a mule or horse, and provisions and food for a month. The redif soldiers are frequently from among those that had been in active service. The government arms them when they join the army. Freehold owners equip them. They send them to service in return for a fee. The regular soldiers of Ethiopia who are always under arms are about two hundred thousand [and] the redif who join the army during campaign are not less than two hundred thousand, either. Military service is not compulsory [and] they enter military service voluntarily given the people's fundamentally abundant tendency and fondness for gunslinging, warfare and combat. Most of the weapons of the regular army are the French Garra, Russian Berdan rifles and besides these they gird curved swords on their waist and right side. Although ammunition is being brought from Europe, the establishment of a cartridge factory is being recommended in Addis Ababa.

They also have weapons like spears, shields, and short spears. Since Ethiopian soldiers are scattered in the regions or states they belong to at present, each state provides for its own soldiers locally. Military movements occur very quickly since there exist provisions and food and arms depots in various places in Ethiopia for periods of campaign.

The speed of mobilization against the Italians in the year one thousand eight hundred and ninety-five had earned the respect of European military circles. The commander-in-chief during campaign is His Imperial Majesty the Emperor and while each ras commands his own division, the commander-in-chief determines the service he will render. There is also a cascade of military ranks below ras and each rank holder commands some number of soldiers. The military ranks after ras are referred to as dejazmach, fitaurari,

---

103 Reserve soldiers

qenazmach, grazmach, balambaras, shaleqa, metoaleqa, and asiraleqa.[104] The importance of the high officials of the army is commensurate with the number of soldiers they command. Although qenazmach is grander than grazmach, sometimes it so happens that a grazmach of the emperor commands more soldiers than the qenazmach of such and such ras and, in this case, his importance is superior to the other.

During combat, the Ethiopian army is on a battle formation. Just as arrangement principles such as right flank, left flank, center, vanguard, rearguard are abided by, they also excessively abide by the arrangement of the headquarters. The tent of the commander-in-chief is the principal one and once the mentioned tent is pitched, they know where and in which direction, at what distance they will pitch the tents of the ras, dejazmach, and other commanders and officers. There is never any disarray. As an example, let me describe the military camp of the Ethiopians during the Battle of Adowa with Italians:

During the Battle of Adowa, the emperor's military camp was arranged in three concentric circles. Namely: in the middlemost, in other words, on the right side of the center of the first circle were the tents of the empress and, on the left side, the emperor's, with the pantries, kitchens, stables, servants and grooms behind these tents, while the perimeter of the circle consisted of the special soldiers of the emperor.

The quarters of Ras Mikael and Ras Welle were between the first circle and the second circle, towards the front. Afa Negus Abon (the spiritual leader) and dejazmach were behind Ras Mikael and two dejazmachs' camps were behind Ras Welle's. Their soldiers constituted the perimeter of the second circle.

Between the second and third circle, in the front, were the right and left fitauraris (vanguard commanders of which there were two arranged in this battle), two qenazmach or right flank commanders were on the right side, two grazmach or left flank commanders were on the left side and rearguard commander Negus Tekla Haymanot's quarters were found at the very back and their soldiers constituted the outer circle of soldiers.

---

104 *The original text refers to dejazmach, fitaurari, qinazmach, garasmach, balambras, ashalaqa, mentualaqa, shalaqa

When the army moved as a whole, it followed the order shown in the second figure. The battalions do not change their location when it is necessary to change direction to turn back, right, or left and the vanguard becomes the rearguard on turning back, the rearguard becomes the vanguard. On changing direction to the right, the right flank becomes vanguard. The left flank becomes rearguard. If the roads are narrow, rugged and the soldiers are sometimes forced to walk scattered and out of order, everyone returns to their position upon passing to suitable terrain and the general position is preserved. Everyone stays in the battalion he is a member of, near the superior they are attached to.

Although the Ethiopian people are not generally burly, very strong men, since they are highly tolerant to hardship and fatigue, their soldier deservedly possesses this trait that is one of the most important traits required for military service. After climbing hills, mountains without eating, drinking from morning until evening, they attack the enemy with great enthusiasm and bravery. They are superior to the European soldier since they are light and fast due to their frugality, patience, barefoot walk.

At times when I tired from sitting on the mule and slipped and fell while walking with boots on some descents, ascents on the road, our servants used to recommend I take off my shoes and walk barefoot like them and would ask how I could walk with shoes.

Just as Ethiopian soldiers attack the enemy with courage, they also do not hesitate to attack a tiger to attain the honor of wearing the hides of the wild animals they kill on their shoulders, their manes on their head.

Just as the people in Ethiopia join the military to attain distinction and honor, distinction and superiority among comrades in arms comes with courage and bravery.

The Italian government had employed a lot of soldiers from the native Ethiopians in Eritrea and those who have been in action and combat with them for a long time praise and laud [them] a lot. When some number of volunteer soldiers is desired, many more aspirants than the number demanded are found. Consequently, these aspirants are made to run a distance of sixty, seventy kilometers within a set few hours with rapid walk, quick march under the supervision of an officer on horseback. Those who go fastest, tire least are separated. The Ethiopian soldier is obedient to and fond of his superiors, loyal to his service and reliable, brave, abstemious and untiring. He preserves order and regularity during training. They have the aptitude for training. The Ethiopian soldier does not like to stay in one place too much. He wants to see action, change of location, new places, prefers climbing mountains to resting and repose, in other words, motion and activity to calm, inherently, and they always preserve their enthusiasm, merriness and cheer. When he sets out on the road, he does not ask where he will go, how much distance he will cover, where he will camp in the evening. He does not stay on the road to rest with various excuses without permission from his superior. He lives on what he finds. He quite likes his weapon. He does not drop it from his hand. Hugging his rifle with his hands, legs, he sleeps with the weapon in his embrace at night. He is always alert, vigilant during movement. His ears hear very well. His eyes are used to seeing far and he picks up the smell from his surroundings quickly. If a soldier gets sick during travel, someone accompanies him. He leaves him in a village or hut. After he is better, he joins his battalion. Upon arrival to a camp location, an Ethiopian soldier begins to build his officers' hut, or pitch his tent, secure his comfort before everything else. They think of themselves after that. If the superior dozes off, one of the soldiers will chase away the flies over him with the branch of a tree, without making him aware. He takes care to try to preserve his comfort. Our soldiers would see to this service when we rested on the road at daytime. In particular, if shrubs, twigs, tree branches came ahead of us, they would either hold it with their hands, or ripping it, they threw it away.

After seeing to his camp duties, the Ethiopian soldier spends some time on entertainment. He is up on his feet early in the morning, fresh, agile, and strong. I have not forgotten at all the diligence, tirelessness of Abu Bakr, one of our soldiers, his rush to all service with great enthusiasm and desire, playing, leaping, and singing folk songs. The Ethiopian soldier likes to hunt a lot. However, he does not like to fire a round in futility. In his mind, a cartridge is the most desirable gift. The Ethiopian soldier does not even grimace, show traces of pain, let alone say "mercy!" when struck on the butt while being punished. Once an Ethiopian soldier in the Italy volunteers had been insulted by his friends so much for screaming while being caned as punishment that he had been forced to resign from his duty.

The perseverance and effort that the Ethiopian soldier will show during battle is proportionate with the bravery and valor of his commanders. So long as their commander perseveres, his soldier will persevere until death. Before battle, the commanders deliver a war ballad or a military speech as a product of their inspiration at that moment. He praises and lauds himself since this will set an example to the soldiers. Here are some examples of the speeches that the commanders deliver before the soldiers enter the battlefield:

The Speech Delivered by Dejaz Debeb One Day Before Fighting the Tigrayans [105]

"O soldiers: Tomorrow you shall know what the man, [whom] you have been serving until today, will be remembered for. Tomorrow I am going to fight until my enemy is defeated or die. Therefore, watch me at all times, and if you see me hesitating... What did I just say? How did I utter the word (hesitation) No! I said it wrong. What I wish to say is that whoever sees a vein trembling upon my face, he may leave me and abandon my service and whoever sees me in retreat, he may pierce my body with his spear and take vengeance on me".

The fact of the matter is that this commander fought valiantly the next day and showed immense courage and braveness.

And This is Another Speech

"I am the one who delivers deadly spear thrusts, I am the one who impales many men with the spear. My name is Kasassa. I am the son of Jababa Fanfel. I am the one whose neck was struck by a bullet that has taken the place of mateb (a blue ribbon that they put around their necks with the cross hanging on their chest). I am the lion and the son of the lion. I am the one who conquered the Alfalala while riding my horse Fanzo. I am the one who killed many Tigrayans with the sword and conquered the Amharans with a rifle. I am the one who threw the Alnaalna with his own hands in the deepest of the abysses. Yes, I am the son of Jababa Fanfel. Yesterday, I was balambaras and today I became a dejazmach, and tomorrow I shall be a ras. I fear no one. Has anyone seen me running

---

105   Translated by Hassana Almuayad Al-Azem and Ghaith Almuayad Al-Azem

away? Can anyone take my shield from me? Should he exist, then let him appear before me".

The Ethiopian soldier has a dissatisfactory custom during battle. They cut the lower genitals of their captives with the goal of cutting, diminishing the posterity of the enemy. The valiant soldier brings glans to his superior as though bringing a head. Saying "I killed men", he throws in front of his superior however many men's glans there are. During a sword-to-sword duel, Ethiopians pay most attention and care to cut that part of their enemy. Most of the Italian prisoners who fell in the hands of the Ethiopians went back home without genitals. While Emperor Menelik has given plenty of orders to discourage this custom, he has not completely succeeded because those who kill an enemy, take an enemy captive hang their glans as signs of victory on their hut and tent doors and hang it on the chest of a horse or mule like an ornament and sign of pride while walking on the road. Some of them used to stuff it with sand to enlarge and hang it wherever he wished.

The tents of Ethiopian soldiers are white, while those of the commanders and high officials are in various colors. Only the emperor's tent is red. The red tent is reserved for His Imperial Majesty the Emperor. Due to this, the red tent is adopted as the basis for the arrangement of the military camp during campaign. In addition, the door of the tent faces whatever direction the army will move to on the next day. And the direction of departure becomes known. This situation is not just prevalent in the military and even the caravans that we come across on the road abide by this principle. Since we always open the doors of the tents towards the opposite of the direction of the wind, it is contrary to the direction we are going most of the time. That is why our muleteers, servants would wonder, "We do not know the place we are going. Or else, are we turning back?"

I saw a four hundred strong battalion of soldiers of His Imperial Majesty the Emperor in Addis Ababa, arranged from black slaves based on the new method. They are being trained and drilled by the French Count Laguie Bourger. They also have a musical band based on the European style. Their uniforms consist of pants, a jacket, and a red cap similar to a fez. They have preserved the general rule of the country, in other words, the custom of being barefooted.

Ethiopian Army Formation During Battle

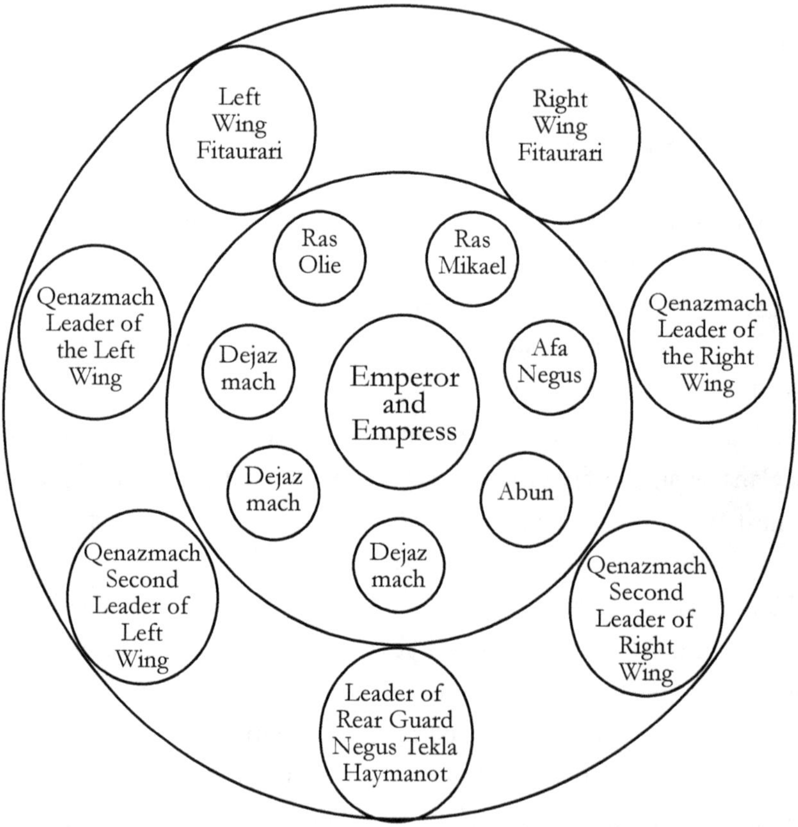

- Emperor and Empress
- Ras Olie
- Ras Mikael
- Dejazmach
- Dejazmach
- Dejazmach
- Afa Negus
- Abun
- Left Wing Fitaurari
- Right Wing Fitaurari
- Qenazmach Leader of the Left Wing
- Qenazmach Leader of the Right Wing
- Qenazmach Second Leader of Left Wing
- Qenazmach Second Leader of Right Wing
- Leader of Rear Guard Negus Tekla Haymanot

Ethiopian Army Formation During Movement

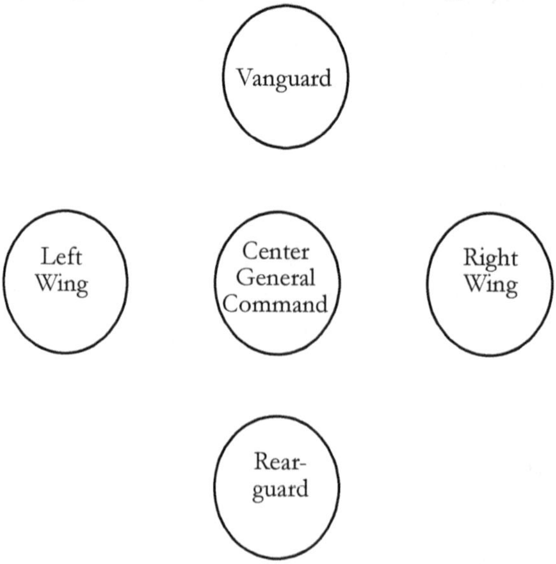

- Vanguard
- Left Wing
- Center General Command
- Right Wing
- Rear-guard

A Warrior from the Imperial Guard[1]

---

1 The Arabic text uses the term 'royal entourage'

Saturday, June 25   Addis Ababa IX

Audience with His Imperial Majesty the Emperor • Visit to the ambassadors, ras • Wezru Desta

We wore our grand uniforms today on waking up in the morning because it was the appointed day for the audience with His Imperial Majesty the Emperor. We sent the imperial gifts with our servants and an accompanying guide, whom Monsieur Ilg added, to the imperial palace. I went out to the balcony. We waited for the delegation that would come to get us. There is a lot of activity in the city, crowds are visible everywhere. Dressed in their grand uniforms and riding on muleback, the ras, dejazmachs and so on are going in droves to the imperial palace with hundreds of their soldiers and slave servants. Some soldiers are lining up on the roads. One should see the variety of uniforms here. The best weapons, spears, short spears and shields of the high officials are going ahead of them in the hands of their slaves. With their soldiers beside them, some commanders had worn tiger manes like a calpac. Their tails are swinging. The soldier's attire is really majestic and awe inspiring. A novice who sees them suddenly will believe them to be half-man, half-tiger.

As we were watching those going to the imperial palace, a large throng from these, in other words about a thousand soldiers, came towards our residence. Then, a delegation composed of Monsieur Ilg, Ras Wolde,

Imperial Palace Chamberlain Azaj Kazu, the Chamberlain of the Empress Fitaurari Irdi and other persons came with their grand uniforms and said that they were assigned to accompany our humble delegation. It was almost three o'clock. We mounted the animals. With a band consisting of clarions longer than flutes as well as pipes that I did not know being played ahead of us, we set out towards the imperial palace with soldiers in the front, to our right, and left.

The roads, roofs, balconies are full of people. They are greeting from everywhere. When we reached the palace, we found it very crowded there, too, with soldiers, officials, and spectators. Some officials were trying to open the way with the sticks in their hands, trying to scatter the people. We entered the palace in a throng through the main gate. We found ourselves in a square such that after this square, which was surrounded by a wall all around, we entered a second square by passing through the gate of another wall. These squares were full of soldiers. A cannon battery is waiting at attention in the second square. I found myself in front of a quite large mirror; this is the grand imperial hall that they refer to as Adarash. While going through its door, His Imperial Majesty the Emperor is visible right at the end of the hall on a big chair and around a hundred of the palace household are seen behind him and on the sides.

The cannons started firing as soon as our humble delegation entered the hall. His Imperial Majesty the Emperor stood up. When I arrived beside him, he stood up again.

After I made a statement regarding my assignment, the aforementioned His Imperial Majesty received the imperial letter and the medal of honor respectfully and expressed his sincere thanks to His Imperial Majesty, the supreme sovereign and showing me a chair prepared in front of him, he made me sit. After first enquiring about the health and welfare of the protector His Imperial Majesty the Padishah and asking about welfare and safety in the imperial countries[106], he asked how the journey had passed. He enquired after us along the lines of whether we had been uncomfortable or not. Later, when I handed over the imperial gifts, he reviewed these one by one, taking each of them in his hand, he declared his satisfaction

---

106 *A reference to the Ottoman Empire

and delight and again declared he was grateful and pleased because His Imperial Majesty the Padishah had remembered him in this way.

All of the officials around the emperor were standing up fully and only three persons were sitting to his right and these were Ras Giorgis, Ras Tesma[107] and Ras Makonen. Monsieur Ilg, who was translating, presented them and hands were shaken with them, too. At this moment, I thanked Ras Makonen for the treatment I received at his residence in Harar. This audience lasted about half an hour. Various subjects were discussed with His Imperial Majesty the Emperor.

His Imperial Majesty the Emperor had worn his official uniform, put on his medals, and his ceremonial crown was right next to him. His head was wrapped with a white keffiyeh. He always wears this, even under a hat. He is sitting cross-legged, leaning with his hands on the pillows beside him. The imperial throne is one and a half times the size of a big bed frame and one climbs on it with a step. Gilded, made from intricate wood, its mat, pillows are embroidered nicely.

When a reception is given to high officials and commanders at the imperial palace, the guests are in clusters around trays. The servants enter into this hall from the outside with the food. They distribute the food with trays. Their principal dish is raw meat. Hundreds of cattle are cut outside, skinned, and their pieces are put on the trays while still hot, fresh. After cutting the piece that they want in the shape of a fillet, lengthwise, everyone holds it with one hand, dips it into red pepper, puts it into his mouth. After biting it, he cuts the piece of the meat that is outside the mouth with a huge dagger or huge knife. In this way, they eat their fill. The Europeans are bewildered when Ethiopians eat in this manner.

The dining hall is eighty arşın[108] long, sixty arşın wide and its ceiling is high in that proportion. There are big posts in two rows from the floor to the ceiling at twenty arşın intervals to support its roof. The building is from stone, the posts of the roof are from wood and it is covered with galvanized, corrugated sheets. The building is solid and strong and constructed modernly.

---

107 *Ras Tessema Nadew

108 *1 arşın = 68 centimeters

Upon the recommendation for us to come to the palace again tomorrow, we parted from there. We returned to our residence with the same persons, same soldiers, and same ceremony. After offering coffee and so on at our residence to these persons, everyone retreated to their places.

We visited the ambassadors in the afternoon, riding mules, with our soldiers and servants bringing weapons together in the front and behind us, based on the country's customs. England, France, Russia, Italy each has an embassy here. The embassies are quite far from each other and located on various hills and only the French embassy and England's have a little proximity to each other. Since there are no macadam and regular roads here yet, transportation is difficult. There is no coming and going to each other at night since there are no carriages. The ambassadors can only meet with each other at daytime. Anyway, it is a frequent occurrence for animals to have their foot slip and fall in rainy weather. [This is] because the surface is rugged, with ascents and descents, and very slippery.

The current embassy residences consist of a ground floor each. Their interiors are very tidy and clean. The English Ambassador Monsieur Harrington[109] has had the embassy built in a quite nice manner, namely: he has connected numerous huts like native huts to each other with corridors and the interior has become quite nice. He had brought craftsmen for the furniture from abroad and had them built on site.

The grand ras had not returned when I stopped by their residences. They were still at the imperial palace. We also went to the residence of Afa Negus. The aforementioned was at a place named Holeta for some business. As we were about to leave a card and return, his spouse declared that she would receive us. They took us to the harem section[110]. A quite beautiful, quite polite, intelligent woman of about forty years age at most, with cheer streaming out of her eyes, appeared in front of us. She had twenty, thirty slave female slaves around her. The spouse of Afa Negus, declaring her name as Wezru Desta, received us with great courtesy. I spoke with the aforementioned through our guide Haji Ahmad Efendi. She had such articulation and manner of expression, such polite sentences

---

109 *Sir John Lane Harrington
110 *Women's quarters

and wise words that she leaves a person in admiration. The most educated European ladies can only say as much. The aforementioned offered us honey sherbets, birz. Since a heavy downpour started while we were there, she did not let us leave until the rain stopped. She was with a headscarf in front of us, not uncovered. She asked for her pitcher to drink to our health. They brought a small one hundred dirhem[111] pitcher, she drank from that. Wezrus, in other words ladies, do not drink from glasses here. They drink directly from the pitcher. Each wezru has a nice, golden gilded, decorated little pitcher reserved for her.

When we returned to our residence they said that Ras Makonen and, on behalf of the emperor, Monsieur Ilg had come to our residence in our absence. His Imperial Majesty the Emperor had declared in the letter that Monsieur Ilg left that he would receive us in private again, tomorrow, Sunday at eight alafranga time.

Besides the durgu coming every day on behalf of His Imperial Majesty the Emperor, sheep, chickens, tej pitchers, oil jars, egg baskets came today as durgu on behalf of Her Imperial Majesty the Empress and, moreover, a palace chamberlain had come to communicate the greetings of the aforementioned, too.

Here I should describe His Majesty the Emperor a little and what I learned about him:

His Imperial Majesty Emperor Menelik

His Imperial Majesty Menelik is a tall, distinguished, modest, dignified man, with a pleasant countenance. He is now sixty years of age, active, and tends to know everything. Through this inclination, he has obtained a command of various things and a lot of knowledge, crafts such as disassembling a clock and assembling it again and laid open a number of rifles and cannons so that these matters became very easy for him. His intelligence and cunning is very high. He treats all his subjects with care equally and rules among them fairly and wishes for their welfare. All the people, Muslims and Christians, like him a lot because of this and they show their gratitude.

---

111 *1 dirhem = 3.2 grams

His Majesty has an immense passion towards the science of architecture and we can say he is the greatest architect in Ethiopia. He draws by hand most of the improvised drawings and describes to those who shall execute the work how to proceed according to these drawings, eliciting the amazement of Europeans and their admiration. He has learned from some doctors and pharmacists how to mix some medicine.

There are craftsmen, engineers and workers in his palace to work on handiworks and engineering. He talks with each of these people about their own craft and personally witnesses the tasks that they do and asks about things he does not understand. He asks them to make some things in front of him.

From what I heard in this regard, he liked the shoes of Europeans who used to visit him while he was the king of the Shewa region. He asked one of the engineers to make shoes in front of him so that he would see how they are made. The engineer answered him apologetically saying that he never made shoes, but this answer was not satisfactory in the eye of Menelik and he insisted on his demand. So, the engineer was obliged to execute the king's order. He started preparing what was needed to make shoes and recommended making a wooden mold. He took out parts from an old shoe to see how it was fixed, then brought the necessary leather and started working on making the shoes in front of Menelik until he made shoes from this leather. The wish of the king was met in this way and he learned how shoes were made. He once ordered an engineer to make him a new style cartridge-firing rifle. He knows that producing these things in Europe takes less effort and less cost, but he asked that it should be done in front of him and in his country to be convinced of the possibility of doing it in his country and to be sure of its metal and wood.

Europeans admit that Menelik has political and military skills as he was commander-in-chief for all Ethiopian army movements during the war with the Italians. He was personally supervising the locations where the army would stay and he also used to supervise the bases before the battle and arrange his army according to inspection and review.

His father, Haile Melekot, was the King of Shewa and his grandfather was the third King of Shewa. When the negus was previously Tewodros, he fought Haile Melekot, father of the current negus. He then brought his son to Magdala and had his daughter marry him and ordered him to stay there.

When the English approached Magdala in the year one thousand eight hundred and sixty-seven, Menelik escaped and crossed difficult valleys and mountains, passing them by himself, and followed several thousand of his father's men, his companions, people, and tribe who were waiting for him. They greeted him with the best welcome and were happy with his arrival. He walked from there with his men, all of whom were Muslims, and attacked Ato Bazaba, ruler of the region of Shewa and the supporter of Tewodros, who lost. He invaded the region of Shewa and sat on the throne of his ancestors and from that date the germ of civil war ended in the region of Shewa and this region became the largest and strongest part of the Ethiopian kingdom from that day. When Dejaz Kasa, ruler of Tigray, became emperor of Ethiopia with the name of Yohannes, rivalry started between him and Menelik, but the latter hated to spill blood and he shut the door on all civil conflict and before he became the subject of Yohannes his victory was not difficult and when Yohannes was killed at the Battle of Qallabat, all Ethiopian princes and ras accepted the emperorship of Menelik. His influence and power increased, then he celebrated his coronation.

After the Battle of Adowa, he sent correspondences to the kings of great powers in Europe.

The first wife of His Imperial Majesty Menelik had passed away, so he married Her Majesty Taytu, the current empress, in the year one thousand eight hundred and eighty-seven and they celebrated her coronation as Empress of Ethiopia in the year one thousand eight hundred and eighty-nine after coronation celebrations for two days.

The One Who Wards Off Misfortunes and Hardships [112]

There is a very important position at the court of the negus called "Lika Makwas". The person nominated for this post must look exactly like

---

112   The two sections that follow have been translated by Sonia Muayad Al Azm

the emperor in every respect including in body build and shape. The holder of this position is to wear what the emperor wears and pins his medals. In general, the most important condition is that there is no difference between him and the emperor. Sometimes, the position is divided between two people resembling the negus. The "Lika Makwas" always stands, during wars and travels, near the emperor and under his umbrella and no one, not even the soldiers, can distinguish between the real emperor from the imposter. In this way, the emperor is able to leave his look alike in his tent and under his umbrella at his official headquarters in time of war, to wander wherever he pleases without being exposed to any harm or least danger, away from enemy bombs and bullets, while the "Lika Makwas" is always exposed to peril instead of the emperor - that is why I called him the one who wards off misfortune.

Her Majesty the Empress Taytu

Her Majesty the Empress Taytu is from a highly distinguished family from Tigray Province and enjoys great influence and respect in the Ethiopian regions for her intelligence, acumen, ability to endure hardships and her wisdom. Even her husband depends on her in many state affairs and listens to her point of view and takes her with him to war.

The empress spends her time inside the harem and rarely appears in public, except during the travels and wars of the negus, when she would be with him. The foreigners claim she is neither fond of Europeans, nor likes them and the reason for this hatred could be due to British and Italian interference in Ethiopian affairs. All the priests in the Ethiopian regions are from the faction of the empress. It is rumored that the empress is very strict in her dealings, unlike the emperor who is renowned for his leniency. Hence, people are more fearful of her than of the negus. Rumor has it that the negus was inclined to pardon the nationals, who were taken prisoner during the war with the Italians, from the punishment of amputation of the leg and the hands, but when he saw her insist on implementing the law of the land on these unfortunate prisoners, he was compelled to enforce it.

The empress has her own private quarters with many servants and a large retinue. During the war with the Italians, she had her retinues and division of guards of fifteen thousand under tents. This army was commanded directly by her and the commanders received their orders straight from her. The Italian officers who were in the Ethiopian wars, reported that Taytu managed military movements of her army as well as any of the greatest commanders who led highly skilled armies in the art of war. Her Majesty was very keen on protecting Ethiopia's honor and reputation. She played a major role in bringing the country up to its present civilized state with her unwavering diligence. She was also the only cause for the war with the Italians and here is the proof:

There is a treaty between Italy and Ethiopia known as the Ucciale Treaty composed of twenty articles that show the borders of the two countries and determine the formal transactions between them. Among the articles of this treaty is article seventeen which engendered a lot of gossip and frequent back and forth exchanges. The following is a translation of the contents of this article from the Italian copy:

"The Emperor of Ethiopia agrees that Ethiopia's communications with the rest of the governments and countries be mediated by Italy".

As for the Amharic copy, the aforementioned article states, "For the negus to benefit from the mediation of Italy", instead of the term, "agrees"; and the difference between the first sentence and the second is very great. So, His Majesty Menelik was compelled to protest against the term used in the aforementioned article. So, Italy sent Count Antonelli to Shewa to resolve this matter. Menelik requested the modification of this article, so as not to leave any scope for humiliating him among European countries. Hence, serious deliberations over this matter got underway. When the Italian delegate completed the modified draft, he presented it to the emperor who did not find anything to adjust or modify again. Governors Makonen, Mengesha and Afa Negus also agreed on how the new amendment was drawn up, but Empress Taytu's opposition to the draft amendment changed the situation.

As Count Antonelli was invited to the palace, he sat after dinner with the emperor and empress deliberating on the modification to the contested article. The empress said to the count that the Italian government had revealed the content of the seventeenth article of the treaty to European countries, [and that] "we also have knowledge of this article as stated in the Amharic copy in which, the aforementioned article has a meaning other than the meaning stated in the Italian version, and we have our honor to uphold". The count replied that he had put another phrase to clarify the aforementioned article. She replied, "Yes, you want to put in a term indicating that Ethiopia is subordinate to you and this will never be. Ethiopia does not accept the protection of anyone", Count Antonelli was affected by this speech and he replied, "Then, Her Majesty the Empress should put forward this article", and Taytu replied, "Yes, that will be". After this short exchange, every one went on his way.

After a few days, Count Antonelli suggested to the emperor to write an amenable placid letter to the King of Italy regarding the contested article, but the emperor refused, due to the objections of the empress and two short articles were sent to the count:

Article "1", The treaty that was concluded on the second day of May in the year one thousand eight hundred and eighty-nine is considered null and revoked.

Article "2", The Emperor of Ethiopia pledges to the King of Italy that he never cedes, to any European government or any other government elsewhere, any territories from his kingdom and that he does not intend a treaty with them, nor does he accept any protection at all.

When this draft reached the count, he considered it as giving him the passport, "ticket to leave", so he severed all his connections and returned to his country.

Emperor Menelik II in Grand Ceremonial Attire

Empress Taytu, the Wife of Emperor Menelik

Sunday, June 26   Addis Ababa X

A private audience with His Imperial Majesty the Emperor and farewell • Imperial gifts

A man came on behalf of Ras Wolde in the morning to inquire about our wellbeing. After wearing our day attire and mounting our animals, we set out towards the imperial palace at two o'clock alaturca time, but with a large number of soldiers and servants. We came across Monsieur Ilg on the way. We first entered his residence. Then, we translated the imperial letter to French to translate it to Amharic. Then, we went to the imperial palace. There was not that much of a crowd today because it was not a formal audience, but a private one. We can see everything since our surroundings are spacious, open. They admitted us into a pavilion that was near the residence of Her Imperial Majesty the Empress and only separated by a wall in between. The name of the pavilion was Shehlabayt and I photographed it with the Kodak machine in my hand.

This pavilion had been built and furnished in the oriental manner. There is a place in the middle like a bed frame for the emperor to sit. The pavillion has been furnished with carpets that are from the imperial gifts and the dais of the emperor has been covered over with a silk carpet from the mentioned gifts and, in this way, His Imperial Majesty the Emperor wants to further show his satisfaction with the imperial grace and favor. Telling us to wait here a little, Monsieur Ilg went to inform His Imperial Majesty the Emperor.

While expecting to be taken elsewhere to go before the emperor, the door between this pavilion and His Imperial Majesty the Emperor opened and His Imperial Majesty the Emperor suddenly came next to us. Immediately running beside the door, we stood to greet him. Shaking hands in a manner of extraordinary compliment and sincerity and coming beside us, we understood that he was making a courtesy visit.

This time he held back only Monsieur Ilg and a chamberlain and dismissed all of his retinue. He gave the audience an informal manner. Taking off his hat, he placed it beside him. He sat in his position. He made my humble self sit in the chair across from him. He also began the discussion today by asking about the health and welfare of the protector His Imperial Majesty the Padishah and declaring his fondness for His Imperial Highness. After conversation about their monastery in Jerusalem, he asked me about the historical relations between Ethiopia and the Muslim world, and I started explaining to His Imperial Majesty, in general, the correspondence and exchange of gifts which occurred between the Prophet, peace be upon him, and Negus Ashama and how the Muslim migrants found the best shelter in Ethiopia, and how many of the companions of our master Mohammad, peace be upon him, were Ethiopians and that there are to our day Ethiopians in high position with our supreme benefactor his imperial majesty the sultan, and they are referred to as companions. His Imperial Majesty was pleased very much and stated that he extraordinarily desired positive relations to continue, and that he loved his Muslim subjects like he loved the Amhara subjects. After our audience continued for half an hour in this way and he gave permission to our request to return due to the onslaught of the rainy season day by day, we bade farewell and parted from the palace.

His Imperial Majesty the Emperor had worn a burnous over a shirt, underwear, and a silk robe from Damascene cloth today, with a castor hat over a white keffiye on his head and a yellow shoe on his feet.

After we left the palace, we started going around in the city. Before going to the residence, we visited Ras Gugsa, the husband of the daughter of the negus, and Ras Tesma to complete the visits that we did not have time to do yesterday. We also saw the thermal bath on our way there. A few sheds have been built over it and those who desire bathe in huts for a small fee or outside for free because water is plenty and runs off into the plain.

I saw two young odalisques with their hands in chains in the vicinity of Ras Gugsa's residence. I asked what their crime was from those around me. One of these was culpable and had been tied from her right ankle for punishment. The one next to her was innocent and was assigned to wait, watch over the culpable one since she had gained the trust and confidence of her master. However, one end of the chain was fixed to her left ankle so as to prevent escape and not lose sight.

At ten o'clock alaturca time, we saw a splendid regiment coming from the imperial palace towards our residence. It approached slowly. A high official is advancing at the front, with fifty, sixty retinue on his side and lots of mules wearing nice tacks in tow behind him. All of them stopped below our residence. The official in the front and ten of his retinue came up to us. Some carried swords, some spears, and some battle attire. We understood that imperial gifts had come to us. The person who had come was the emperor's clothier Ato Mogna and after communicating the greetings of the emperor, he fit the medals that the emperor bestowed depending on our ranks with his own hands and also delivered their warrants written over gazelle leather and the gifts. To my humble self, an Order of Solomon Medal of the first rank, a uniform for ras, two spears from weapons reserved for ras, a sword, a shield and one of the mules reserved for imperial ride with its tack. To Talip Bey, medal of the third rank, uniform belonging to dejazmachs, two spears, one sword, one shield and a mule with its tack from the imperial stable. And they gave the sergeant master a medal for officers, a weapon and a horse (as you can see, a mule is more valued than a horse in Ethiopia). A mule each was also sent to the five soldiers accompanying us from the imperial stable, together with their tacks. Our soldiers became so happy that they drank tej until they started seeing their mules as camels because it is a rare award for a soldier to have the honor of receiving a mule with its tack from the emperor.

In the evening, the deputy of the Italian ambassador and embassy clerks came to visit us. Their ambassador was headed to Europe while I was on the way. Since it had been decided for us to return on the following Tuesday, travel preparations were being seen to in the meantime.

Monday, June 27   Addis Ababa XI

The return visit of the embassy • Is it an umbrella? Is it a shield?
• Meeting with Ras Makonen

In the morning, the English Ambassador Monsieur Harrington and the embassy first secretary came to my side to return our visit. Before arrival to Addis Ababa, my plan was not to return to the Red Sea coast again, but cross Ethiopia westward towards the shores of the White Nile and following the Nile Valley via Fashoda, Oum Durman, Khartoum to go to Cairo, [and] Alexandria. [This was] because more places would have thereby been seen. Whoever I consulted about this idea among those who knew the region, they stated that this was not possible for now because the rainy season was starting and the shores of the Sobat River would turn into a swamp, and it would likely be necessary to stop for weeks next to a stream since there were no bridges over the streams on the way and nobody came and went there from here.

Knowing the shrewdness of the English on these matters, I revealed my plan to Monsieur Harrington on our first meeting yesterday. He approved of it. However, he stated the unsuitability of the season and the possibility of having to stop a lot on the way. Nonetheless, if I was set on the idea of returning from that direction no matter what, he stated that he would communicate with Fashoda via telegraph, and given that there was a small boat coming and going to and from Itanga, located on the banks of the Sobat River, [to and] from the Nile once a month, he could learn the arrival time of this boat and was ready to perform all kinds of facilitation. However, since it was not possible to eliminate the biggest impediment, namely the season, and all the experts unanimously stated it would be quite arduous for us to return even from the way we came let alone descend to the Nile Valley, we were forced to decide on returning via the Asebot road located between the Chercher road and Adal road. Still, we engaged in the research of courses with Monsieur Harrington on the map today and the determination of routes and distances. We calculated it would be possible to arrive in thirty-five, forty days to the ship pier if the weather was favorable and in one month if one walks fast and with a light load. While the aforementioned was still at my side, His Excellency the French Ambassador Monsieur Lagarde, his military attaché Captain Martin de Cain, Lieutenant Collat came. The routes were also discussed with the aforementioned. They unanimously stated that the Asebot road was better in this season. In the afternoon, I went to Ras Makonen.

I had described the rainbow colored umbrellas in Harar. I believe I also said that some gentlewomen and men carry for decoration some local umbrellas woven from thin wicker that are not collapsible. I saw quite a strange and crude umbrella today, too, such that it must have been woven not so much for rain, but against hail the size of a stone. It is woven from the broad wood sticks that bread baskets are woven with in Istanbul and it is one and a half arşın long, one arşın wide and instead of a grip it has a handle at its center like enarmes in the middle of a shield so that it is held from there. Without any doubt, it can also shield its owner against the attack of wild animals if necessary.

A few hundred soldiers met us outside with full due honor and respect when I arrived at the residence of Ras Makonen. He stated that he had come to visit us yesterday, regretted not finding us, and was pleased that we could speak today. The aforementioned is a quite polite, modest, humble, respected, hospitable and pious person. He had coffee, milk, birz, tej brought to us. We drank coffee and birz. The deliciousness of the honey from which birz is made is equal to the deliciousness of the honey that I had eaten in Ankara, the taste of which still lingers in my mouth. It resembles Taif honey. It is as though the bees have only fed on nice scented flowers and created it with this. Understanding we liked birz, the aforementioned sent some to our residence without our knowledge.

During the chat, he said he regretted not being in Harar when we came there and inquired that God willing we were not uncomfortable there. He is more influential than other ras on account of his virtues of intelligence, prudence, courage, and benevolence. He is of medium height, thin, calm, proud, light colored, long visaged, but with quite bright and active eyes and smiling countenance and instills respect and affection in the hearts of those who see him. He is very rich. While his military fame is known, he is a diplomat more than a soldier. As he is one of the ras who mingle with Europeans the most and since he has seen Europe, he possesses a lot of knowledge of circumstances in Europe. Since he is famous for piety and courage, he has gained the affection and respect of Ethiopians with these virtues.

Aside from Christians, I heard his praise and plaudit from all the Muslims I met. I heard that some rogues among Greeks in Harar used to torment [Muslims] and saw them as inferior during the Ottoman Greek war and Muslims used to endure these torments with patience. And when it became apparent that they were defeated by the victorious Ottoman soldiers, Muslims started to decorate their homes and shops and prayed for further victories of His Imperial Majesty the Sultan. When the Greeks went to the ras and complained and said that the Muslims were insulting and trying to belittle them, he answered them "When you used to insult and hurt them they did not raise their voice, not even a word. When they started showing their happiness without attacking you, you started complaining. You are the offending people".

The character of the ras is quite good. He eats, drinks in moderation. He had extraordinary love for his wife. He had pledged not to get married at all after her death and has still remained true to his oath and fidelity. Although I did not ask his age, it can be guessed as fifty.

Ras Makonen had been sent to Italy by His Imperial Majesty Emperor Menelik in the year one thousand eight hundred and eighty-nine to sign the annex to the Treaty of Ucciale.[113] There, they had shown him around quite a bit. Military arrangements and training attracted his attention most. Commanding the Somalis and Gallas within Harar, Ras Makonen had defeated the Toselli regiment in the Amba Alagi locality in the battle with

---

113 *Treaty of Ucciale in Italian named after Wuchele in Ethiopia where it was signed

the Italians, shown his courage and valiance by actually being at the Mekelle siege and Battle of Adowa. After chatting with the aforementioned for a while, we bid farewell sincerely and parted. He saw us off to the door, while the household retinue [came] until quite a distance.

Upon return to the residence, I found a paper from Baron Rothschild.[114] The aforementioned had come to visit [and] left a paper since he could not find [me]. Although the aforementioned had come here to go to the Nile Valley, they said that he had given up on this idea and would return to the coast. The Russian ambassador had also come for a return visit in my absence and left his business card. We finished here describing the emperor and Ras Makonen, so I must recount what I learned in describing some of the officials and important people of the Ethiopian state.

The Princes of Shewa Province

Upon the death of the Governor of the Gojjam Province Tekla Haymanot, all authority was initially transferred to his son Dejazmach Bazab and a small part was given to Ras Mengesha Atikim, and another part to Dejazmach Dams the son of Afa Negus.

Ras Welle Betul

Ras Welle Betul comes from a prominent family in the province of Tigray in the Land of Seh and he is the brother of Empress Taytu. He ruled the provinces of Ginfio, Zobril, Adala, Guino, and Talanta with great prestige and dignity. A tyrant who was even feared by his own followers and had hated the people of Tigray. It was alleged that he had hoped to become the Emperor of Ethiopia after Menelik.

Nonetheless, he loved the sister of the empress so much that he was totally under her spell. Despite his famously deep-seated hatred of the people of Tigray, he nevertheless let his stunningly beautiful daughter marry Ras Mengesha Yohannes from Tigray, at the desire of the empress. He was also famous to have been the biggest foe of Italians.

Ras Mengesha Atikim

A descendant from the largest family of the Zion clan from the Land of Amhara, he captured a part of the Land of Gojjam. Armed with the

---

114 *Maurice de Rothschild

full blessing, trust and reliance of the emperor, he managed to have a vast and overreaching grip on power, ruling and expanding his influence to parts outside of the Zion domain to the outskirts of Lake Tsana like Begemder, Khuana as well as other parts. Over the age of fifty, he was extremely wealthy, famous in political shrewdness and a man of his time. He also won the blessing of the empress and has a really high position with a limited number of soldiers. He participated in the Battle of Adowa against the Italians.

Ras Gugsa

He was the nephew of Empress Taytu and the husband of Princess Wezru Zewditu, the daughter of the emperor from his first deceased wife. This ras is a handsome and good-hearted young man. He was accused by his countrymen of having been a womanizer, but this was seen as a forgivable inclination! Those who lack such inclination, let them continue with their accusations if they want. He ruled the Provinces of Semien that encompassed the Lands of Wanhaghm, Slimt, Izaghadi, Waldeba, Qabet and other parts as well. Ras Gugsa loved his aunt a lot and followed in her footsteps in the tenacity of dealing. He also participated in the Battle of Adowa.

Ras Mengesha, Son of Yohannes

The son of the Emperor Yohannes who was killed in the battle of Qallabat with the Dervishes. He had a great passion for adornment, uncontrollable affinity of the opposite gender and immersion in life's pleasures and excesses. Nonetheless, he always aspired to capture the Ethiopian royal throne till the Pact of Maareb was sealed in the year one thousand eight hundred and ninty-one when the Italians were defeated and Menelik seized on the opportunity to consolidate his grip on the empire. Although Ras Mengesha joined the victor, he was quickly exiled by Menelik to Ankober where he lived. The son of Ras Mengesha Dejach Seyoum, he started a revolution in the Province of Tigray in order to redeem his father that caused Menelik some pain. Later, Menelik managed to bring the son to his side whereby he became a resident of Addis Ababa.

Tuesday, June 28 Akaki

Telegraph and post • Return from Addis Ababa • Heavy rain

I sent a telegram to Istanbul today, advising of [our] departure. Telegrams are sent in two ways from Addis Ababa to Europe. First, through the government's telegraph, in other words Addis Ababa, Harar, Dire Dawa, Djibouti. From Djibouti to Europe via Berim and each word is five francs. One word to Harar is sixty para[115]. It is three kuruş[116] to Djibouti. However, a person who is going to send a telegram to Europe with this line can send his telegram via someone he knows to Djibouti and have it reach Europe since the cable has no agency here. [This is] because the cable fee is paid in Djibouti. The Italians have a telegraph line here which separates to two after reaching Asmara from Addis Ababa. One goes to Massawa. It is connected from Massawa to Europe through the Berim route. The second is from Asmara via Kesla. It goes to Egyptian Sudan, from there to Cairo and to Europe via Alexandria. With the Massawa line, three francs and sixty-two and a half centimes fee is charged for each word and two francs and forty-five centimes for each word with the Kesla, Egypt line. I sent my telegram with this line.

---

115 *Coin equivalent to one fortieth of a kuruş

116 *1 lira = 5 mecidiye, 1 lira = 100 kuruş, 1 lira = 4000 para

While the government and embassies have postal service to send letters to the coast, it only comes and goes to Djibouti by means of a traveler since it does not go with the range method, in other words animals, people do not change at intervals. I spoke to someone who travels in this way at length. He said that when people in Ethiopia understand that time is valuable that is when rapid post can be operated.

Coming before my humble self in the morning today, Monsieur Ilg communicated the greetings of their majesties the emperor and empress and entrusted the aforementioned's petitions to His Imperial Majesty, the supreme sovereign and gave a note sealed with the emperor's seal to be honored with obedience everywhere and bade farewell to our humble delegation. The military attaché of the French embassy, his deputy and numerous other persons came to see us off. This time the mules and muleteers were arranged by Haji Ahmad Efendi to ensure greater comfort on the road, [and] to have the muleteers move in the manner we wanted.

We decided to stay at Ahmad Efendi's residence at Akaki today since it is always customary for the first travel day to be short. We transferred our belongings there ahead of us. Since our long bags are heavy for the mules, this time there are two camels between the mules. It will be possible to go with camels since Chercher way is not going to be used.[117]

Just as we have been riding these mules since the day they were gifted by the emperor, we set out riding them at alaturca quarter past five o'clock today, too. Just like every day, heavy rain started today, too. We continued on our way since there was not a roof to shelter under. We reached Akaki at half past eight o'clock. We came across our baggages, which we had sent from before, on the road. We entered the residence there until our tents arrived and were pitched. The residence consists of a large hut without separate sections, with fifteen meters length, ten meters width and a round egg shape.

Haji Ahmad Efendi had sent a few concubines, slaves here three days ago to cook food. Some of them speak Galla, some Amharic. Cattle, goats that have escaped from the ferocity of the rain have also taken refuge here.

---

117 *The Arabic version of the book has the following sentence: " ...we are going on the Asbot road on which camels travel instead of the Chercher road"

I sat on a high barrier on one side of the hut, watching the surroundings. Concubines are cooking food. The slaves are taking the tack from our mules. They are piling them to one side. Our soldiers and servants hung their shemma that had become soaking wet by stretching long straps from one mast of the hut to the other so that they dry. A kid[118] is looking for its mother. A calf is suckling from the teats of a cow. Tired mules are rolling on the ground. Two dwarf monkeys that were tied on two different animals became very happy when they were set on the ground here. They hugged each other. The male is picking the fleas of its female. I thought I was on Noah's Ark alright, because the rain that is continuing outside is reminiscent of the rain of the great flood. Each of our soldiers is separating the softest grass and giving it to his mule. A commotion is going on. We are all under one roof. Since it is the first stop, we have not yet gotten into a routine yet. Everything will settle down in a day or two.

Although our big tents came, it is unknown where their posts have remained. I had my small tent pitched outside. After spreading a lot of dry grass on top of a quite wet ground and spreading a rug on top, I entered my tent. I had the things that needed to always be at our side during the journey placed in saddlebags, travel baskets for the next day. Our dinner consisted of sheep, cow, chicken meats with vegetable, rice, a type of pastry and box of desserts.

A banquet for about two hundred and fifty people had been held here yesterday night. A notable person from the Muslims was coming. A lot of people had come out for his reception and met him here. The concubines of the hospitable Ahmad Efendi had cooked for all these people. The concubines had cooked the meats of a few sheep, a few cattle. If the sisters in Istanbul see the difficulty that the odalisques suffer here, they would appreciate how fortunate they are. The ones here have no monthly, yearly [wages]. They serve for their board, for one or two robes a year. If they receive an occasional tip, this is the money that comes into their hand. While quite heavy rain continued during the night, it did not penetrate my small tent. However, since its sheets struck the tent like a whip, I could not sleep. We made it to morning chatting with Sergeant Yasin Efendi.

---

118 *Baby goat

Wednesday, June 29   Dubbi Base

Rain • Wolves • Hyenas

I went from the tent to the hut before sunrise. Fire is burning there. Coffee, milk is boiling. We drank our morning coffees until our mules were loaded and our animals were ready. We had breakfast. Saying goodbye to those who came to bid us farewell here and briefly to Bekir and Haji Ahmad Efendis at half past two o'clock, we set out with the intent to camp in Dubbi in the evening. Since our camels could not go down from the path that the mules were descending from in order to descend to Akaki Valley, we took them on a quite circuitous and lightly sloped path. The roads are quite muddy, the animals are sinking to their heels. Where it does not sink, their hooves are sticking to the ground as though sticking with a gum. I have not seen such firm earth, such sticky mud in my life. The mud under their feet is making a snapping sound when the animals are walking as though gum, candy is being ripped.

We arrived to Tchefe Donsa with a lot of difficulty at half past six o'clock. We camped there to eat beside the stream and under a big tree. A lot of Ethiopian village girls, women surrounded us. They had come to sell bread, barley, flour and so on. They all have leather pouches, bags from goat leather instead of a sack. They do not demand money. They want [rifle] cartridges. We bought some barley for the animals, treated flour, bread for the soldiers. They give two, three okka injira bread for a Garra cartridge.

The sky began to thunder again. Butterflies, ants, spiders and similar insects surrounded us. They are attacking our food. They are going into our saddlebags. After resting for an hour and a half since rain had started due to the thunder, we continued on our way. Our pack mules had passed without stopping. [And] what do I see a while after passing the stream? Contrary to my warning, the muleteers had unloaded the baggages. They had piled them one on top of another, covered them with leather. They have dispersed the animals around the grass. Meanwhile, they are pitching tents and sitting. They had told themselves, "Once the general sees that we have camped, naturally he is not going to makes us get up, load the baggages again under the rain, is he? He will, of course, stay here today". When I saw this situation, I told them, "You camped wrong. Dubbi is not here. It is ahead. Catch up quickly!" and continued on our way. They started to load the animals willy-nilly. Because if one makes a concession to them from the first day, then they would never listen. We reached Dubbi after an hour and a half.

We started waiting there for our baggage on top of a high rock, with our tarpaulin on our heads, umbrellas at hand. The mules came, settled. Since the camels had not yet caught up, we sent word to the cameleers to definitely come here. We shot a wild duck the size of a turkey at the stream. Since there was no wood here, we heated our food on top of dung fire and ate. The camels could only come at half past one o'clock at night. Henceforth, I warned the cameleers to set out on the road before us. We dispatched them at nine o'clock at night.

Wolf, hyena sounds were not absent during the night. However, they could not even get close to the dung fire. Nonetheless, when an animal from the pack caravan that camped right next to us drifted away from the base a little, they tore off a huge piece of flesh from the wretch's leg. The animal barely escaped with its life. I examined it in the morning. They had torn off about a handsbreadth of the skin of its thigh, too.

Sunday, June 30   Menabella Base

Monkeys • Threshing by villagers

At twelve o'clock, we set out on the road together with our pack mules. We first came to the Chankura Stream from the direction of Balchi at three o'clock. Since our pack mules had not come with us, we stopped here to wait for them and eat and grazed our passenger mules. There was a pavilion like gazebo here, covered with shrub and high from the ground [and so] we sat below it. We ate and rested. At this moment, an Ethiopian carrying a fiddle with a single cord came and started playing in front of us. When he understood that I was going to photograph him, he became more eager and started singing a folk song, too, so that his voice is heard in the photograph together with his instrument. Continuing on our way at four o'clock, we arrived at the Burka Stream at six.

We rested under the tree where we had taken a break when we were going to Addis Ababa this time, too. The numerous monkeys which came to drink water on the other side of the stream started hooting stridently when they saw the grivet monkeys beside us and our's began to respond to them. They were obviously encouraging them to escape because our grivets showed the desire to escape from their leashes and run towards their fellow kind. After filling our water canisters here, we continued on our way under heavy rain and came out to the Menjar Plain. Although we shot four pej chicken the size of a turkey with two rounds, one disappeared among the shrubs. Game is abundant to such a degree here that a person is not content with shooting one bird with one round. The pej, wild chicken, gazelles, rabbits are plenty and roaming in herds.

In the first village we came across in Menjar, they were beating grains. Such a strange scene that it was worthy of seeing. Eight [to] ten cattle, tied side-by-side from their horns, are being made to walk on the grains on a bounded circle. Youths, young girls have taken sticks in their hands and, singing folk songs, leaping, stamping their feet, shaking their heads right and left, are raining their sticks on the grains in a great hurry. After observing these people for a while and taking their photograph, we continued on our way. Arriving at Menabella at eleven o'clock, we camped there.

Friday, July 1   Tadecha Malka

We bought a forty okka talla jar for the soldiers, muleteers and servants beside us since there was no water until Tadecha Malka ahead of us. We gave glasses since there was no gourd to drink from. It looked very small in their eyes. They all want to drink from the jar to their hearts content. Everyone wants to drink first. Sergeant Yasin lined them up in a row and began to have them drink in turns. Those who have drunk four, five times do not want to get away from the jar. They drank it in a few minutes until not a single drop was left in the jar. Their desire for talla, tej is more than the fondness of Germans for beer. We departed at twelve o'clock.

We arrived at Choba at half past three. The official in the telephone cabin here is examining the passports of the travelers that are coming and going. When he saw our paper with the huge seal of His Imperial Majesty the Emperor, he joined his hands on his chest and paid respect by bowing all the way to the ground. Spreading a rug under the trees here, we rested and ate for a while. Although our pack mules caught up later, they look very tired and exhausted since it is very hot and they have not drunk water the whole day. As one of the camels squatted and would in no way get up with the baggage, we exchanged his load with a lighter one and continued it on its way. With the animals weary from thirst, we arrived at the Tadecha Malka Stream towards the evening. The wretched animals threw themselves into the water with their loads. They cannot quench their thirst [despite drinking]. One of the monkeys that were at our side started howling stridently as soon as seeing the water even though we had occasionally given it water on the road. Getting down from the animal, it jumped into the water like crazy. It drank thirstily. Its other friend had stayed behind with the baggage. They have not given it water. It has perished from thirst. The wretched grivet is left without a female, a friend. It became very sad when evening fell and its mate did not come.

We climbed up from this valley to the plateau and a distance of about seven hundred meters from the stream since there was no grass for the animals to graze on next to the stream. We camped at a place with quite dry grass. After the load of the animals was lowered, we sent them to the stream again so that they drink in comfort. The animals are quite tired; the pasture is very abundant. We have little barley. I decided to stay here until noon tomorrow since there is no barley here.

It appears we are covering double the distance we covered on a single day while going to Addis Ababa because we want to arrive in Djibouti by July 12th so as not to miss the ship. Since it would be necessary to wait fifteen days in Djibouti if we missed the boat, each day in July would be a hellish torture for us, God forbid. I had mentioned that Djibouti's heat was very severe. The temperature that will be seen there will be declared upon our arrival.

We could not pitch the big tent because of a strong wind tonight. We made do with the small tent. Pouring the whole night, rain continued to strike our tents like whips. I was preoccupied since the camels had not caught up and camped far. As four mules were lost at night, the muleteers that we sent around searched and found and brought them.

Saturday, July 2   Fantalle

Poisonous snake • Poisonous scorpion

Our camels came in the morning. We sent all the animals to a place with more abundant grass half an hour's distance from here. While we had given them barley in the evening, they needed to graze. Even though it is not the custom to give barley to animals here, we are feeding them barley because we are covering long distances.

I advised the muleteers, servants to make their bread at daytime before noon. We also cooked our meals from the morning because we would depart in the afternoon and camp at night. The waters were so murky from the abundance of rain that the color of our rice looks like rice with tomato, zerde[119] with saffron. The breads were also in the color of mud. Since we had one canister of the more still and less murky Burka water, we earmarked it for only drinking to be used sparingly.

We found a mule that we had lost here while going to Addis Ababa. One of the locals had kept it alongside. We gave him some tip. Later, we took it with us to be sent to Addis Ababa with the other mules. The crafty mule had softened, fattened, and become naughty. It had gotten used to grazing in comfort for about a month. He looked for an opportunity to escape as soon as he saw the loads. He could not find [one]. He began looking at the loads sadly. He understood what would fall on his back, not his fate.

Loading the camels at six o'clock, we got them underway. We departed, too, at half past eight, together with the pack mules. The muleteers, servants mixed roasted sesame flour in water to a boza[120] consistency and drank it abundantly before departure. Apparently, this boza quenched the heat and kept one full. It was just the thing especially for thirst, apparently. After getting on the way, our servants asked those they came across, "Is there water on the way?" [This was] because the temperature started to rise from Tadecha Malka onwards. Our men, however, are not used to carrying pitchers, flasks, gourds. They drink when they find water, stay patient when they do not.

---

119 *A dessert made from rice with saffron
120 *Thick, fermented millet drink popular in Turkey in winter

We arrived in Fantalle at twelve o'clock. We found some water deposits in the pits of rocks in the valley. Our men drank from this. While some of the water had moss and was in a stagnant state, they did not hold back. Their stomachs are in harmony with every part of their body. Just as they do not get sunstroke, their wounds heal quickly [and] they easily digest everything. However, they beware a lot from harmful insects because the insects here are very poisonous. They all started shouting, "ganad ganad ganad" beside our kitchen before departure today. I ran to see what there was. A kind of rather big scorpion, but it had worried all of them. They killed it. Apparently, this type of scorpion would kill immediately if it stung a person. I had seen of its type live in the vicinity of Diyarbakır and in Van in an ethyl alcohol preservative. They had said that it was poisonous there, too. It is somewhat large, rather yellow.

Lighting lanterns when night fell, we continued moving with a lantern until moonlight emerged. We camped in the middle of the plain, at a place with abundant grass at four o'clock at night. We only had the small tent pitched since the wind was quite strong [and] on one side my bedframe and on the other Talip Bey's were set up. Although we offered Sergeant Yasin Efendi to sleep in the middle, he stayed out in the open. Talip Bey had placed one of his long bags to the front of the bed and had the bedframe lean against that. The whole night there is a rustle, a light noise behind the chest. We were not curious to understand the cause, assuming that the wind was striking the skirt of the tent to the bag. Do we not find a poisonous snake between the two bedframes when we wake up in the morning! It escaped behind the chest when it saw that we made a move. Just then, one of the poisonous scorpions from yesterday is running around. After killing this one, we lifted the chest and killed the snake, too. These had not come to our side at night. We had camped where their nest was in the darkness. Just as God protected us, it was a good thing that Yasin Efendi did not stay in the tent because the aforementioned does not sleep on a bed, but spreads his rug and sleeps on the floor. Our camels came at nine at night and continued moving towards Katyinwaha without stopping at all.

Sunday, July 3   Laga Arba

We could only depart at one in the morning. When we reached the Awash River, we found it very murky. Crossing the bridge, we continued on our way. It was quite hot today and the temperature kept on rising after Awash. We were dying to reach Katyinwaha at earliest by crossing the bridge because the sun was quite scorching and unbearable.

At six o'clock, we finally arrived to the Katyinwaha Stream that was almost like heaven in the middle of that quite beautiful, quite cool and humid desert. Upon arrival, we thought we reached heaven when we stepped on the grass under those big, big trees and washed our faces with the rapidly flowing cold water. The same sudden, rapid change felt by a traveler coming by road from Beirut to Damascus in the summer season, when suddenly entering the Rabwe Strait after the Dimas Desert, the sudden coolness one feels, the freshness and spirituality are felt here, too. Mind you, this place does not resemble the Rabwe Strait in terms of charm because the terrain is flat. However, the freshness that is felt there is also felt here. A person does not want to leave the waterfront at all. Everyone occupied himself with a task in the shade, in the cool. After drinking a lot of water, the animals began grazing. After preparing lunch, our cook occupied himself with cooking dinner. The soldiers, servants washed their shemmas, clother afar, laid them. I bathed with a loofah and soap, too. Everbody used the water to whatever degree that water could be used. Our men baked their bread, cooked their food. While we were going to stay two hours, we sat close to four hours. With our eyes still on the stream, we continued on our way at quarter to ten o'clock.

After following the old road, in other words the Chercher road, for another two full hours, we left the telegraph poles and the Chercher road on our right and started following the Asebot road. While the terrain cannot be made out well on account of the darkness of the evening, it can be seen that it is quite flat, covered with both dry and green grass, with the rare big and small trees.

At two o'clock in the night, two shots were heard coming from the front of the caravan. It is the sign that we had come to a waterfront. The watercourse we reached was a river named Laga Arba and originates at a place located some distance from here and reaches the Awash River. After crossing to the other side of the stream as always, we camped five minutes away from the water at a location with grass. After eating and resting under the light of the full moon, we retired to sleep. Although the weather had been nice and clear at the start of the night, a heavy rain made a mess of the surroundings after midnight.

While the rain did not penetrate the tent, water seeped in from the sides so the inside of the tent became like a swamp. All our items on the floor got wet. Since I was on a bed, the water did not rise up to my side. Yasin Efendi, who does not like beds, regretted it this evening and climbed on top of a very small wood chest that was on my bedside and perched on top of this until morning.

Outside, our native soldiers and servants who are staying in the open are sleeping deeply, snoring, with only their heads above water on a saddle, while they are completely soaked in water. Since our provision chests were out in the open and they were not covered, our provisions such as sugar, salt, flour were completely ruined.

Monday, July 4   Laga Masu

Itus wed seven, eight women • Heavy rain

    I had made the cook soak beans in a big copper bucket from yesterday night so that it would be easier to prepare today. Our soldiers and servants knew that these beans were for them. When it was morning, they emptied it in a canister before the beans were placed over a fire. They surrounded it and started eating it with a great appetite like eating roasted chickpeas. They finished it until not even one was left. I had not been able to make out the terrain we had camped at night. I am now watching the surroundings. As far as the eye can see, the surface is covered with green grass and shrubs, while trees are wide apart from one another. It is quite suitable for development, and housing, and cattle grazing. We set out on the road at two o'clock. The nature of the terrain is continuing like the way described. However, it is sometimes flat, sometimes undulating. One comes across occasional blacks known with the name Itu here. These people do not reside in a single place and travel and camp here and there with their cattle. They live from the milk of their cattle. Except for their genitals, their body is naked. Besides their loincloth, some also have a cloth on their shoulder. Their appearance is terrifying because they are semisavage. They do not practice a religion. A man takes as many women as he can feed. Some of them have seven, eight wives. Their weapons consist of a short spear in their hand and a big knife at their waist. These people are not of Ethiopian kind, but a people of their own. Today, we continued on the road until two o'clock at night. At two [o'clock], Private Osman, walking ahead of us, fired two rifle shots to report that we had come to a stream. After camping, we understood that we were not that close to water. Obviously, either Osman's mule was excessively tired and Osman now wanted to camp, or he was mistaken. The name of the stream ahead of us is Laga Masu. We had water brought by sending our servants with canisters. Fires were lit. Dishes were cooked. The food was eaten. Everyone retreated to the rest that they needed. Only the guards are waiting by the fireside. Although a quite heavy rain began at four o'clock at night, this time the water could not seep inside the tent because the ditch that I had had dug was quite deep.

Tuesday, July 5   Lost in the Forest

Laga Masu • Mulun Stream • Quite a lot of desert animals
• Two kicks by a mule

The sun comes out, then stays under clouds in turn. The rainfall at night had soaked a lot of our belongings. Especially some of the cartridges of the double barrel rifle had swollen so much that it does not go into the rifle. We loaded them one by one. We separated the ones that were spoiled. While these were under a tent, we only have one small tent that is impervious to rain and we have been bringing that since Addis Ababa. Our other tents are manufacture of Istanbul and cannot hold back the rain here.

While we were drinking our coffee, our soldiers and servants had their breakfast by dipping their bread in red pepper paste as though dipping in molasses. We waited until half past three o'clock so that both our tents and the shemma of our men dried. We set out at half past three.

We arrived to the Laga Masu Stream at five. The Laga Masu Stream is sufficient to turn a millstone and, originating from Chercher Mountains, it becomes a tributary of the Awash River. We have not come across a village, town since Choba, from now on we are traveling in the desert and an almost empty terrain. We arrived to the Mulun Stream at half past seven o'clock. This stream flows towards Ogaden territory. It disperses in the sand there, disappears. The joy, exhiliration that rivers give here do not resemble any other exhiliration because the land between the streams consists of hot desert. We rested and ate in the shade of large trees beside this stream. Since the current of the stream is strong, its rustle is giving the ear a pleasure aside from the coolness and shade. It cheers the heart.

At this moment, Sergeant Yasin Efendi gave Idris, one of the servants in our retinue, rusk, stewed fruit pulp, olives, and soujuk. Not knowing to eat these in order, Idris first ate the soujuk. Then drank the stewed fruit pulp. Later, he ate the rusk with a crackling sound. Afterwards gulped down the olives like grape.

We set out on the road again at nine o'clock. The nature of the land changed after the stream. With dry grass starting rather than green grass, the trees are also sparse, small and dry like. A lot of deer and gazelle herds can be seen afar. The odd rabbits stand here and there. Even wolves are occasionally cheeky, passing us at a little distance. Pej and wild chicken are very abundant. We shot as much pej and wild chicken as necessary for the evening. Our pack mules passed when we were resting at the stream. They continued on their way. We cautioned the muleteers to camp wherever they would be at sunset in case we had not caught up with them before then. While moving about, chasing game, we lost our way. The soldiers who are with us pointed to various directions, some saying, "the way is here", some "the way is there". The trail cannot be found since darkness has fallen.

Some of the trees in the forest that we are in now are large, its surface is rugged, hilly. We wanted to go in the direction that was being followed without using the path. It was not possible because dense shrubs, thorns are impeding. We walked around inside the forest until half past one o'clock at night. We could not find the trail, no matter what. It is not possible to get out when the trail cannot be found. We fired a few rounds to get a sign, response from our caravan. We could not get a response. We had men climb to the top of tall trees. They shouted, called out. They fired shots. There is no sound at all.

To determine "do the soldiers, one, two muleteers and servants really know the direction that we need to go to, or not?" and to be assured, I lit a candle under a tree and took out my pocket map. I placed it in its natural position with the compass. I approximately determined the point where we were. I asked the direction we would go. They pointed correctly. I understood that they would be able to find the trail in the morning. However, it is not possible at night. Consequently, we decided to spend the night in the forest. We camped under a big tree. We tied our mules to its roots that had burst out of the ground in turns.

Abu Bakr and his friends collected piles of dry grass for us within a quarter [hour]. We spread some of these under us. We spread the pads of the animals, our rugs over it instead of a bed. We put our saddlebags instead of a pillow. A large part of the grass was piled in front of the animals. The animals started to eat with a great appetite. Meanwhile, gathering a lot of dry logs, tree trunks, our servants lit four, five big fires around us so that we are protected from the wild animals that are present here in plenty. Juma'a, one of the servants, is asking, "Do you have this much abundant wood in Istanbul?" to console us in a proud tone.

We counted each other after camping. We checked our ammunition and weapons. We consisted of eight persons in total, my humble self, Talip Bey, Sergeant Yasin, Abu Bakr, Omar, Juma'a, Hasan, Idris Agha. Our ammunition is plenty; our weapons are excellent. We have no fear of animals. However, we do not have food. We checked the morning meal basket. We found a bottle of stewed grape, a little coffee, a coffee pot, a teapot inside it. We found a small box of biscuits in Sergeant Yasin's saddlebag, one pot of meat stock extract in my saddlebag. Better than nothing. Everyone ate a little. Our flasks were full. The most important thing is water.

Since I had received two mule kicks in the afternoon at daytime, one to my neck and one to my chest, my jaw cannot open. My neck had swollen. I did not need anything other than rest. Fortunately, the hooves of the mules are not shod. Otherwise, it would have broken my jaw, neck, and chest.

The servants stood guard. We slept as much as we could by pulling our tarpaulin above our head. Supremely glorious Allah must have pitied us so that it did not rain tonight. With the sound of a rifle in the middle of the night fired by the muleteer Omar from the top of a tree at a distance being heard at the location of our caravan, they responded with a rifle. We understood that we were near each other. We waited for the morning. In the morning, we drank our coffee and some meat broth and got ready for the road until Abu Bakr found the way by walking around. With the aforementioned finding the trail, we reached our caravan after an hour by following him. Praise God for safety.[121]

---

121 *'Alhamdulillah al salameh' is an Arabic expression to welcome travelers

Wednesday, July 6   In the Middle of the Desert

Since the muleteers had not watched the mules with the panic of searching for us at night, most had run far away and most of the men had gone after them. Consequently, we were forced to wait for them. I warned those who were present to cook food, bake bread until the mules and the men came because I understood that we would leave late and camp at night. We will not be able to reach Dire Dawa, Djibouti on time if we do not cover a long distance.

The weather is quite hot today, the sun scorching because the Asebot road that we are following is not high in the mountains like the Chercher road, but relatively lower. With great difficulty, the mules started coming in twos, threes. Having gotten lost while searching for mules, Omar, one of our muleteers, had come close to almost perishing because of a lack of water and one of the Itus had caught up with him and rescued him and brought him to our side. Although one of the mules could not be found, we did not wait for it anymore and we could depart at half past seven o'clock. Since one of the animals that Bekir Efendi had added to escort the caravan with a baggage consignment no longer had the strength to move, its load was distributed to the other mules and we set this one free in the plain. It can preserve its life for a while if it reaches water without falling into the hands of wild animals and grazes to restore its strength.

As we had come to a place with plenty of grass at half past eleven o'clock, we camped here. We got wet a few times during the journey and since we had filled water from a suspect well, we boiled the water when we came to the base.

Thursday, July 7   Gota Base

Taking out water with a bucket from a well without a rope or pulley • Smart animals • Strange birds • Bracelet with notches

We woke up at half past seven o'clock at night so as to set out at full moon. The baggage could only be prepared by ten o'clock and we could depart. The surroundings are very nice at sunrise. The trees, grass have been washed perfectly with the night rains. Raindrops are shining brightly like pearl pieces on each leaf, each twig with sunlight. Flying from one tree to the next, the birds are singing morning songs.

We arrived to a village like place named Darayle at half past twelve o'clock. The brother of Negadras[122] Mohammed Abu Bakr, whom I met in Addis Ababa, a few of his relatives and their families are residing here with their children, sheep and goats. Their foremost came and invited us to drink coffee, have breakfast. We dismounted from the animals. We sat under a tree. While drinking coffee, one of them began to criticize the Iyessas, Itus, explaining that they shed blood. While he was chatting and pointing, the copper bracelet on his hand attracted my attention. I asked, "Do your men wear bracelets?" He said that he did not wear the bracelet as ornament, but as sign that he had killed men from his enemies. Then, showing the notches on the bracelet, he explained that each notch meant was an enemy killed. There were five notches on the bracelet. The man told me that he had killed five persons from the Itus. Those beside him confirmed. They offered yogurt after the coffee. We drank some. It is very sooty. The reason is that they clean containers woven from grass with soot, as I had described before.

Two of our mules were left behind here. With one being a pack mule, we distributed its load to the other mules. The other is the mule His Imperial Majesty the Emperor gifted my humble self. This mule had grown in the imperial stable with full comfort and pampering [and] was quite beautiful, large [and] those who saw it in Addis Ababa would be jealous.

---

122 *Literally 'head of the merchants'

They estimated it at forty, fifty lira there. Since it was not possible to take it with us, we gifted it to someone together with the mule that His Imperial Majesty the Emperor gave Talip Bey. Declaring that he would accept these after reaching Dire Dawa, the aforementioned insisted. Nothing happened to Talip Bey's mule. My mule stopped eating two days after getting on the road. It started walking slowly. We led it without burden. It perished here today. Our muleteers who knew said, "It had put on fat, it could not cope with the road, that is why it died".

We came to Iylabella Village at seven o'clock. The people here are of the Iyessa clan of the Somalis. Their women, men are walking with a waistcloth each. The bearing and gait of all of them is quite serious and proud. We came to the head of the well on the flood basin to give water to our animals, fill water in our flasks. The community has opened numerous wells on the flood basin since there is no running water here.

The wells are funnel shaped since the flood basin is composed of thin sand. Although the well is four, five meters deep, the width of its mouth is five, six meters, its bottom is just one arşın. Since it was not possible to take out water with pulleys, ropes here, the method that the people have invented is quite strange and worthy of attention. One of the Somalis descends to the bottom of the well. He stands in the water. Somebody from the head of the well throws him a bucket without a handle, a stem, woven from grass, glazed with soot inside. The one below fills it in an instant. The moment he throws it up filled with water, the guy above throws another bucket. He catches the full bucket. He empties it into the small pool at the head of the well. In short, buckets are flying - one down empty, another up full - with such speed and such skill that a person is dazzled. A person admires the guys' skill and that the bucket does not turn upside down when the water is going up and spill. The buckets are masterfully made in terms of balance and not completely cylindrical, with half and bottom side a cut cone, while the other half, or the top side, cylinder shaped and half a meter long, and thirty centimeters in diameter at the top, in other words, the shape and size of the containers they use in Istanbul for toilet taps.

Besides skill, throwing this four, five meters up full of water also requires brute force. To tell the truth, both the guys' wrists and their bodies are like steel. Their veins, nerves are seen below the skin like ropes, thick strings. Besides the men, their women, girls also take out water in this manner. Once the pool at the head of the well was full, one of the men turned his face towards the sheep, goats that were grazing about a kilometer away from the well on a crest and called with a strange sound. They came galloping at full speed altogether, like soldiers obeying the sound of a bugle. After they drank their water and withdrew, another guy called the ones that were in the other direction and they came running, too. They drank. In short, each herd came in turns with the sign and sound given by their owner to them and drank their water, without a stampede by the cattle.

We are hearing two kinds of strange bird sounds from the trees while we are resting here. One is shrieking exactly like a crying child saying "wa wa wa wa". The other is calling "pa pa pa pa pa pa pa". Anyway, the plants and birds of Ethiopia are really strange and supposedly only found in this region. Just as the German Monsieur Schimper who resided in Arabia and especially Ethiopia for a long time and became famous in Europe for his scientific inquiries sent six thousand plant varieties unknown there to botanical museums in London, Berlin, Paris a few years ago, they told me here that a German expert in ornithology had come to Ethiopia with his hunter friends and, after removing the flesh of the strange birds they had shot, stuffed their insides with some drugged cotton that prevented rotting and packed them in chests and took away many bird samples that were not known in Europe.

After stopping and resting for about three hours at the head of a well, under a tree at Iylabella Stream, we continued on our way. Coming to the place named Erer Gota at two o'clock at night, we camped at a rather high location one hundred meters away from the water. We had water carried from the stream. We had big fires lit around us as usual. We had our meals cooked. After the meal, the guards went in front of the fire, while the others retired for a rest of sleep.

Friday, July 8   Tuma Base

Big Turtle

I looked around the surroundings when we woke up this morning. Although the streams were quite murky due to the rains, the water running through here was quite pure and clear. While the location of our base is quite hot even in the morning because of the scorching sun, it is quite cool, nice and shady beside the stream because big, big trees next to the water are extending along the sides of the stream.

In Gota, there are the farms of Haji Mohammad Efendi, the sibling of Negadras Mohammed Abu Bakr, and Haji Ahmad Abdulqadir Efendi from Jeddah. They grow grapes, coffee, banana, sugar cane, a fruit named babay, like citron, and many other fruits such as this here and it is quite suitable to grow various grains.

Although the owners want to develop this place, they cannot do it since attacks by Iyessas are not absent. It is possible to establish a big city here with its orchards, gardens, and farms. So much water is flowing and going in vain. Our passenger and pack mules were very tired now because we had been covering long, long distances every day without interruption since Addis Ababa and a few of them were in a state of not having the capacity to take another step forward. Anyway, with two stops left to Dire Dawa that was the terminus of the railroad, I was forced to leave the provision chests and gear that were no longer necessary at Haji Ahmad Efendi's farm and procure as many mules as possible from here. Setting aside two days' food, we left the rest. In brief, we cast out a lot of onions, garlic. Dropping the sugar canes in their hands, our servants surrounded the onions, garlic that were cast out and began to eat these crunchily like fruit. Warning them that they would feel thirsty on the road, that they would look for water and not find it, I forbade them.

With Mohammed Efendi procuring two mules and two horses for us and adding his slave Feda to our side, we set out on the road at half past three o'clock. We arrived to Erer at half past five o'clock. The heat was very harsh. A water of life[123], covered with trees, sufficient to turn a few millstones is flowing with a burble here, too. Upon seeing this, we felt as though we had reached heaven. We descended below the trees. We left our mules to graze in one corner. We bathed in the stream until our meals were ready. I wore my underwear inside out after bathing because I did not have [clean] underwear with me. This method is very good if a person does not have underwear alongside and has sweated. A person feels as though it is new underwear. The body is comforted.

At this moment, our pack mules caught up [and] after the mules, muleteers drank water, they continued forward. We ate our lunch with a great appetite and desire after bathing. Shepherd girls, half naked above the waist, were spending noontime under the trees with their sheep. While there are also ten, fifteen huts in Erer, this is nothing relative to the capacity and ability of the land. A great city could be established here, too. The community are only living with the produce of animals when water, forest, pasture, cultivable fields are so plentiful. We departed from here at half past seven o'clock.

We arrived to Kermam Valley at quarter past ten. Replenishing the shortfall in our flasks, giving water to our animals from the pits dug in flood beds, we continued on our way. With the weather quite hot today, we are drinking a lot of water since we ate plenty of flour halwa at lunch.

---

123 *An allusion to the fountain of youth

At half past eleven o'clock, finding our baggage being lowered and caravan camping about two kilometers' distance from the foothills of the Tuma Mountain, we descended there. The mules made do with gnawing roots since there is no grass here. However, we had fed them as much barley, corn, millet, grass as we could find in Gota.

Sergeant Yasin Efendi gave his servant a shoe here. The guy wore it. He stood up. Like a little child getting used to walking for the first time, he took a few steps, then stopped. His friends laughed out loud. Saying that he could not get used to shoes, he took it off.

It rained at night. We got quite wet since we left the quite firm and waterproof tent that we had brought from Addis Ababa in Erer with the excess gear and stayed in Talip Bey's tent.

Saturday, July 9   Arrival to Dire Dawa

We could only depart at half past ten even though we acted early in the morning in order to reach Dire Dawa as soon as possible so that we could now complete our journey with means such as railroad and ship, shelter under a proper room, a roof, in short, start benefiting from the facilities and comforts that civilization provides.

We had no more need on the road for a caravan, in other words, pack mules and chests. We started departing with the guidance of Mohammed Efendi's slave Feda who was walking ahead of us as our guide. The terrain that we are traveling on is forested and cannot be crossed without a guide because there are numerous tracks. The tracks are sometimes disappearing.

Besides the gazelles, rabbits and various birds in the forest, we came across a big turtle for the first time today. I estimated its length at eighty centimeters, its height fifty-five centimeters. One of our servants, Alamu wanted to ride the turtle for a while and tour around. He settled for climbing and staying on it a little since there was no time.

Both our servants and our mules have a swiftness, a hurry since this was the last stage. Our servants are going as far as possible with rapid steps in front of us, our mules at pace. We stopped under a tree at four o'clock for a little food and rest. We continued on our way after replenishing the shortfall in our flasks from the fresh rainwater among the rocks. The speed of our servants and mules is increasing as we near the city.

We finally reached Dire Dawa at seven o'clock. We felt we were almost approaching Istanbul and were in the world we are used to when we saw the locomotives and wagons at the railway station.

While travel by road is enjoyable, its hardship, toil, heartache cannot be denied. The days are sometimes very hot, the nights very cold. Heavy rains pour at night, at daytime, in turns. Sometimes mules cannot go on. Some get lost. Wild animals rove around the base at night. The muleteers never pay attention when loading and unloading baggage. They mostly load the chests upside down, or haphazardly. They turn the belongings inside upside down. They drop the provision chests when lowering them. The oil canister bursts. It is both wasted and spreads to other provisions. These require cleaning, wiping. In particular, if there are fragile goods, most are broken. The goods on the back of the animal get chipped by being shaken, rubbing against each other. Each of these conditions disturbs a person.

Anyway, we arrived to Dire Dawa, thank God. It seems to my humble self that if it were necessary to go with a mule another two hours, I might not be able to go on. We directly checked into the Michaelidis Hotel, named after its owner, where we had stayed when we were going to Addis Ababa. Taking our belongings, we put them in our rooms.

We sent the mules to the representative of Haji Ahmad Abdulqadir here. We pointed out where our chests coming with pack mules and camels should be placed. Everyone retired to his room. I had put clean wear into my saddlebag from the evening. My first benefit out of the hotel rest was to get into the hamam and shower and bathe very cleanly with soap and change clothes. After that, I sat on a swing chair in front of the door of my room, facing the hotel garden and began resting. Getting a narghile filled, I smoked it with great desire.

It is very hot here. A lot of European ladies are walking around in the hotel in plain clothes. I asked the waiter, "Where are they going, where are they coming from?" He said, "They are the wives of some officials in Djibouti and escaping from the harshness of the heat, they have come here to cool for a few days". When it is hot like this here, God knows how hot Djibouti is.

According to the inquiry I performed from both the post office and the French Ambassador Monsieur Lagarde when I was in Addis Ababa, the Messageries ship that would come from Madagascar would arrive in Djibouti on the morning of the twelfth day of July and depart towards Suez in the afternoon. We arranged our movements from there according to this. According to that calculation, Dire Dawa would be reached on Sunday. We would go from Dire Dawa to Djibouti on Monday. With the ship to be embarked on the next day, Tuesday, we would only stay one night in Djibouti in this case.

So, you see, we arrived in Dire Dawa a day earlier than our calculation. However, upon our arrival here, they informed us that the ship would come on Wednesday, not Tuesday. We will probably stay here tomorrow because the train does not come and go on Sunday [since] it is a holiday. On the other six days of the week, the train goes one day to Djibouti [and] departs one day from Djibouti to here. We will stay here two days since we will depart from here on Monday.

Our baggage came towards evening and were tied again because the animal saddles, tents, travel bedframes, beds, kitchen, dining sets, these were all placed in sacks, chests to be opened in Istanbul since it would not be possible to move with mules from now on.

Ato Biyana, the son of the ruler of the region Ato Mersha, other Ethiopian officials, Ethiopia's Djibouti Consul Ato Joseph, who was here for some business, and the Consul of the great French state Monsieur Nouman Khouri came and welcomed us. We had been school friends with Nouman Khouri Efendi thirty-three years ago at Beirut schools. We had not met since then. We chatted quite a bit remembering and reminescing about school and the childhood world. He gave me a lot of information about circumstances in Ethiopia since he had been here for a few years. As he is a person who is scholarly, open-minded, intelligent, fluent in four, five languages, possessing a nice library, sociable and cheerful, one both benefits from discussions with him and does not get bored at all. Our visits to each other were friendly and sincere rather than being official. He invited our humble delegation for dinner the following day.

Sunday, July 10   Medal Warrant, Letters

When Ato Joseph came to my side today, I had both the warrant of the medal that His Imperial Majesty the Emperor bestowed and the passport that he had given for the road translated by the aforementioned.[124] As a few letters had also come to my humble self while I was in Addis Ababa, brief copies and translations are included:

The Translation of the Medal Warrant

"Menelik II, who became ruler of Ethiopia with the help and favor of God, salutes all those who read this document and all those who love him. Just as great rulers bestow medals to their loyal soldiers and to those who engage in the progress of science and wisdom, we also bestow medals. We gifted our government's foremost medal to our friend from His Imperial Majesty the Padishah's Aides-de-Camp, Sadık el-Müeyyed Pasha and gave permission for him to wear it".

19 June Year 1896 [1904]

---

124 *The Arabic version has the following: "Ato Joseph arrived to the hotel today and delivered to each on of us the warrants which permit us, with the grace of His Majesty the Negus, medals which were mentioned before. So, I took the opportunity of Ato being present with me and I asked him to translate for me the aforementioned warrants and the passport which was given to us on behalf of the emperor and some letters in Ethiopian that came to me while I was in Addis Ababa and here is the translation:"

The Translation of the Passport
"The Ruler of Ethiopia, Menelik II

As Sadık el-Müeyyed Pasha, Talip Bey and Yasin Efendi are returning to their country, let no one harm them. Let them be honored with respect and welcomed".

21 June

Upon his request to His Imperial Majesty the Emperor before our arrival to Addis Ababa to host our humble delegation at his residence, the letter that includes the imperial order that was communicated to Haji Abdulqadir Efendi of Jeddah by the imperial palace chamberlain in this regard:

"Let this reach Haji Abdulqadir Efendi.

How are you? I am in health and well, thank God. I submitted your request to host the honorable Ottoman delegation, which is a guest of the Emperor, at your residence to His Imperial Majesty the Emperor by telegraph yesterday. I came to your residence in the evening to communicate the response I received. I could not find you. His Imperial Majesty the Emperor, who was extraordinarily pleased with you regarding your offer which came about of your own accord, allowed your request and prayed for you saying, "May God reward him" and "God bless him".

8 June 1896 [1904]
Negadras Haile Giorgis

I left a visiting card to her highness the daughter of the emperor when I visited her husband, so Her Imperial Highness the Princess honored [me] and sent a correspondence of which this is the translation:

From Wezru Zewditu, the daughter of Emperor Menelik the second, to his Excellency Sadık el-Müeyyed Pasha, the Ottoman general:

How are you? I hope you are well. We are well thank God. I received your greetings and also received your note and was very pleased. God bless you always and stay well and in health. I am sending you this with my greetings and salutations.

Wezru Zewditu

This is the Translation of the Letter that Came from Afa Negus: "From Afa Negus Nesibu to the Envoy of His Imperial Majesty Sultan Abdulhamid Khan, His Excellency Azmzâde Sadık el-Müeyyed Pasha:

How are you, how is your spirit? Are you well? If you inquire us, we are fine and in health, thank God. I received your valuable card. I could not be present on your honoring my humble residence since I was at Cennet[125] (This is the name of the imperial pavilion being built at the location named Holeta) by the order of their majesties the emperor and empress. I regretted this excessively. I heard of your arrival to Addis Ababa. I thought you would come to the palace that is being built here. I did not send a message to ask your welfare. If there is something that saddens my humbleself, it is that we could not meet. If you are really about to depart, may God facilitate our meeting at another time".

19 June 1896 [1904] in Cennet
Afa Negus Nesibu

The Letter that Came from Wezru Desta the Wife of Afa Negus:
"From Wezru Desta to our dear friend, His Excellency Sadık el-Müeyyed Pasha:

How are you? How is your spirit? If you ask us, I am in good health, thank God; The gift that you sent has arrived. I was extremely pleased that you thought of me while you were about to set out. May God be with you".

20 June 1896 [1904]   Wezru Desta

It can be seen from the dates of the letters that there is an eight year difference between the Ethiopians and Europeans and this was stated during the calendar discussion. The sentence "Triumph and Victory of the Lion of the Judah Tribe" exists at the start of all royal correspondence, and its origin is taken from the Torah. It is taken after Judah, one of the sons of Jacob, peace be upon him. The forefather of Judah the Lion referred to him with this nickname. It is known that Judah is the father of

---

125 *Literally 'paradise'

David and David is the father of Solomon, peace be upon them, and the Ethiopians claim Solomon is the forefather of the royal family which is now in Ethiopia. All the children of our master Jacob used to make a coat of arms for their family and their tribe and draw the picture of an animal on top and if Jacob had named his son Judah as lion, it was necessary to draw the picture of the lion on the flag of Judah. It is the emblem of the Ethiopians to this day. They draw it on their currency and all their flags. In this regard, the rest of the children of our master Jacob drew distinguishing signs on their flags, so the emblem of Joseph was the picture of a bull and the emblem of Benjamin was the wolf and the emblem of Naphtali was the gazelle and the emblem of Issachar was the donkey and the emblem of Dan was the snake and the emblem of Reuben was fish.

Today, we delivered all our belongings to the railway company. We obtained our tickets. We attended the banquet of the French Consul Monsieur Nouman Khouri Efendi in the evening. The aforementioned had had Ottoman dishes and especially Syrian dishes cooked to please us. After the meal was had with full appetite and a friendly chat, we all retired to our places.

Monday, July 11　　Departure to Djibouti

We woke up early. Handing our handbags to our servants, we went to the station. The French Consul Monsieur Nouman Khouri, Ato Joseph, Ato Mersha, Ato Biyana and many more officials came to see us off.

The train departed at six o'clock alafranga time. At each station during the journey, the Somalis who are present beside the station are coming and giving prayers for our mighty master His Imperial Majesty and greeting us and inquiring after us. I received the welcome telegram and invitation of respected merchants named Ghaleb brothers who are located in Djibouti at a station during the journey.

The train stopped a little at the French border since the French border officer in Ali Sahib was going to Djibouti with his family. The railway Chief Engineer and Chief Inspector Monsieur La Cornique came with a special train to Ambuli to welcome our humble delegation. At the Djibouti station, persons such as the Chief Secretary[126] Monsieur Antoine, other officials, the Russian Consul and principal agent of the Messageries Maritimes Company Monsieur Marechal, Ghaleb brothers, and the owner

---

126 *Chief secretary of the province

of Arcades Hotel Monsieur Wijbiya came to meet and welcome us. Following their invitation, we went to the residence of Ghaleb brothers that had been prepared. The aforementioned had been mentioned in the Djibouti discussion before.

On account of the Ghaleb brothers being from the Exalted State's[127] subjects and Syrian, their treatment and hospitality to us was of the utmost degree. Although they had prepared living rooms, bedrooms for us, we could not sleep in the rooms at night. We were forced to sleep in the wide balcony like them because the temperature is close to forty degrees even at night. Although they put bed frames, mattresses in the balcony for our humble delegation, they did not spread a mattress for themselves, as is the custom in Djibouti. They lay on the bed frame consisting of wood and linen by only putting a pillow.

Everybody sleeps like this in Djibouti. Mattress, blanket, covers are intolerable. In addition, the bed frame is set up towards whichever direction the wind is blowing from. If the wind stops from that side at night and begins to blow from another, the owner of the bed frame pulls his bed frame and lies there. Some people set up two, three bed frames on numerous sides of the balcony. Depending on the direction of the wind at night, he gets up from one and lies on another. With the motivation of travel fatigue, we drifted into sleep, waking up sweating at night and drinking water continuously, dozing off again in turns and made it to morning. I thought I was taking a bath. We first took a shower before everything else when it was morning. However, God knows, the cold water of this place is no different than bath water.

---

127 *Ottoman Empire

Tuesday, July 12

While we are waiting for the Messageries ship to come today, even the agency does not know yet that it will arrive. In the morning, the notables among the Muslims came to our side and prayed for the longevity and health of the protector, our benefactor, our mighty master, His Imperial Majesty. Since Governor Monsieur Bonhoure had been designated as governor to Martinique, visits were exchanged with Monsieur Dubary who was the acting governor. The aforementioned arranged an official banquet at the government mansion to honor our humble delegation. I conducted some return visits in the afternoon. Fortunately, European shirts, a collar, formal suits, frock coats are not worn here in this season. The heat of the season has beaten ceremonies here to a degree. So, we wore our white military uniforms. Those dressing European style here just wear pants and a jacket. Although some are wearing a thin shirt, it is doubtful that they are wearing anything else.

I went for a return visit to a respected chairman of a board. He was embarrassed of his attire. He apologized. However, he is right. The poor man had only worn pants and a jacket from a quite thin calico. He had slippers without socks on his feet and his head was naturally bare. He is busy with his work in this way. He apologized since his garb was quite thin and without lining.

Later, I went to the residence of the Russian Consul and the agent of the Messageries Company Monsieur Marechal with Bashar Ghaleb Efendi. It was afternoon. The aforementioned had not yet come from the office to his house. His wife received us. Although the house where they reside has been constructed by the company and is quite solid, durable and equipped against the heat, I pitied the state of the wretched lady.

She is stretched out on a couch with a white dress, with a slave outside the living room pulling and shaking the ropes of a fan called beranqar that is attached a few meters above her head so that the lady can breathe. Having resided in Istanbul for a while, the aforementioned recalled the beauty of Bosphorus, the coolness of Tarabya, Büyükdere with longing.

I had gained the acquaintance of the aforementioned and her husband when I came to Djibouti two months ago. I was present beside her at the official banquet last time. Most of the words of the aforementioned were about Istanbul. She is a quite polite, intelligent, pleasant to chat, hospitable, considerate, informed lady and discussions with her are rightly of benefit. The Monsieur also arrived during the chat and after talking to the aforementioned for a while as well, we left to meet at the banquet at the government mansion.

The hall has been decorated with various flags since the banquet this evening is official and two large Ottoman and French flags have been brought together at its door. Officials are with their ladies in formal dress. The table, hall, candles had been mentioned in the previous banquet. Only this time the heat is harsher and it is being adjusted by means of big fans.

While everybody in Djibouti has been drinking hot water because the ice factory has not been working for a few days, it is possible to drink cold water at the table this evening due to the ice that the railway director gifted to the acting governor. The railway company has a special small ice counter for its officials and employees. Everyone is thanking the director. In truth, the value of ice here cannot be compared with anything else. When I also thanked him, he made me happy saying that he would send my humble self a few kilos of ice tomorrow for lunch.

After standing up and giving a polite speech at the end of the meal, the representative of the province Monsieur Dubary[128] gave wishes for the health and welfare of His Majesty, the supreme sovereign. This was reciprocated in multiple from my humble side. After consuming coffee, cigarette, and drinks and chatting for a while in the balcony outside the hall, everyone retired to his place.

Since the Madagascar ship belonging to the Haver Peninsular Company came here today and will go to Suez tomorrow, we decided to depart with this one even though this ship is not as orderly as the Messageries ships. While we lay in beds at night with this desire, we could not sleep that much.

---

128 *The original text refers to M.Bonheure, but this is likely to be an error since M. Bonheure was assigned to Martinique and it was M. Dubary who organized the banquet

Wednesday, July 13   Departure to Suez

Obtaining our tickets through Ghaleb brothers, we dispatched our belongings to the shore. After having lunch and bidding farewell to the acting governor, we embarked on the ship at alafranga two o'clock. The weather is hot to such a degree that it is not possible to go down to the cabin. There are a few passengers who are coming from further to the south in the ship. Thank God they too are unable to adhere to formal clothes. Thin pants from calico each, a thin jacket each, not even socks.

Having actually done active military service in Indo-China, the captain of our ship likes soldiers. He always addresses my humble self with a soldierly demeanor saying mon général. He is hospitable, lively, and pleasant to chat with and the mirth and gaieté specific to French seaman is embodied in the aforementioned.

Seeing that we would not be able to eat and sleep in our cabins, he had a section made for us above, from tents. He had all the arrangements carried out for us to eat and sleep there. He did not lose any opportunity to please us. It is possible to shelter in the guardroom located above, which he showed to my humble self for reading and rest at daytime, because this cabin is high up relative to the others and so is breezy. Our sweat is

The Ethiopia Book of Travels

dripping from our jaw even though wind is blowing in the sea. The Ghaleb brothers stayed on the ship for a while to see us off. We departed from Djibouti in the direction of Suez at four o'clock alafranga time. Even the hope of nearing the north a little more every day is consoling us from the heat we felt.

Just like we could not go to Djibouti directly with the Messageries ship even though we went from Istanbul to Marseilles, this time, too, acting on our plans, we wanted to return with the service mentioned before, but could not since the ship did not catch up on time.

The wind blows not according to the wishes of the ships.[i] There is a long distance between us and Suez, so we must spend some time looking at the incidents of war that occurred between the Ethiopians and Italians:

Incidents of War Between the Italians and Ethiopians

Occupation of Massawa [129]

The Italian government wanted to occupy a large region in Africa and make it a gateway access to enter this great continent, as European states do in colonizing, by taking advantage of the opportunity of the Ethiopians being busy with the Dervishes and they occupied Massawa. The English knew that Massawa and its vicinity was not suitable for inhabitation by Europeans and Italian colonization, [but] they encouraged them. There was no cause and pretext for the Italians to do this deed and take it from [a show of] power to action. For this, the Italians took advantage of the death of Gustavo Bianchi the Italian and his companions in the year 1885 in Dangali in the same place which where Galliani and his companions were killed in the year 1884. Public opinion in Italy at that time supported and approved this occupation. Italy sent a regiment of its soldiers for that and occupied the Bay of Massawa on the fourth day of the month of February in the year 1885 and the Italian soldiers spread on lands of Samhara and Rashiku and Monkullo and Saati and all of them belonged to the Ethiopian government. Then, the Italian soldiers started to advance slowly to north Massawa, and south, and west until they occupied all the region of Eritrea.

---

129   Translated by Amina Sanaa Al Muayad Al Azm

The Italians colonized the land and formed a regiment from volunteer paid native soldiers. When Emperor Yohannes, the Ethiopian negus at that time, saw this, he wanted to stop the advance of the Italians up to the known extent. So, he sent Ras Alula and five thousand soldiers to push the Italians to the coast. This news reached the Italians who started to fortify Saati to defend it if necessary.

Battle of Dogali on the Twenty-Sixth of January, 1887 [130]

A battalion consisting of five hundred Italian soldiers loaded with gear and ammunition was heading to Saati under the command of Lieutenant Colonel De Cristoforis. It came across a battalion of soldiers of Ras Alula on the road and fighting ensued between them at a location called Dogali, at ten kilometers' distance from Saati. The Italians defended very heroically, but that defense was not enough to prevent their doomed faith that dealt them a major defeat, so that not even one of the Italian soldiers survived and their arms and ammunition were spoils in the hands of Ethiopians.

Concurrently, there was another battalion in the aforementioned Saati comprised of five hundred soldiers under the command of Major Burati waiting for the anticipated arrival of the battalion of Cristoforis that the Ethiopians had annihilated. As the wait dragged on and the battalion did not arrive to Saati, the major immediately dispatched a scouting team to probe the cause of the alarming delay. The scouts returned and told him the calamity that was inflicted on the battalion of Christoforis by the Ethiopians who were camping on the foothills of the mountain located in front of Saati. Major Burati learned of an impending assault on Saati by the Ethiopians the following day and hence he ordered a retreat to Massawa in the thick of darkness and unnoticed by the Ethiopians. As he and his soldiers retreated from Saati at night, they left most of their gear behind and only carried their arms and ammunition. When the Ethiopians attacked the city at the crack of dawn, they found it deserted and empty at which point they gained more spoils from what the Italians had left behind in ammunition and military gear.

---

130   Translation: Omar Khoja, Amina Sanaa Al Muayad Al Azm

Calamity that Befell Monsieur Salimbeni and His Companions

An Italian delegation headed by Count Salimbeni went to Massawa in the year 1887. The mission of this delegation was to go to Shewa, where Emperor Yohannes resided, via Asmara, Adowa, Mekelle, and Antalo under the pretext of doing a drawing of the Mareb River Bridge which they were planning to build. The delegation was also joined by an Italian person by the name of Count Savoiroux who was an officer with the rank of lieutenant in the Italian army. He came to Massawa to see his fellow officers present in these regions, so he accompanied the aforementioned Salimbeni. After going around with the men of the delegation in the region of Monkullo for the purpose of hunting, he headed to the aforementioned Saati. Another officer with the rank of major named Piano and his son, who was twenty years of age, also departed with them from Massawa, giving the impression that the delegation was peaceful in purpose and [that they] considered this a pleasant trip. The number of people in the delegation was four persons.

The delegation used to hunt during the day as they trekked and went to the homes of the natives at night where they stayed as guests. Upon the arrival of Count Salimbeni with his men to the camp of Ras Alula, the Ethiopian commander kept them at his residence for a few days under the pretext that there were many bandits and brigands on the road.

When the men of the delegation returned from hunting one evening on the day of the incident, they were treated with excessive generosity and pampering by Ras Alula at the table and after they finished eating some men approached from the Ethiopians at the sign of the ras and put chains and shackles on the necks of the men of the delegation and on their hands and legs and told them that they were captives of the ras. They imprisoned each one of them in solitary in a hut. Ras Alula wanted to execute them, but his wife, whom he loved so much, pleaded for leniency on behalf of the Italian officers and hence spared them from death.

Two months afterwards, for the purpose of sending his mother in Italy a letter to inform her of his whereabouts and his welfare, on the condition he would return, Lieutenant Savoiroux succeeded in securing a permit to travel to Monkullo for the stated purpose. He delivered on his promise and his oath of honor to Ras Alula and returned to captivity.

The Italian government requested the return of these captives from Ethiopia and Ras Alula responded in agreement on the condition that the Italian government returned five Ethiopians held as captives by the Italian army. Upon that the Italian commander released four out of the five captives and kept one with him because he had accepted Italian citizenship, so it was incorrect to return him to his previous government. When Ras Alula learned about this, he ordered the Italian captives to be brought in front of him and informed them that there was an Ethiopian captive in Italy and as a result he had decided to reciprocate and keep one captive. He asked them to nominate one of their own to be kept as captive until the Ethiopian was released. He let them meet and caucus on the matter.

At that point, Count Salimbeni suggested conducting a toss, but Lieutenant Savoiroux objected on the premise that it was not appropriate in case the candidate was, for example, Count Salimbeni because he was old, or the major, or his son out of concern of family separation and the son was a child. Therefore, Salimbeni affirmed that he be the one since he was young and single which made it easier to be a captive. The lieutenant persuaded his companions that it was incumbent upon them to depart and he be left behind. Based on this decision, Count Salimbeni, the major and his son were all released the following day. In parallel, Lieutenant Savoiroux's paternal uncle wanted to pay a ransom of one million francs to Ras Alula, but the Italian government rejected the idea fearing this would set a bad precedent in the future. The lieutenant was treated harshly and violently by his prison guards. On the other hand, Ras Alula's wife used to visit the lieutenant in his prison cell in secret sometimes, bringing him food and entertainment.

This poor captive used to be often taken to a square there for execution, placed in front of a firing squad with their guns pointed at him for a while, only for them to change plan at the last minute and return him to his cell, bragging that he was granted amnesty by the ras this time around. As this psychological torture dragged on, one day the lieutenant told his jailers, "Go to your boss the ras and inform him that I do not need his amnesty and to expedite my execution". The jailer replied, "The actions of the ras stemmed from his desire to test whether you were a coward or brave. You were ignorant of the fact that the ras is a man of compassion and mercy and there exists no other commander like him. Is it conceivable in such a case that he orders your execution? If you were to be punished, he may order the amputation of your right hand and left leg only. That is because our ras is extremely merciful to people, as I told you".

That said, this poor man stayed captive for nine months, while Italian diplomacy failed to gain his release. This caught the attention of a French Catholic Lazarist monk who lived in Ethiopia and brokered a deal to release the lieutenant in exchange for a sum that would be paid to Ras Alula. Agreement was reached in the amount of a hundred thousand francs. The monk reached out to the family and relatives of Lieutenant Savoiroux. They sent the sum at once and he was released thereafter.

Occupation of Eritrea [131]

Twenty thousand soldiers under the command of San Marzano[ii] went on an Italian expedition to Massawa on the eighth of November, 1887. This expedition was made up of four brigades led by Generals Jana, Lanza, Gani and Baldiserra.

Italy had already come to the realization that fighting Ethiopians was not an easy task and so requested England to send a delegation to Emperor Yohannes in order to settle the differences between Italy and Ethiopia in a peaceful manner and without spilling any blood. England responded and sent someone to present this request to Yohannes. Therefore, an order was issued to General San Marzano to stand still until the messenger sent to Ethiopia returned with an answer to the request. When the English delegate returned with an unsatisfactory solution, orders were issued to General San Marzano to conduct military action as he saw fit and so the Italian soldiers in Monkullo situated near Massawa marched forward and controlled the important positions on their path, and then they seized Saati and fortified to defend it, and embarked on the construction of a railroad from Massawa to Saati. The Ethiopians, who had withdrawn to the highlands after the Battle of Dogali, returned this time under the

---

131   Translated by Hassana Almuayad Al-Azem and Ghaith Almuayad Al-Azem

leadership of Yohannes and descended through Ganida and Sabergorma and made camp in the plains of Sabergorma and scattered their forward forces all the way to the hills of Defneh, situated a few kilometers from Saati. Ras Alula[iii] was inciting Emperor Yohannes to attack the Italian camp. However, the emperor refused to listen to the Ras and refrained from attacking the Italian army because he was afraid of the Italian cannons, balloons, night rockets, and especially the electric light at night to the point that he once told Ras Alula "Yes, attacking the enemy is the least of our concern, but these people with white skin have the strange ability to even create suns at night and they have machines and demonic tools that astonish and bewilder our brain".

Thus, he stood still without moving, neither forwards, nor backwards. After a little while, epidemics like the plague and typhoid fever broke out among Ethiopian soldiers and starvation took its toll on the army, while deadly diseases were killing cattle and animals, and so Yohannes withdrew his army to the interior and left the Italians alone. As for General San Marzano, he did not wish to follow the Ethiopian army and so he returned with a part of his army to Italy and the rest remained near Massawa.

In April 1888, General Baldissera was appointed commander of Italian forces located in this area. One year later, in the year 1889, Yohannes was killed in the war with the Dervishes in Qallabat as mentioned earlier and when Menelik succeeded him as Emperor of Ethiopia, the people of Tigray revolted against him on the basis of the right of Ras Menghesha, son of Yohannes who was the prince of the aforementioned district, to the Imperial throne. When Menelik saw this, he requested the Italian commander to occupy Asmara with his Italian soldiers to force the Tigrayans to return to his allegiance.

In the meantime, deliberations and memoranda were exchanged between Italy and Ethiopia pertaining to defining the border and the relations between the two governments and this set the border to be Asmara.

The Treaty of Ucciale was signed on the second of May, 1889 between Menelik and Count Antonelli and the name of Empress Taytu, the wife of Menelik, was mentioned in the treaty.

Meanwhile, General Baldissera, who was active and young, managed to conquer the city of Keren situation in the Bogos district that he took from its Governor Balambaras Nahafe without resistance. This city possessed strong fortifications that were constructed by the Egyptians when they had it and three hundred thousand Muslims inhabited the city. The weather of Keren was very nice and its water sweet. After taking control of Keren, the general, with the Italian regulars, and local volunteers marched from Ghinda on Asmara. As the general was approaching, the Ethiopians were withdrawing, so as he reached Asmara in the third day of August of the same year, he found Ras Alula had withdrawn to Godofelassi and from there to Adowa.

As these events were underway, Menelik sent Ras Makonen to Italy as his delegate to sign the treaty agreed upon by Monsieur Crispi the Italian Prime Minister and Ras Makonen and it was annexed to the Treaty of Ucciale and the two delegates signed on the first of October and the nations were informed on the eleventh.

At the end of that year General Baldissera was called back to Italy and General Orero[iv] was appointed in his place to command the Italian soldiers. Upon arrival, the new commander prepared an expedition of two columns, one comprising Italian soldiers and the other locals, a group of cavalries and a few batteries of artillery which he sent to the very rich district of Hamasen to execute the Treaty of Ucciale to impose the influence and the rule of Italy on the aforementioned district. The commander of this expedition was informed by his scouts that the Ethiopians had withdrawn beyond Mekelle.

Due to the weakness inflicted on the country because of the consequences of war, epidemics which spread among the cattle and animals, which killed most of it, and the poverty arising from the taxes imposed by the "ras" on the population in order to finance the military and feed the soldiers, the population leaned towards the Italian, so that even the gentlefolk of Ethiopians vowed obedience to the Italian. General Orero started appointing employees and servants who vowed obedience, and conquered more territories until he reached the region of Mareb, Belesa, and Muna. Following these conquests, Menelik sent on the twenty-second of March 1890 a protest to Italy against this act and informed them that he did not accept such an act. Official correspondence was exchanged back and forth, but to no avail.

Three months later, General Orero was discharged and replaced by General Gandolfi[v] in the position of the Governor of Eritrea colony and commander of its soldiers. In the meantime, an Ethiopian prince by the name of Balambaras[vi] Ilma, the commander of Dembelas Province revolted against the Italians after his submission to them. The aforementioned was defeated in the third battle between him and the Italians and fell with his men to the hands of the Italians. In that same year, a battle took place between the Dervishes and the Italians which resulted in the expansion of the territory which fell under the rule of the Italians and control of the land of Agordat, and when the expansion of Italy by colonization had reached this boundary, Menelik sent another protest on the twenty-eighth of September of the same year against the Treaty of Ucciale and he reiterated his refusal that the borders would be beyond Mareb, Belesa and Muna. During this period, the Italians established regular paid soldiers instead of volunteer irregular soldiers. These were trained according to Western military protocols and they benefited with very good results.

Ras Mengesha could not accede the throne of his father Yohannes and was waiting for an opportunity to change the title of "ras" with the title of negus (king).

The Italians had two political plans in Eritrea. The first policy was on Shewa and Menelik, and the second on Tigray and Ras Mengesha. They used to look for ways to benefit from the division and rivalry between these two provinces. When they received Menelik's rejection, they headed towards Ras Mengesha and wanted to bring him to their side and get an agreement with him on the basis of Mareb.

Oral Treaty of Mareb [132]

General Gandolfi, the governor of the colony of Eritrea, and the chief of his entourage sent several soldiers under the command of two officers

---

132   Translated by Amina Sanaa Al Muayad Al Azm
*Convention

with the rank of captain and another with the rank of lieutenant to Adowa, the center of government of Ras Mengesha, to meet and discuss with him the issue of the governing general meeting with the aforementioned ras and to decide the necessary arrangements for this. After the two sides agreed to this meeting and arranged what was needed for that, the general traveled officially at the end of the month of November with several cavalry of native soldiers and a regiment of Italian soldiers and a cannon battery, heading to the Mareb River located near Adigula where the Italian and Ethiopian leaders had decided to meet.[vii] Ras Mengesha and Ras Alula camped on the shores of the mentioned river from the other side and had three thousand soldiers with them. So, General Gandolfi arrived and spent two days there with the Ethiopians. They were working on preparing what was needed for a treaty and, on the third day, the two sides swore on the Bible in front of Italian soldiers and their priest and generals and the Ethiopian priests whom they brought especially from Aksum that the two sides always stay friends and promised orally and each side gave the other side the treaty and the two charters to clench their alliance on what they agreed. This is what the Italian general pledged:

"I pledge that I will always be a friend to Ras Mengesha and I will consider his enemy my enemy and his friend my friend. I will extend a helping hand and assist him at every time and period". Ras Alula asked the general another pledge for himself because he knew that the Italians did not ever forget their defeat in Dogali and would want to take their revenge from him one day. So, the general swore again saying "I swear I will consider Ras Alula our friend and not do anything to undermine him" and Ras Mengesha and Ras Alula also swore. After the celebration, Ras Mengesha gave General Gandolfi and District Governor Nafa the title of Dejazmach and he also gave all the men of the Italian army medals of Solomon of different ranks and hung those with his hands on their chest. Their general also gave presents that were sent from his government to the ras and the leaders and their men. Europeans say in their proverb that "Promises of love are written on pages of rose and when the wind blows, they disappear" and I say how right this proverb is regarding these oaths and pacts because the following incidents showed that that these pacts were of no importance or account.

The Reason for the Announcement of Martial Law in Hamasen

There was a young man from the Ethiopian nobles and a relative of Ras Mengesha named Asmasak Abarra who entered an Italian seminary and studied and graduated from there after he learned the Italian language very well. Following his graduation from school, he enlisted in the Italian army and studied Italian customs and their ways there. After he gained the rank of an officer, he ran away with native Muslim soldiers under his command and allied with Fitaurari Gairu who served in the Italian army for a while and his brother. Fitaurari saw him and they revolted against the Italians with many Ethiopians who joined them. At that time, or fifteenth of March 1892, there was an Italian officer, Captain Batini, coming from Mulai Sataya to Asmara who had six soldiers with him. The men of the aforementioned Asmasak and his companions came out and killed the captain and the soldiers with him.

General Gandolfi sent two regiments on March seventeenth to catch Abarra and his companions, but they took refuge in high mountains that were difficult to climb. So, they could not succeed in their drive to catch them. At the end of April, the regiment of the captain met Asmasak Abarra the aforementioned who shot with firearms on them. Despite this Abarra was saved from the hands of this regiment and went hiding in the Tigray region this time. Ras Mengesha did not want to accept Abarra, but he changed his mind because of the insistence of his mother and after the deeds of Abarra some matters and developments appeared that led to revolution and rebellion in some areas of Hamasen. So, the general was obliged to announce martial law in these regions and arranged in each city from the mentioned region a war council of three officers who started punishing all bandits and Muslim rebels and hung them. The sentence was executed immediately. So, they stopped the revolution in Eritrea temporarily, but this violence that the Italians adopted against the native rebels was the reason for the grave harm that occurred to the Italians as will be explained later.

Announcement of the Annulment of the Treaty of Ucciale

Three years passed from the objection of His Majesty Menelik against the Italian seizure of the region of the Mareb and Belz border between them and Ethiopia. The Italians did not pay any attention to the objection of the emperor and kept considering the mentioned countries the end of the border to their colony. So, His Majesty Menelik announced the revocation of the Treaty of Ucciale on the eleventh day of May in the year 1893 so that the articles of this mentioned treaty became void from the mentioned day. However, the Italians did not care about this announcement and continued in their plan. The coming incidents showed that the Ethiopians were not asleep in this period, but were working and striving secretly to bring and prepare what was necessary to have their word listened to.

Battle of Halaya[viii] with Batha Agos [133]

Prior to the occupation of the colony of Eritrea by the Italians, the so-called Dezajmach Batha Agos, the Prince of the Province of Okule Kusai[ix] of Eritrea, had fought Ras Mengesha and, afterwards, Ras Alula. He lost against them and his property was seized. However, when the Italians arrived and occupied these territories, he showed obedience and submission to them. He asked the Italians to reinstate him in the province. The Italians responded favorably and seconded him with one thousand and two hundred indigenous soldiers under the command of Italian officers. He regained the province. Moreover, the Italians endowed him with sufficient funds.

Concurrently, Ras Mengesha, son of Yohannes -whose father was killed at the Battle of Qallabat with the Dervishes- showed friendliness and inclination towards the Italians. He promised the Italians to help them in preparing a campaign against the Dervishes to avenge his father's death. Meanwhile, simultaneously and secretly, he kept in touch with Batha Agos. Thus, he informed the Italians of the details of Batha Agos' disposition. The commander [of the Italians] secretly inquired with Lieutenant

---

133   Translated by Sufian M. Azm

Saningueti, the aide-de-camps of Batha Agos in Saganeiti. The lieutenant answered that he had no reasons to doubt Batha Agos.

However, on the fifteenth of December 1893, telegraphic communication suddenly ceased with Saganeiti, the capital of the Province of Okule Kusai. The Italians attributed the disruption to natural incidental causes. However, it was soon revealed that Batha Agos had gained the allegiance of the indigenous soldiers who were under the command of the Italian Lieutenant Saningueti. He had put the lieutenant in custody together with three telegraph operators and a few Italian soldiers. Whereupon General Baratieri, who was in Keren, ordered Major Toselli and his regiment in Asmara to march with his troops to Saganeiti. The next day, when Batha Agos sent his Italian prisoners to the camp of Ras Mengesha, it became crystal clear that these Ethiopians were totally in cohort in creating an organized insurrection against the Italians. This demonstrates that enemies would never become friends. Meanwhile, Major Toselli left Asmara on the fifteenth of the month and arrived on the sixteenth to the village of Maharba, adjacent to Saganeiti. He contacted the military base of Halaya, eighteen kilometers away from Saganeiti, asking for and awaiting the arrival of reinforcements. Concurrently, he sent a message to Batha Agos asking for the release of the Italian prisoners. However, Batha Agos procrastinated since the prisoners were already on their way to the camp of Ras Mengesha. On the night of the seventeenth, Batha Agos moved on Halaya to take over its defences, and to kill its defenders. The aim was to open the way for Ras Mengesha to the heart of the Italian colony. On the eighteenth, Major Toselli attacked Saganeiti only to find it void of Batha Agos' forces, who had vacated it a day earlier.

The major became aware of the intention of Batha Agos to gain Halaya. Immediately, and without informing anyone, the major moved on Halaya to save its few Italian defendants from the ravages of Batha Agos.

Meanwhile, Batha Agos arrived to Halaya with one thousand nine hundred riflemen. Once he arrived, he sent for Captain Castallazi, commander of Halaya defense forces, asking him to vacate the area and to withdraw unhindered to anywhere he wished. The captain procrastinated to gain time. However, Batha Agos understood his ruse and the importance of swiftness to open the way for the inhabitants of Aswarati, who were waiting his arrival to join his forces. So, he hastily attacked and almost prevailed over the Italians, were it not for the Italian reinforcements that arrived under the command of Major Toselli. They turned the tide and the Italians were victorious. Batha Agos was shot dead. The Ethiopian soldiers were dispersed. One of the sons of Batha Agos disappeared with a few of his father's soldiers into the mountains. While his other son, together with other soldiers, joined the camp of Ras Mengesha.

When news of the Italian victory reached the ears of the guards of Lieutenant Saningueti and his companions, they headed towards Ras Mengesha. The guards [then] returned them to Saganeiti, on condition that the guards should not be harmed.

Battle of Koatit [134]

Ras Mengesha was congratulating the Italians on their victory in Halaya, ostensibly showing sincerity, while concealing the ill intentions inside him towards them because while he was on the one hand demonstrating the extremes of the wrongdoings of Batha Agos and tarnishing his legacy, he was preparing for an attack on the Italian army on the other hand. The reason behind the above is that when Ras Mengesha could not attain his objective after pledging obedience and allegiance to the Italians, he left to Entoto where Menelik took residence, and he reconciled with him while pledging allegiance to him in order to at least maintain the Kingdom of Tigray for himself. He had already talked to Menelik before the Mareb Convention with regard to the royal title and Menelik had replied by saying, "In order for you to become a prince or a king, you must have a government. So, where is your government and your domain which you have inherited from your ancestors to appoint you a prince or a governor? You must regain this lost domain and honor to deserve the ruling crown on your head". So, when Ras Mengesha saw that he did not gain anything from the Italians, he turned back to his kinsmen and second, took refuge in the stronger of his enemies and that is Menelik.

---

134   Translated by Ghaith Almuayad Al-Azem and Hassana Almuayad Al-Azem

While General Baratieri received the letter from Ras Mengesha congratulating him on his win in Halaya, he sent back a letter to the ras demanding him to disperse the soldiers whom he had been busy gathering in Antskew, situated at the border of the colony, and hand over the revolutionaries who had rebelled against Italy and to whom he had provided shelter, and to issue an order to Ras Magos to attack the Dervishes in accordance with the Convention and the understanding exchanged by both parties. Ras Mengesha did not cater to the demand of the general. He had an Italian officer in Adowa at the time, a lieutenant called Mulazzani. When this officer saw that the ras did not respond to the demand of the general, he feared the same fate as Lieutenant Saningueti. So, he left Adowa at once. Upon that, General Baratieri started to mass in Adi Ugri. This strategic position overlooked the Sauria Plain and was situated in the middle of the road between Massawa and Adowa and these locations were very helpful for the defense of Asmara and an army can be entrenched very well and can perform very effective battle maneuvers with few soldiers due to the unassailability of its position.

When General Baratieri completed the preparation of his equipment and gathering soldiers, he marched in the direction of Adowa which he entered on the afternoon of the twenty-eighth of December 1894 without spilling any blood so as to renew and affirm the Mareb Convention. A few people who were there and the Aksum clergy visited General Baratieri. However, he was not visited by Ras Mengesha and the Ethiopians who were fit to fight and attack because the only people present in Adowa at the time were the feeble, the elderly, and the priests.

Since the general did not find anyone with whom he could renew the Mareb Convention, and he also feared a sudden attack by the Dervishes, he was forced to return with the soldiers on the third of January to Adi Ugri without getting any of his demands from the Ethiopians. The whereabouts of Ras Mengesha was not known to the Italians until noon on the tenth day of January when he and Ras Alula appeared in Okule Kusai, threatening the Italian lines of defense in Massawa, Asmara, and Ghinda and under their command was an army consisting of ten thousand men with whom they crossed the Belz River and crossed the Zama Plain arriving in Okule Kusai. When General Baratieri saw this, he decided to attack them and ordered the soldiers to perform military maneuvers. Major Toselli quickly occupied Koatit with six infantry platoons. Lieutenant Saningueti and Lieutenant Mulazzani marched with other forces behind the major, and on the twelfth of January all the Italian forces took their positions and were ready. On the thirteenth day, at three thirty in the morning, an order was issued to the Galliano Battalion to stand in line to the north of the Toselli Battalion. The Hidalgo Battalion stood behind the other two battalions as army reserves. The night was calm with a full moon lighting the land like daylight. The Italian soldiers were scouting the fires of the Ethiopians in front of them. The Italian army implemented all military tactics followed by soldiers at night. Instructions and orders were issued to every platoon and battalion with the required duties.

When dawn started to break, the battery of Captain Cicco di Cola started shelling the Ethiopians, and the Ethiopians answered with their own fire. Shelling from both sides intensified. The Ethiopian soldiers attempted to besiege the Italians several times, but to no avail. The fighting continued until the evening. However, the shelling stopped at nightfall and the two armies spent the night in close proximity to each other.

In the morning of the fourteenth, the Ethiopians started shelling the Italians and the fighting continued for a few hours after which the Ethiopians were forced to retreat after running out of ammunition. In the two days of fighting, the Italians lost two officers, one petty officer, and ninety-seven soldiers dead, as well as two hundred and thirty-one soldiers wounded.

The Senafe Incident [135]

Several indigenous soldiers of the Italian army fell captive to the Ethiopians in the aforementioned incident. Some of them succeeded in escaping in the evening and returned to their regiment in the mentioned army. They said that the Ethiopians were retreating in disorder and that fear and terror had very much taken hold of them. When General Baratieri heard this, he gathered his officers and general staff and, after discussion

---

135   The following sections have been translated by Amina Sanaa Al Muayad Al Azm

and consideration with them, decided to pursue the Ethiopians. The next day, he distributed ammunition and rations sufficient for four days to each soldier and ordered them to move. So, [the force] composed of Italian and indigenous soldiers started to move in the morning. After they crossed difficult lands and very difficult, rough terrain, they arrived at noontime to Tegonda where the commander learned that the Ethiopians had passed from there before heading to Senafe. The Italians then rested an hour here and headed to the aforementioned Senafe and arrived before sunset to a hill overlooking Senafe in front of the camp of the Ethiopians. When they arrived, their cannons started to bombard the Ethiopians. The first bomb of the Italians fell on the tent of Ras Mengesha, but he was not inside because he had left it a few minutes before to encourage his soldiers to fight the Italians. Several people were killed from the men of the ras. When darkness fell, both armies were obliged to interrupt the war until the second day.

The Italians came down to the foothills the next day, but found it empty of Ethiopians who withdrew from there during the night, albeit leaving some belongings. One of these was the tent of Ras Mengesha where they found some documents of correspondence taking place between the ras and Menelik and Batha Agos and the head of the French Lazarist Church. So, they learned from these documents that what emerged from the rebellion and insurgency of Batha Agos was with the support of the ras and his consent and the aforementioned priests were busier with political matters than with religious matters.

Some who were present in these incidents say that the retreat of the army of Ras Mengesha in front of the Italians in this way was because of the cowardice of the ras and lack of determination and his limited knowledge in military matters. Another enemy of his fellow countrymen attacked the ras while retreating. So, he fought him and the ras suffered great losses. Here is the report of that incident:

There is a very important province in the region of Tigray called Agame whose governance is in the hands of the eldest from a very old family in terms of origin and the name of this family is Sagabadi. When the ruler of this province died before the aforementioned incidents, conflict stirred up within a few years over governing between Ras Sebat and Dejazmach Agos Tafari, both from the aforementioned family. When Ras Mengesha saw this, he appointed a person outside the Sagabadi family as the ruler of the province instead of appointing the most deserving and the oldest from the ancient ruling family there. This new ruler named Ras Antalu, whose only virtue was that he had the approval of the ras, was appointed by Ras Mengesha. The people started complaining about Ras Mengesha's action in this manner and both Ras Sebat and Dejaz Tafari, who were mentioned before, became very angry. A great civil war was about to occur, but influential men of religion intervened. They asked them to come to Ras Mengesha to settle the issue between them and the ras, and Ras Sebat accepted. When he went to Ras Mengesha, he treated him well, then caught him and put him in prison in Amba Alagi. However, Dejaz Agos Tafari knew about the situation in the country and flattered Ras Mengesha because he suspected malice from this reception more than his relative Ras Sebat did. He did not accept the invitation and hid with his men in Belz Mountain and declared his defiance and rebellion to Ras Mengesha.

When war started between Ras Mengesha and the Italians this time, Dejaz Tafari was watching his movements and waiting to take advantage of this opportunity. When Ras Mengesha retreated from Senafe, Dejaz Tafari attacked him and killed many of his men and took a lot of cattle and other loot from his army. After that, he went and bowed to the Italians and the Italians accepted his submission. Since the members of this family have entitlements in the Agame Province and have clout and influence and status, they appointed him as the ruler of the province and put the soldiers of Dejaz Tafari under the command of Major Toselli, commander of the Agame region, as regular troops.

Dejaz Agos Tafari stayed subject to the Italians until the thirteenth day of February 1896, then joined with Ras Sebat the enemies of the Italians and his fellows.

Occupation of Tigray

After the two small victories of Coatit and Senafe, General Baratieri wanted to invade all the lands of Ras Mengesha, in other words, the lands of Tigray. So, he sent Toselli and the fourth regiment that consisted of native soldiers and the soldiers of Dejaz Agos Tafari, who was mentioned before, and ordered him to occupy Adigrat, the capital of Agame. He sent the fifth regiment of Major Amagulio, comprising native soldiers, to Adowa, the capital of Tigray. At that time, Ras Mengesha was retreating to the south. So, the Italians thought that they could occupy Tigray by invading these two cities and started arranging the affairs of the cities and taking the helm of government in them. However, the rulers of Tigray like Ras Alula and Ras Antalu and others were retreating to the south to gather soldiers and complete preparations. When General Baratieri was entering Rome, the capital of Italy, he asked its government for an order in the month of July to allow a triumphal entry by acclamation and applause of the people and while he was honored with a banquet and drinking champagne to toast his victories, the Ethiopians were busy working on preparing the necessary tools to recover the land of their fathers and their forefathers from the hand of those who occupied them.

When the soldiers of the Ras Mengesha were sufficient, they joined the forces of Ras Alula and Ras Mikail and they all gathered in the south of Lake Ashenge. When this news reached Rome, General Baratieri was ordered to immediately travel to Africa and when he arrived to his duty station he considered it better to attack the Ethiopians and reduce their numbers. Therefore, he ordered the soldiers to mobilize in Adigrat. When the soldiers gathered in the mentioned city, he headed to Ras Mengesha's camp on the fourth of October. He sent an expedition to the camp comprising four troops from infantry and another expedition of Carabinieris and a battery of cannons and this expedition crossed the difficult Mount Debra Ailat route. It arrived on the ninth of the mentioned month to where the Ethiopian Tigray soldiers were camping. The expedition started to attack them and inflicted heavy losses. The Ethiopians lost the battle in a short time and escaped defeated, leaving behind them a lot of cattle and ammunition for firearms as booty for the Italians.

The retreat of the Ethiopians in front of the Italians in Debra Ailat is not a victory and is not important, but it encouraged General Baratieri. He ordered for the remnants of the Ethiopians to be pursued and separated his forces to two parts. They started marching slowly to pursue the Ethiopians, but the bulk of the Italian army could not follow them. So, he divided his soldiers to small parties and distributed them to the surroundings. In the end, all the Italians met in Amba Alagi where Ras Sebat had been captive for five years. They let him go and when he saw himself free out of prison, he showed his ease in the presence of the Italians there. However, we shall see that he joined Ras Mengesha with his soldiers after a year. These Ethiopian princes look like brothers who quarrel several times every day, then reconcile. The internal conflicts that take place among them have no importance. They consider these fights like exercises and national games, or games of chess.

While we see them fighting among themselves, you can find them become brothers who love each other and united as if they are one man if an enemy comes from the outside. However, when the Italians did not see any defence from the Ethiopians while following them this time, they also assumed that the country had become theirs and started looking at Tigray as a colony of Italian Eritrea. It did not cross their minds that there was a crouching lion, gearing up and gathering his soldiers to pounce on them in a quick strike, that was Menelik the second in Shewa [and that] while Ras Makonen was showing his affection and fondness for the Italians, he was, on the other hand, expelling their merchants and community from Harar.

Defeat of Amba Alagi

The army of Ras Makonen, which was ahead of the army of Menelik, was camping on the shores of Lake Ashenge. When this news reached the Italian general, he ordered Major Toselli to march with two thousand five hundred soldiers and several cannons to the camp of the aforementioned Ras Makonen first, to stop the Ethiopians from marching forward second, to discover the situation of forces who were descending to the border of that mentioned lake, and third, to give enough time for the commander to be able to gather his general forces in Adigrat. It arrived to a hill named Amba Alagi and stayed camping there. On the third day of its arrival, the Ethiopians attacked and a clash started between both sides. Major Toselli did his best to keep his line of retreat so as to make the road on which the General Arimondi was arriving with help safe, but this help did not reach him. Most of the Italian officers fell among the dead and wounded, so that most of them were among the ranks of those who perished. When the commander saw this, he ordered Captain Risi to attack the Ethiopians with his battalion. So, they attacked with a really heavy charge and cannons were giving cover from behind, spreading terror and destruction among the ranks of the Ethiopians who were bringing others immediately each time they lost some of their soldiers and defending like heroes without heed of the heavy Italian fire and regard to a quick death. At eleven o'clock before noon alafranga time, the battalion under the command of Ras Alula marched to stop the line of retreat of the Italians. When Toselli saw this, he was obliged to retreat to be able to at least save the remainder of his forces. Despite this, the road that he was obliged to retreat from was fraught with danger on both sides. One side was situated on the edge of a great ravine of about four hundred meters and the other side was exposed to the fire of the soldiers of Ras Alula who were standing on lookout on cliffs fifty meters above the road. What made matters worse and critical was that the road was crowded with mules and wounded and heavy weights. With all this danger and difficulty, the rest of the Toselli battalion started to pass from this road while fire was descending on them from above and the abyss below was ready to swallow whoever fell, so the losses of the Italian battalion were really great.

The battery which was under the command of Lieutenant Manfredi was firing from a close distance on the Ethiopians, but the soldiers of the second battery which was under the command of Lieutenant Scala threw everything, cannons and mules and ammunition and all military equipment in a deep pit so that the Ethiopians would not benefit from them. The company did not reach the bottom of the hill. Only three officers remained alive from the twenty-six officers who were leaving and Major Toselli the commander of this battalion was killed by a bullet that struck him after his battalion reached the bottom of the hill. In brief, this defeat was a disaster and a great calamity on Italian soldiers because only three hundred persons survived from the whole battalion.

Following the bravery of Major Toselli and the skill and courage and resourcefulness he showed during the battle, Ras Makonen ordered that he be buried in one of the churches there and his burial be celebrated with a military ceremony with military honor and fitting a commander like him.

Mekelle Siege [136]

General Arimondi arrived with his soldiers a long while after the battle of Amba Alagi and found out that the battle had ended and was joined by those who had fled and most were wounded. According to a book written by an Italian officer, the delay in the arrival of General Arimondi and the disaster and defeat which were inflicted on the Toselli expedition were the result of the jealousy on the part of General Baratieri of General Arimondi to the point that even the late victory in Adigrat did not appeal to General Baratieri. This time General Arimondi requested permission from Baratieri to depart in order to provide support to Major Toselli. However, permission was not granted which forced Arimondi to send an order to the major to retreat, but the order never reached the major. Since he did not receive any news from Toselli, he took responsibility upon himself, to put his mind at ease, and departed without permission from the general commander only to arrive in Amba Alagi and witness the miserable conditions suffered by anyone who fled from the hands of the Ethiopians.

On that same day, an order was issued to the Italian commander in Adowa to retreat to Adigrat, but not before burning the city which forced the officers there to evacuate the population in order to execute the general commander's order. The people fled the city, women, men and children leaving their homes and belongings to the fire. The sight of them was gut wrenching, seeing their despair and hearing their cries and wails. The Italian officers, in charge of burning the city, admitted the savagery of this act. After the Italian retreat, a band of Ras Mengesha's soldiers entered Adowa and tried their best to extinguish the fire. However, it did not succeed and the city was in ashes and in ruins in a few hours. The order to withdraw from Adowa was issued to the Italian soldiers in a hurry. Therefore, the soldiers and officers fled with only the clothes that they wore. The remainder of clothing and belongings of the soldiers and the officers were left to burn in the fire.

While these events were taking place in Adowa and General Arimondi was returning to Adigrat, the third column, which was made up of natives,

---

136   Translated by Ghaith Almuayad Al-Azem and Hassana Almuayad Al-Azem

was in Mekelle under the command of Major Galliano. Mekelle was the capital of the Andarte State of the region of Tigray and was renowned for the fertility of its land and had been the capital of the government of Ras Mengesha in the past. Mekelle was the Ethiopian army base for military movements. When the Italians occupied the Tigray region, they built fortifications and castles and when the battle of Amba Alagi occurred, these fortifications were not yet complete. However, the Italians had massed a lot of supplies and ammunition there. There were no wells or tanks for drinking water inside the city. People took their supplies of water from two springs. One had little water, located outside the city near the gate of the great wall. The second was at a place further from the first spring. Therefore, the commander of the garrison there erected two tanks that he filled with water for reserves. A few days after the departure of General Arimondi from Mekelle, telegraph wires were cut and communications were interrupted. The major sent a platoon to fix the wires. However, they returned without executing the order after being attacked by Ethiopian soldiers near the hills of Masabut and the garrison in Mekelle could only hope to depend on themselves and their small force. While General Baratieri was ordering troops from Italy and massing them near Adigrat, news came on the fifth day of January that a great force under the command of Ras Makonen and Ras Mengesha occupied the hills on the outskirts of Mekelle and a day before that day, Emperor Menelik and Empress Taytu arrived with their camp to a place called Chalacot near Mekelle.

Negus, ruler of the region of Gojjam, joined the camp of the Emperor. On the seventh day of the month, soldiers arrived in Chalacot in large numbers and camped eight kilometers away from Mekelle. When the Italians inside the city saw the red pavilion in the middle of the camp, they realized the emperor and the empress arrived with their horses and men. On the same day, Ethiopians sent their cannons to the Enda Eyesus Hill located eight hundred meters from Mekelle. Most of the Ethiopian cannons were mountain cannons and of several calibers and among them were four cannons of Mitrailleuse model, and twenty-eight cannons of Hotchkiss rapid fire model that could launch its bombs to a distance of three thousand five hundred meters; and of these cannons there are always five in the private army of the empress.

The Ethiopians started the war against the Italians today. However, they only inflicted a few losses. In the morning of day eight of the same month, the Ethiopians started shelling the Mekelle fortifications with their cannons from three different locations, and they sent a force to the aforementioned springs and blocked the water supply. The water in the tanks erected by the commander of the garrison could only provide drinking water for the besieged for two days. The cattle, horses and mules inside Mekelle perished of thirst. On the ninth, the Ethiopians fortified their military positions and, in addition to the shelling with cannons, they attacked the city with their rifles and heavy fighting persisted on the tenth and the eleventh. The leaders and commanders of the Ethiopian army suffered heavy losses as they marched at the forefront, ahead of their attacking soldiers. Hence, twenty-two commanders and senior officers died, and both Ras Makonen and Alula were wounded. The reason behind these heavy losses was that the attackers' shells hit rocks and dirt (fortifications), whereas the shells of the besieged defendants hit men, that is to say the Ethiopians.

When the Ethiopians saw the futility of capturing such a fortified city like Mekelle, they changed their strategy and persisted on besieging the city and so they increased the number of soldiers near the springs, and sent plenty of soldiers to the hills around the city to reinforce the already present soldiers. From time to time, they dropped bombs on the Italians. As for the Italians, they persevered in their positions, as they were sure help would be on its way in the near future.

On the thirteenth, a delegate of the emperor arrived in Mekelle demanding a truce for a few hours during which the dead would be buried. The commander of the Italian garrison accepted on the condition that the number of soldiers approaching the city was limited. The delegate returned in order to present this condition to the negus. The besieged hoped they could fill their tanks during the truce proposed by the Ethiopians. However, to their disappointment, the delegate never returned. The commander would usually give each person seven hundred and fifty milliliters a day. However, he cut this ration to five hundred milliliters on that day, and he only gave two hundred and fifty milliliters on the following day. In short, the condition of the besieged deteriorated drastically and on any specific day no one would get more than one glass of water. On the eighteenth, water was completely depleted. The major summoned his officers and after deliberation they decided to wait for one more day without water. If the expected help did not arrive on the twentieth, they would deactivate their cannons, blow up their military ammunition and charge through enemy ranks either opening their way to safety, or die defending themselves. While the besieged were preparing to leave on the nineteenth, an order was received from General Baratieri to surrender Mekelle to the Ethiopians. This order impacted the officers and the commander of the garrison in a very bad way, and they started crying like children.

On the next day, the Italian merchant, and old friend of Emperor Menelik, Monsieur Felter[x] arrived at ten o'clock to mediate the surrender of Mekelle between the emperor and General Baratieri. A few minutes after his arrival, the Italian flag was lowered and a white flag was raised instead. People ran towards the springs out of thirst. On the twenty-first of the same month, the major went to the emperor's camp to discuss the exit of the soldiers from Mekelle. He was received very well by the Ethiopians and the emperor presented him with a mule and a mare saddled and ready, and promised him a thousand mules to help him and his soldiers leave Mekelle. Evacuation of the city began at two o'clock in the afternoon and while the Italian soldiers were leaving from one gate, the soldiers of Ras Makonen entered from the other gate. When the city was handed over, the white flag was lowered, and the Ethiopian flag was raised in its place. At that very moment, the Italian soldiers who just got out of the city saw the raising of the Ethiopian flag on the flagpole had their eyes fill with tears for the loss of the city. The soldiers rested in a place two hours away from the city and waited until Ethiopian soldiers arrived whereby everyone marched towards the destination of Hawazen on the twenty-fourth of January. A regiment of soldiers belonging to Ras Mengesha and Ras Alula marched in front of the Italian battalion. A regiment of soldiers belonging to Ras Makonen marched in the rear, and to the right and north, a regiment of soldiers belonging to the emperor and Negus of Gojjam Province. They continued marching until they reached Hawazen on the twenty-ninth. While the Ethiopian soldiers remained there, the Italian battalion continued its march accompanied by Ras Makonen until they reached a particular location on the road. Ras Makonen stopped and told the commander of the battalion that the emperor agreed that they can leave Mekelle without suffering any harm based on the condition that General Baratieri was to send the Major Salsa to the emperor's camp to discuss the terms of the truce. In view of the fact that the aforementioned major had not presented himself until that moment, the emperor had issued an order to take ten officers as hostages of the Ethiopian army. After Ras Makonen conveyed the order of the emperor, he picked ten from among the officers and then allowed the battalion to depart and so it did. General Baratieri had already ordered Major Salsa to travel to the Ethiopian camp. However, when the news of Menelik holding ten of his officers hostage reached him, he ordered the return of aforementioned major.

As a result of General Baratieri not fulfilling his promise, Empress Taytu and her entourage demanded the execution of the officers held hostages. However, the emperor ordered their release just when they where about to be executed saying that it was unfitting to execute them for someone else's fault. Ras Makonen advised the officers to depart at once from the Ethiopian camp and explain to General Baratieri the need to send the major, or at least Monsieur Felter, because the ras and the emperor were leaning toward reconciliation.

The ten Italian officers reached their camp located in Mai Ghayna after a five hour walk. When spotted by the forward Italian posts they started shooting at them with their rifles thinking they were Ethiopians. So, they killed a sergeant and a mule, then realized that these were the Italian officers held by the Ethiopians. The Italian officers themselves admitted that Emperor Menelik was a man of peace and hated to spill blood and he had proven that when accepting the mediation of Monsieur Felter to allow Italian soldiers besieged in Mekelle to leave after they almost died from thirst.

One more matter that indicated the shrewdness of the emperor and his mastery of the art of politics and war is that when the Italian battalion left Mekelle, it was accompanied by him and his army as a display of honor. However, by so doing, he managed to seize a big amount of land from within the influence of Italy and crossed quite a distance inside Italian territory. This move was quite an achievement in the art of military movement and mobilization. The Italian soldiers and officers were surprised at General Baratieri for not sending the major to the Ethiopian camp for a truce agreement.

The Agame Revolution [137]

After the return of ten officers, who had been taken as hostages, to the camp of General Baratieri on the fifth of February, Balambaras Emmanuel informed him, on behalf of Emperor Menelik, that the emperor was moving his camp from Hamasen to Gandapata and would wait there for six days to sign a truce. This strange general agreed to send Major Salsa and ordered him to conclude a truce according to the following conditions:

1- Renewal of the Ucciale Treaty

2- Total recognition of the territories that Italy seized in the latest period as an Italian colony

It was no secret that these conditions neither satisfied the emperor, who preferred to make peace, nor the empress and her faction. For these conditions, which were unbearable, raised the anger of the empress, her brother Ras Welle, Ras Mengesha, and Ras Alula. Accordingly, the emperor demanded from the general a change to the peace agreement, first - The evacuation of all the territories that the Italians had last occupied. Second – Amendment of the Ucciale Treaty. The negus issued this demand as a final ultimatum and sent it with Major Salsa, the Italian delegate. When the demands of the emperor reached General Baratieri, he immediately sent a correspondence with strong language to the emperor informing him that both sides were free in their military operations.

On the same day that Major Salsa arrived to the camp of General Baratieri, Ras Sebat and Agos Tafari, who were in the service of the Italian army, left the camp of the general and joined the army of their fellow Ethiopians with five hundred soldiers. They were received with great pleasure and respect. Yes, the joining of five hundred Ethiopian soldiers does not count as a great loss for the Italian fighting army, but the importance of it was because these were two leaders of influence

---

137   The following sections have been translated by Amina Sanaa Al Muayad Al Azm

in their country and that was where the war would take place. In fact, it so happened that the people in the country were against the Italians and started attacking military caravans carrying food and ammunition and the forward positions of the Italian army and its troops. The maintenance of Italian soldiers had been very difficult, but it now became impossible. As a result, General Baratieri was obliged to retreat with his camp to the hills of Tizala. In particular, the Italian soldiers, who had come from their country, were not used to fatigue and hardship and eating a little flour mixed with water and long stretches and distances, climbing mountains that were more challenging than the mountains of the Alps. The soldiers were extremely tired due to all this and disease spread among the cattle and horses and mules of the camp, so that most of them perished.

Meanwhile, the Ethiopian army started heading to Adowa after preparations. At the time, the general commander of the Italian army was coming down with his forces to the hill dominating Enticho and settled for sending small parties every day to discover what was around the hills. They came across a large number of Ethiopian detachments and clashed, then returned to where they came from after losing many of their men.

The Lina Incident

Among the incidents of these regiments, the Lina incident occurred when Lieutenant Sizini went to scout with sixty Italian soldiers and fifty native soldiers in the evening of February the fourteenth. While he was climbing a rugged foothill with his soldiers during return to the camp, Ethiopian soldiers attacked them and started firing on them with rifles and this continued until darkness fell. Many of his soldiers were killed. The sound of the rifle shots were heard from Adigrat, so they sent help comprising thirty-five Italian soldiers under the command of Lieutenant Conselli, but because of the darkness they could not find the place where their friend Lieutenant Sizini was in and they were obliged to spend the whole night on the mountain. In the morning, they came across an Ethiopian battalion and fighting started between them and the Italian detachment perished to the last.

Meanwhile, Lieutenant Sizini did not know about the help that came until he heard the sound of the rifles. He wanted to help his companions, but saw an Ethiopian battalion consisting of five hundred soldiers surrounding him. He was afraid the line of retreat would be cut, so he ordered his soldiers to retreat. Only a few persons from his soldiers remained with him when he arrived to Adigrat and the rest perished under Ethiopian fire.

The Alekeye Incident

Lieutenant Simeone set off from Adigrat on the sixteenth of February and had one hundred cavalry troops with him to join the protectors of the big caravan carrying war equipment. When this Italian company arrived to Alekeye, they met the Italian company of Lieutenant Nifritti and joined them. After a while, a regiment of Ethiopian of soldiers consisting of a thousand soldiers appeared. They surrounded the two Italian companies and killed all their men and Lieutenants Simeone and Nifritti were among the dead.

When news of the attack of the Ethiopians on the two aforementioned companies reached the Italian camp, Captain Moccagatta and one hundred and forty soldiers immediately went to rescue the companies, but the battle was finished by the time he arrived to the location of the incident. When the Ethiopians saw this company, they attacked it from all sides. Thus, it was obliged to retreat when they were about to be annihilated to the last, as only nine of them, eight soldiers and the officer, survived. As for the caravan, it all fell to the hands of the Ethiopians. It is necessary to tell you here about an event that occurred during that incident which is a sample of the bravery and loyalty of officers and soldiers:

While the fight was on, some of the Ethiopians surrounded an officer with the rank of lieutenant named Caputu and asked him to surrender, but the officer refused and killed six of the Ethiopians with his gun. Then, a bullet struck him and he fell dead to the ground. The Ethiopians thought that he was dead and burned his leg with fire to be certain and left. However, the officer had fainted from his wounds and when he woke up from his blackout, he found himself in the arms of an Ethiopian soldier, looked in his face and knew him. This Ethiopian soldier had enlisted in the

Italian army as a volunteer and so had joined the battalion of the lieutenant. When the incident was over and the Ethiopians left, the soldier returned to the location of the incident and he started to treat the mentioned officer with first aid until he woke up. Then, he carried him to the Italian camp on his back. How great this deed and noble soul this simple soldier has, who, after having served his duty as a soldier with his natives on the battlefield, fulfilled his duty as a human being and obligation of loyalty and friendship and being an old acquaintance. May this noble feeling be blessed and may this generous human being be blessed.

On February seventeenth, General Baratieri left his camp accompanied by three regiments to conduct a reconnaissance himself. He saw the Ethiopian army descending from the foothills of the Silasit Mountain, which was fifteen kilometers' distance from the location of the Italian camp. So, he could not attack the Ethiopians at this place and ordered arriving caravans that were coming to his camp to change their way and come from the Mai-Marat-Debra-Damo route from now on. The general did not know that this road was more perilous and dangerous than the first because Ras Sebat was coming down with his soldiers from the hills overlooking this road.

There is an Ethiopian monastery built on a hill (Amba Damo) at this place and it is famous among Ethiopians. Damo territories consist of sixty villages with four hundred families in them and all these villages are the property of the mentioned monastery. So, every priest among the priests owns a village from these aforementioned villages with everything from the land, people, and cattle. The priests follow the rules of the leader of the monastery of the Damo region and the mentioned monastery belongs to hardened offenders and bandits because it is sacred, so officials are forbidden from entering. It is above the law and government. The hills that are referred to as amba in Ethiopian territories is a hill surrounded on all sides by very high rocks standing like columns or walls that are impossible to climb except for a very narrow path that only animals such as goats and sheep can traverse. However, the top consists of a flat field and fertile, productive land. So, these hills are a natural impregnable fortress within which a small, fortified platoon can cast failure on the ranks of a large force and make its base one of the most critical. From the hills that I saw in Ottoman territories, these hills look like the hill on which Van Castle is built, located at the top of a hill that has only one narrow path and in the middle of a wide meadow. Whoever looks from the top can see the region as if he is looking from high fire towers of Istanbul.

There is a big, standing rock like a pillar on top of the Amba Damo hill on which the monastery has been constructed. A person cannot climb to the monastery and get down except by rope because the height of the monastery is thirty meters from the surface of the amba. The monastery has servants charged with helping those who want to climb up the mountain. There are sixty priests in this monastery and their water comes from a cistern constructed earlier. While the monastery has a story for the reason why it has been built, we are not going to mention it here.

Altogether the surroundings of the monastery and beside it are more dangerous for caravans than the old road as mentioned before. Due to this, the Italian general commander ordered Colonel Stevani who was in Mai Marat to occupy this amba named Piza Ragania with his company. When the colonel arrived to Damo Monastery, he brought the head of the monastery and kept him as a hostage to prevent aggression by the people on Italian soldiers for one and having this chief help the Ethiopians reach the hill for another.

On the twenty-sixth of the mentioned month Colonel Stevani attacked the camp of Ras Sebat and obliged him to evacuate his position and retreat. In this way, he opened the line of movement for the Italian army and the road that caravans came from carrying ammunition and rations for the Italian army. If the colonel had not succeeded in doing this, the Italian army would have been obliged to retreat to Adi Qeyh or Asmara.

When the Ethiopians saw this, they pulled back their soldiers who were descending to the Mareb River and its borders to behind Adowa to pull the Italians to them.

Battle of Adowa [138]

While General Baratieri was preparing to withdraw from Sauria to Adigrat, he received a telegram from Italy informing him of the departure from Napoli of General Hoche with an entire army and a few columns with the destination of Massawa. The Italian government had informed him of the departure of General Hoche, but concealed his discharge from leadership and the appointment of General Baldissera in his place effective from the twenty-third. The latter departed from Brindisi to his post of assignment. However, the rumor of this appointment spread on the twenty-seventh of the month among officers in Asmara. During this time General Baratieri was in Sauria, far away from Asmara, and it was not known whether or not the news had reached him. General Baratieri did not wish to wait for the arrival of soldiers who were traveling from Napoli, so he established an advisory council with members from his high-ranking officers and his commanders of the armed forces, and they deliberated on whether to retreat or attack the Ethiopians. The result of the deliberation was to attack the Ethiopians.

On the twenty-ninth of the month, General Baratieri was informed by the teams scouting the position of the Ethiopians that a small part of the Ethiopians' army, numbering about twenty-thousand, was located on the plains of Aba'azyma and that the big part consisting of about a hundred-thousand soldiers camped beyond Adowa. The general commander decided to attack the camp, so he ordered all Italian armed forces to travel on the evening of the same day. His strategy was to conduct a surprise attack with his army early in the morning on the next day and seize the camp by surprise.

The following are the number of forces of General Baratieri as described by Italian officers:

1- One brigade of local volunteers under the leadership of General Albertone: [xi]

Four battalions of natives	3,700 rifles
Soldiers of the native chief named Okula Kusani[xii]	376 rifles

---

138   Translated by Ghaith Almuayad Al-Azem and Hassana Almuayad Al-Azem

One battery of national artillery	6 cannons
Two batteries of Italian artillery	8 cannons
2- Infantry brigade led by General Dabormida: [xiii]	
Six battalions Italian soldiers	2,640 rifles
One battalion of natives	650 rifles
Soldiers of Asmara	218 rifles
Three Italian artillery batteries	18 cannons
3- Infantry brigade led by General Ellena: [xiv]	
Six Battalions of Italian infantry soldiers	2,930 rifles
One infantry battalion of native volunteer soldiers	1150 rifles
Half a company of soldiers from the Engineering Corps	70 rifles
Two batteries of Italian artillery	12 cannons
4- Infantry brigade led by General Arimondi: [xv]	
Five battalions of Italian infantry	2,273 rifles
One company of native infantry soldiers	230 rifles
Two batteries of Italian artillery	12 cannons

If we add to the aforementioned forces five hundred officers and five hundred of the gendarmerie soldiers and others, the total number of the Italian soldiers will add up to sixteen thousand five hundred soldiers.

This Italian expedition embarked on an excursion to the Ethiopian camp near Adowa at nine o'clock alafranga in the evening on the twenty-ninth of February, 1896 and it moved steadily under full moonlight, and it followed the road of Sauriabouny, crossing the Entiseio Plains and the rugged Juha[xvi] Mountains with their many steep slopes where the soldiers at times had to walk hand in hand in order to be able to continue their march. General Albertone's brigade was at the forefront followed by the brigades of Generals Arimondi and Dabormida, General Ellena's brigade was in the rear. The expedition, which lasted eight hours, suffered all kinds of hardship and arrived at the crack of dawn at a place called Ruba Arin[xvii] where it rendezvoused with the Italian general commander and the commanders of his armed forces. Here the battle tactics were changed and soldiers were aligned as follows:

The brigade of Albertone was to walk forward on the Shidan Warna road with two other brigades and occupy the points of Ruba Arin and Raio and the reserve brigade of Ellena was to occupy the northeastern side of

Ruba Boumi where the general commander established headquarters.[xviii] These forces executed their orders and occupied the aforementioned points and the brigade of Albertone descended the left side of Mount Raio, while three other brigades also descended behind that mountain. As for General Albertone, he sent forward the first and second battalions of local infantry soldiers under the command of Lieutenant Colonel Turitto. This brigade arrived at six o'clock in the morning in front of the Ethiopian camp and took them by surprise and started firing their weapons at the Ethiopians who fired back and launched a fierce attack against the brigade and, in no time, the brigade was annihilated to the last man with no survivors, not one man. They extended their attack to the brigade of Albertone who was marching behind the Turitto battalion and fought fiercely. However, the hordes of Ethiopians kept marching on it from all sides like ant swarms and they besieged the brigade. At seven o'clock, General Albertone sent for backup from the general commander. However, his message was not received until nine o'clock. General Baratieri ordered the other two brigades to march forward to strengthen and supply [the other forces]. The brigade marched under the order of General Dabormida, but lost the way leading to the headquarters of General Albertone and walked in Mariam and Shavitu Valleys and so was completely separated from the army. As for the second brigade, which marched aiming toward Arissen, they had discovered that the Ethiopians occupied all the hills located in parallel with the Italian forces.

General Albertone continued to fight and resist the Ethiopians until all his forces were defeated and outnumbered and so, he was defeated. He then retreated with the survivors from his brigade. However, in spite of that, Ethiopian soldiers did not leave them alone and followed their tracks and no one was spared from the beating and the stabbing until all the officers perished and General Albertone himself fell in the hands of the Ethiopians.

So much for General Albertone; and as for Generals Arimondi and Ellena, their brigades were surrounded by the Ethiopians like the "bracelet around the wrist" and the two armies got so entangled that hand to hand combat was inevitable to the point that these two generals failed to gather their soldiers in any way and retreat in order to escape the carnage. The losses among the Italians were great, especially among artillery soldiers and their officers who could not use their cannons and did not wish to leave them in the hands of the enemy. So, they all perished defending their batteries. The Italians had fifty-six cannons, of which fifty-four fell to the hands of the Ethiopians. The ranks of the Italian soldiers were annihilated and the efforts of the officers to lessen the burden of defeat were in vain and so General Arimondi was killed and many other officers as well, and what increased the losses of the Italians while retreating was the attack of the local population on the retreating forces. So, this is what became of Albertone's brigade that was killed to the last man, while the Arimondi brigade was badly defeated. As for the Dabormida brigade, which lost its way and got separated from the rest of the army, while it was marching in the Mariam and Shavitu Valley it met with an Ethiopian company and a battle ensued. The Ethiopians retreated to the valley however at half past two o'clock in the afternoon the brigade found itself suddenly in front of the Ethiopian army chasing the other defeated Italian forces. General Dabormida resisted valiantly against these huge forces, but he was defeated and killed with the majority of his officers and his ranks were defeated. This brigade was also in shambles and suffered the same fate as General Arimondi's brigade.

Whoever managed to escape death ran in the direction Adi Ogri and the Ethiopians continued to follow the tracks of the defeated all day. In the evening, some of the officers who survived pulled the rest of the Italian forces and returned to Asmara. As for General Commander Baratieri, he had been watching from the hill that he took as his headquarters what became of his army from defeats and calamities. When the army was completely annihilated, he returned in the evening to Asmara through the road of Enticho and when he counted the losses of Italian troops, he found that it exceeded seven thousand dead and wounded. The general commander was brought to trial before the military tribunal due to this. However, he was found not guilty.

After the war ended, Emperor Menelik held a council with the ras to decide on the punishment to be exacted on the local prisoners of war who served in the Italian army. The merciful emperor wanted a soft punishment, but on the insistence of the empress and the ras, it was decided that they should be treated as traitors and so the verdict was issued to cut their right hands and left foot as dictated by the law (fata negus) for a traitor. The verdict was executed at once. As for the Italian prisoners of war, some of them were assigned to serve the high ranking officers of the army as was the custom in this country.

As a result of this defeat, Italy paid the army a huge sum in military reparations and gave up all bases and regions that Italy occupied in Tigray province.

Wednesday, July 20

It was Wednesday, the twentieth day of July. Crossing the Red Sea, our ship had come to Suez. Bidding farewell to the captain and fellow travelers, we checked into the Continental Hotel located on the shore of the canal.

Thursday, July 21

The next day, Thursday, we went to Alexandria via Ismailiye and Banha, getting on the train an hour before noon. Staying there until Saturday, we embarked on the Russian ship named Chikhachev on the mentioned day and came to Istanbul on Friday.

Endnotes

i   Arabic proverb 'Ma kullu ma yetemenna almari idrikuhu tejri ilriaju bimala teshtahi al sufunu'

ii   Alessandro di San Marzano

iii   Ras Alula Engida

iv   Baldassare Orero

v   Antonio Gandolfi

vi   Commander of an Amba or fortress

vii   Tishreen thani is the ninth month of the Rumi calendar

viii   Halai or Halay

ix   Akkele Guzay is in modern day Eritrea

x   Pietro Felter

xi   Matteo Albertone

xii   Likely an error in the Arabic script since Okule-Kasai or Akkule Guzay is a province in modern day Eritrea where Batha Agos was from

xiii   Vittorio Dabormida

xiv   Giuseppe Ellena

xv   Giuseppe Arimondi

xvi   Likely Mount Yeha

xvii   Rebbi Arienni

xviii   This may be a reference to Chidane Meret

Famous Ethiopians

Lokman the Ethiopian[139]

He was famous by his prudence and wisdom. God mentioned in the holy Qur'an the sermons that Lokman gave to his son. Some persons took judgment of Lokman as proof of him being a prophet, but most interpreters said that this judgment is eloquence and fluency of tongue and proof of wisdom and favor and sagacity. In fact, people were debating whether he was a prophet or saint. The last word is the more accurate. One of those who spoke is Ibn Marduba who said he is related to Abu Huraira. Ibn Asaker relates him to Abdurrahman bin Yazid and Jabber says that Lokman is Ethiopian.

Bilal, the Ethiopian, the Muezzin[140] of Our Prophet Mohammed (PBUH)

He was the slave of Abdullah bin Jadaan in Mecca when he became Muslim at the hands of the Prophet, peace be upon him, and because of that his owner used to torture him as revenge. When this news reached Abu Bakr Al Siddiq, he bought him and freed him in the name of God. Bilal, the Ethiopian, is one of the companions of our Prophet Mohammad and he would perform the call to prayer in front of him and many stories were told about him. He participated with the Prophet in most of his battles. After the demise of the Prophet, peace be upon him, he went with the Ethiopian who was sent by Omar, God bless him, at the time of his caliphate in the conquest of Damascus and after it was conquered, he settled there. He died at more than sixty years of age and was buried at the small gate cemetery. His tomb is known and to this day people go visit it and obtain blessings, God bless him and all the esteemed companions, too.

---

139   Translated by Amina Sanaa Al Muayad Al Azm and Ghassan Aidi

140 *One who calls the faithful to prayer

Mahja the Ethiopian

He was the servant of Omar bin Khattab, God bless him, who became Muslim and companion of the Prophet, peace be upon him, and was killed in the Battle of Badr.

Nafia bin Maruh the Ethiopian

He was the servant of Al Harith bin Kalada Al Thaqafi. When Taif was under siege, Nafia was there and lowered himself from the wall with rope and went to the Prophet and became Muslim and was honored to accompany the Prophet. They called him Abu Bakara. He stayed, God bless him, neutral during the Jamil incident and he did not take part in battles with any of the fighters. He died in Basra in the year six hundred and seventy-six and was buried there and had two sons, one was Abdullah and the other Selim.

Shakran the Ethiopian

His real name is Salih bin Udey and his nickname is Shakran. In the beginning, he was the servant of Abdul Rahman bin Auf. Then, our Prophet, peace be upon him, bought and freed him after the Battle of Badr and this companion, God bless him, was present at the demise of the Prophet, peace be upon him. He was one of the persons who shrouded, prepared and buried him. His offspring continued to the time of Haroon Rashed Al Abbasi.

Zumahjer the Ethiopian

He is the son of the brother of Negus Ashama the Ethiopian and was among seventy-two Ethiopians who came from Ethiopia with our master Jaafar. This companion used to love the Prophet, peace be upon him, and was beside him. They used to think he was one of the companions. He did not leave the [side of the] Prophet even for a second and was always at his service. He used to tell some of the hadith. He died in Damascus at sixty years of age.

Zumehdem the Ethiopian

He is one of the Ethiopians who came with our master Jaafar and they were honored with the company of the Prophet. This companion used to tell poems in front of the Prophet on the origin of Ethiopians from the children of Hud who crossed from the Arabian Peninsula to the coast of Africa.

Khaled bin Ribah the Ethiopian

He is the brother of Bilal the Ethiopian and used to live in the village of Darayaa near Damascus.

Zudjen the Ethiopian and others

He is one of the Ethiopians who came with our master Jaafar and also accompanied the Prophet. Those who came with Jaafar from Ethiopia who were honored to accompany the Prophet were Zumenasib the Ethiopian and Khaled bin al Hawarni the Ethiopian.

Islam the Ethiopian

He was with one of the Jews of Khaybar in the day this city was under siege and during the siege this person arrived beside the Prophet, peace be upon him, and he became Muslim. He participated in the Khaybar Battle and was killed. There were only two hours between his announcement of being a Muslim and his demise.

Yasar the Ethiopian

He was with one of the Jews of Khaybar. His name was Amer. He became Muslim and was killed during the siege, too.

Wahshi bin Harb the Ethiopian

He was Jubeir bin Mataam's servant before he became Muslim. He was in the Battle of Uhud among the polytheists who killed Hamza bin Abd Al Mutalleb who was the uncle of the Prophet. After that he came to Madina and became Muslim and killed Musaylima the Liar who claimed prophecy in Yamamah during the caliphate of Abu Bakr.

Asem the Ethiopian

His master gave him to the Prophet, peace be upon him, as a gift.

Nael the Ethiopian

He is the father of Ayman, one of the esteemed companions, and one of the persons who told the hadith.

Laqeet the Ethiopian

One of the servants of the Prophet, peace be upon him.

Yasaar the Ethiopian

He was the person responsible for cleaning and wiping the masjid. Abu Huraira said that the Prophet praised Yasaar in front of him.

Jamal the Ethiopian

He is one of the persons who participated in several battles and was killed in one of those.

Abraha bin Sabah the Ethiopian

The mother of this companion is the daughter of Abraha Al Ashram, the owner of the famous elephant and King of Yemen. He was one of the men of the Negus Asmaha and came to the Prophet with seven of his friends and all of them became Muslims.

Islam Abu Khaled the Ethiopian

He was the servant of Omar bin Al Khattab and told many hadith from many esteemed companions. He lived the longest of the companions because he reached one hundred and eleven years of age and died in the time of Marwan bin Al Hakam.

Ayman the Ethiopian

The father of Abdul Wahid and servant of Abdullah Ibn Amr Al Makhzumi had narrated after Jabber bin Abdullah Al Ansari.

Injashe the Ethiopian

His nickname was Abu Maria and he is among the people who won the honor of being a companion when he attended the farewell pilgrimage with the glory of the Prophet our master Mohammad and he was next to him wherever he went and he herded the camels faster. There are many

Ethiopians other than the ones mentioned who were honored to be companions of the Prophet, but the names were not kept.

Here [are] the names of virtuous Ethiopian female companions:

Barakah Oum Ayman the Ethiopian

The concubine of our master Abdullah bin Abd Al Mutalleb. She served the Prophet, peace be upon him, after he was born and raised him until he became young. Our master Mohammad freed her after he got married with Lady Hatija, God bless her. He used to love her like his mother and used to say this in front of people. After he emancipated her, the Prophet, peace be upon him, married her with Zaid bin Harisa, one of his servants, so she gave birth to Usama bin Zaid. Our master Mohammad used to frequently visit the home of Barakah Oum Ayman and, after the Prophet passed away, the four caliphs visited her following the practice of the Prophet himself visiting.

Saatra the Ethiopian

She was one of the slaves of Bani Asad. [When] she was sick, she came and complained to the Prophet, peace be upon him, and so he wished her to be healed.

Barakah the Ethiopian

She is the slave of Oum Habiba one of the wives of the Prophet and she came with her from Ethiopia.

Afira Bint Rabah the Ethiopian

Sister of Bilal the Ethiopian the muezzin of the Prophet, peace be upon him.

Nabaa the Ethiopian

She is the slave of Oum Hani, one of the wives of the Prophet, and daughter of Abi Taleb. She was in the service of the Prophet, peace be upon him.

And here are the names of some his male and female companions among the Ethiopians:

Abdullah the Ethiopian

He is the son of Negus Asmaha, the contemporary of the Prophet, peace be upon him. He was born in Ethiopia and Jaafar named him after his son Abdullah, the newborn. The wife of Jaafar nursed him and when Abdullah bin Jaafar and Abdullah the Ethiopian grew up, they loved each other and the friendship between them was mutual.

Hamis the Ethiopian

Historians wrote of Hamis as being one of the virtuous companions and some others mentioned that he was one of the followers.

Al Faqih Ataa bin Rabah the Ethiopian

He is the servant of Abi Misara Al Fahri and he was one of the best scholars and ascetics. Many stories were told about him. He was the Mufti of Mecca in his time, and Imam Abu Hanife and Hasan Al Basri and Imam ibn Malik praised him. Suleiman bin Abdul Malik, who was the Umayyad caliph, attended his lessons and his son was one of his students. He died in Mecca in the year seven hundred and thirty-two and he was ninety years of age when he died. He spent his life spreading knowledge and teaching.

Abraha the Ethiopian

She was the slave of Negus Asmaha and was the intermediary in communicating between the aforementioned negus and Habiba the mother of believers. At the time of the solemnization of her marriage to the Prophet, Oum Habiba presented her very precious gifts, [but] she did not accept them.

The names of the companions whose mothers were Ethiopian:

Usama bin Zaid

He is one of the most famous Arab poets and one of his grandchildren is Imru Al Qais the famous. His mother was Barakah Oum Ayman, the nanny of the Prophet, peace be upon him. There are many hadith that indicate how great the affection of the Prophet was towards Usama. He was entrusted with the command of the army that was marching to the Levant and Usama was eighteen years old at that time. One day Usama fell down and hurt his face. Our Prophet treated him until he was healed. Once he also had him ride behind him on the horse he was on.

Usama did not participate in Ali's wars, God bless him because he had a grudge towards one of the polytheists and when the polytheist saw this he recited the shahadah and yet Usama struck him with a blow that took him out, so the Prophet rebuked him for this deed. Abu Osman Al Hindi and Abdullah bin Abdullah and many other hadith scholars narrated many hadith about Usama. He died in the fifty-fourth year after the Hijra in a place called Al Jarf near Medina and was buried in Medina.

Ayman bin Obeid bin Amr

The son of Barakah the Ethiopian who was mentioned before. He is the brother of Usama, but from the mother's side. He was assigned to bring what was necessary for the Prophet, peace be upon him, to perform ablution. He died in the Battle of Hunayn.

Fayrouz Al Daylami

He is the son of the sister of Negus Asmaha and his nickname Abi Abdullah and Abi Abdulrahman. He killed Aswad Ansi who was claiming himself a prophet in Yemen. He died during the caliphate of Osman bin Afaan.

And here the names of some Muslim notables who were born from Ethiopian mothers:

Abdullah bin Qais bin Abdullah bin Zubair, Mohammad bin Ali bin Musa bin Jaafar bin Mohammad, the son of Ali bin Al-Hussain bin Ali bin Abi Taleb, Jaafar bin Ismail bin Musa bin Jaafar Al Sadiq, Abdullah bin Hamza bin Musa bin Jaafar, Suleiman bin Hasan bin Aqeel bin Abi Taleb, Ibrahim bin Hasan bin Aqeel bin Abi Taleb, Mohammad bin Ibrahim bin Hasan bin Abi Taleb, Jaafar bin Ibrahim bin Aqeel bin Abi Taleb, Al Abbas bin Mohammad bin Ali bin Abdullah bin Al Abbas, Isa bin Jaafar Al Mansur, Jaafar bin Jaafar Al Mansur, Hibatullah bin Ibrahim bin Al Mahdi,

Al Abbas bin Al Maatasim, Al Khalifa Muqtadi Lamrallah and there are many others whose mothers are Ethiopians.

And here [are] the names of the daughters of the virtuous companions who migrated to Ethiopia and were born there:

Amna Oum Khaled Al Quraishiyah

She is the daughter of Khaled bin Said bin Alaasi. She was born in Ethiopia and returned to Medina with some of the companions. She married Al Zubair bin Al Awwam and gave birth to Omar and Khaled. Her nickname was Oum Khaled. [Persons] like Musa bin Uqba and Ibrahim bin Uqba and Kuraib bin Suleiman Al Kindi and Musaab bin Abdullah and others told many stories about her.

Zainab bint Al Harith

She was born in Ethiopia and also died there after drinking water.

Zainab bint Abdullah Abi Salma

She is the daughter of Oum Salma, one of the virtuous wives of our Prophet. She was born in Ethiopia. Her nickname was Barra, but our Prophet peace be upon him changed her name and named her Zainab. She was famous in the study of Islamic jurisprudence.

Aishah bint Al Harith

She was born in Ethiopia and was one of the virtuous companions who returned to Medina.

Here are the names of the male children of the aforementioned companions born in Ethiopia:

From Bani Hashem Ghouth bin Jaafar bin Abi Taleb and Abdullah bin Jaafar bin Abi Taleb and Mohammad bin Jaafar bin Abi Taleb and from Bani Abd Shams Mohammad bin Abi Hudhaifa bin Utbah and Abdullah bin Osman bin Affan.

And here are the names of the virtuous companions who passed away in Ethiopia:

From Bani Asad, Ibn Abd al-Azizi bin Qusay. And Amr bin Umayyah bin al-Harith bin Asad, one of Bani Jahm - Hatib bin Murthe and brother of Khattab bin al-Harith. And from Bani Sahem - Abdullah bin Al-Harith bin Qais, and from Bani Adi - Farwa bin Abdul Ashari bin Harthan. And Uday bin Fadla. And from Bani Zahra - al-Muttalib bin Azhar bin Auf and his brother Labab bin Azhar bin Auf. And from the Bani Taym, Musa bin al-Harith bin Khalid, his mother Rita bint al-Harith bin Jabalah, and her sister Aisha bint al-Harith, Zainab bint al-Harith, Zainab Safran bin Umayya al-Kutabi, Fatimah, wife of Urwa bin Saeed bin al-Aas, Oum Harmala bint Abd al-Asad and wife of Jaham bin Qais.

From Bani Abd Shams - Sa'id bin Khalid bin Saeed and his sister Amna bint Khalid bin Saeed and from Bani Makhzoum - Zaynab bint Abi Salamah Abdullah bin Abd al-Asad, Abdullah bin Abbas bin Abi Rabi'a and Omar bin Abdullah, and from Bani Zahra, Abdullah bin Abdul Muttalib bin Azhar and from Bani Tim - Musa bin al-Harith bin Khalid and his sisters Aisha, Fatima and Zainab. And from Bani Jamah - Al-Harith bin Hatib bin Al-Harith, Alharat bin Sufian bin Maamur and Muhammad bin Khattab Harith, and from Bani Amir, Salit bin Salit bin Amr.

The Voyage is Complete

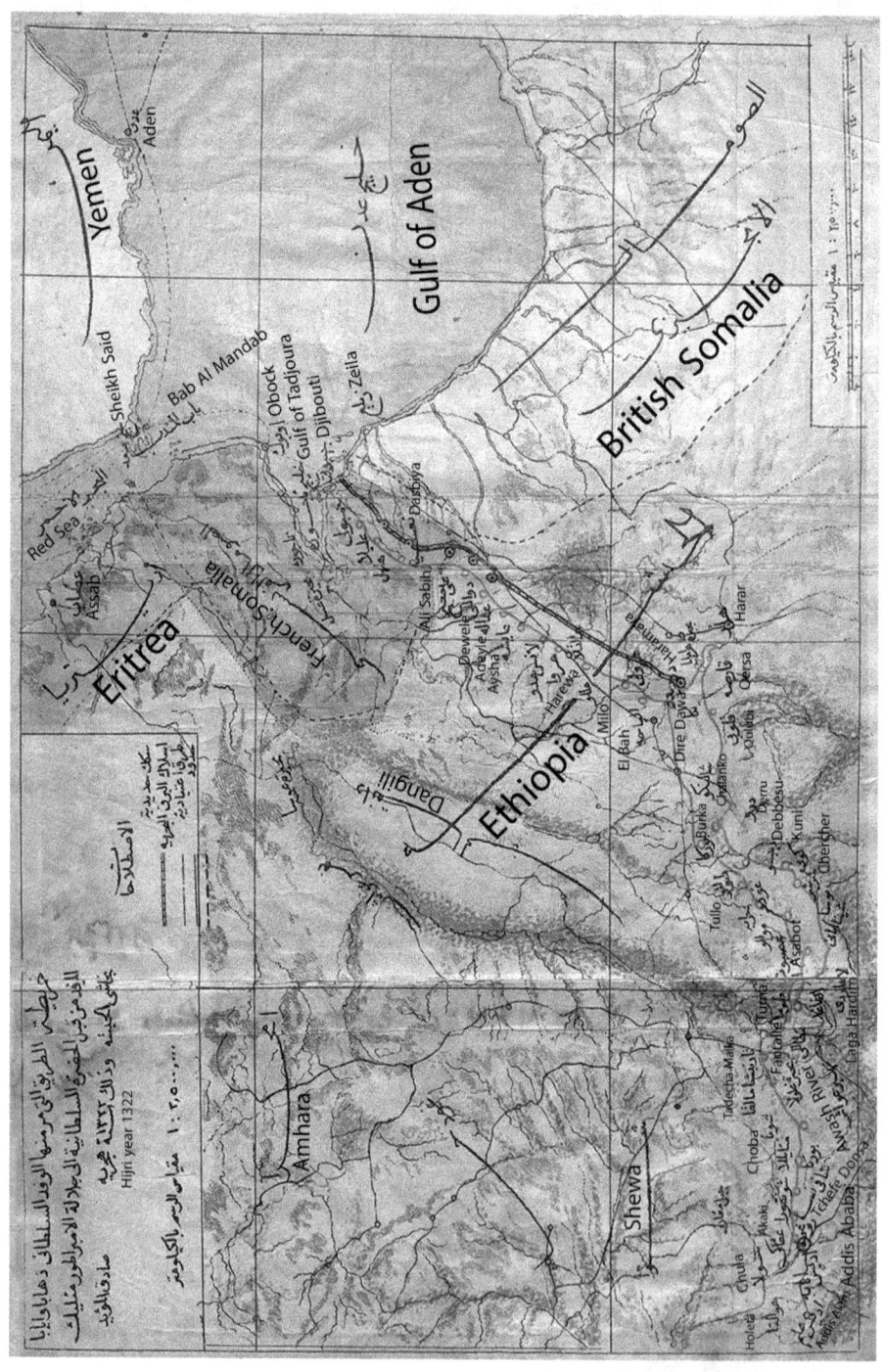

Sadık Pasha's Map - from the Arabic Translation of Habeş Seyahatnamesi

*Warrant of the Order of Solomon Medal of the First Rank
Bestowed upon
Sadık el-Müeyyed Pasha by Emperor Menelik II
19 June Year 1896 [1904]*
Copyright © İklil Azmzâde 2000

www.ingramcontent.com/pod-product-compliance
Lightning Source LLC
Chambersburg PA
CBHW051857160426
43209CB00039B/1974/J